COSMO
World
POLITAN
Citizens
HABITAT
Living Space

A Research Agenda for Urban Resilience

Edited by Jörg Schröder
Maurizio Carta
Federica Scaffidi
Annalisa Contato

CONTENTS

page 52–119

02 ACTIONS

case studies *

page 120–263

03 EXPLORATIONS

Cosmopolitan Atmosphere

*motif 01

Cosmopolitan Accelerators

*motif 02

Cosmopolitan Makers

*motif 03

COSMOPOLITAN HABITAT

JÖRG SCHRÖDER, MAURIZIO CARTA

In order to achieve resilience and sustainability goals within the framework of the European Green Deal, Europe is advancing ideas and actions for manifesting change and long-term strategies in its cities. At the same time, we are facing the impact of the Covid-19 pandemic on our cities, ambitions, and ways of imagining and constructing the cities of the future. *Cosmopolitan Habitat* aims to contribute to this current debate from a research perspective, addressing cities as main stages for the crucial political, economic, and social topics of our time, and as multi-places and multi-communities on the front lines of the global challenges of climate change, migration, and health. A specific focus is placed on addressing social inequalities, including in the context of the United Nations Sustainable Development Goals.

How can cities become new, concrete places to invent, explore, experiment, and live in open communities? Places that are able to simultaneously face global challenges and enhance urban inclusiveness and urban economies? *Cosmopolitan* (from the classical Greek *kosmos*: world and *politai*: citizens) *Habitat* (from Latin *habitare*: to dwell) focuses on the city as the laboratory of civilisation. *Cosmopolitan Habitat* is an international dialogue for a new paradigm in urbanism in Europe: conceptual models, urban strategies, and spatial practices of the Open and Inclusive City.

The book is organised into three parts, which each display approaches from different modalities of research: visions, actions, and explorations. The aim of the first part, **visions,** addresses the evolvement of questions to articulate and discuss whether and how *Cosmopolitan Habitat* can become a new—and crisis-proof—urban paradigm. In reference to several academic and societal discussions, the backgrounds, lines of argumentation, and perspectives of *Cosmopolitan Habitat* are directed towards a renewal of urbanistic concepts and methodologies. Voices collected by students in the form of postcards and on Instagram form a parallel, subjective way of grasping current social and spatial change in cities.

As a *catalogue raisonné* of 6 research and design projects, developed together with PhD candidates and master's students, the second part, **actions,** offers a comprehensive debate on the impact of cosmopolitan topics in urban analysis, conceptualisation, and strategy building. Through the lens of *Habitat*, the interaction between cultural and social phenomena and processes of spatial change is brought in focus: it is discussed with regard to new research and learning modes in urbanism, with regard to interdisciplinary cooperation, and in dialogue with society. The concept of *Habitat,* too, points to the interrelation of human living spaces and nature. The city of Palermo, venue of the 2018 *Manifesta* biennial entitled "Cultivating Co-existence" and a hotspot of political and cultural innovation in Italy, is put forward as an exemplary case and possible laboratory for contemporary urban change in the Mediterranean. Perspectives on the cities of Hanover, Halle, and Flensburg are orchestrated into a discussion of the urban shift towards *Cosmopolitan Habitat* in Germany.

The third part, **explorations,** collects a range of current research perspectives and projects shedding light on the topic of *Cosmopolitan Habitat* in urban design, urban planning, and urban studies, as well as in the social sciences and humanities. This lively debate between twenty-four researchers from Germany, Italy, Germany, Italy, Cyprus, Greece, Portugal, Slovenia, Spain, and the US involves prominent figures on the cosmopolitan stage and evolved research projects and pathways as well as emerging young researchers. The twenty-four explorations are structured across three motifs:

Cosmopolitan atmospheres: triggering innovative spirit
How can cosmopolitan atmospheres be defined, enhanced, and formed using urban planning and design frameworks? In what ways can they create value that is an asset to cultural, economic and social innovation, and liveable and safe habitats?

Cosmopolitan accelerators: activating spaces and networks
How can processes of activation that lead to attractive places, new uses for abandoned space, and new urban networks be configured and framed? What innovations can be introduced to urban planning and design processes?

Cosmopolitan makers: co-creating urban change
How can the engagement of stakeholders and active citizenship of *Cosmopolitan Habitats* be conceptualised in order to develop new models of co-creation? What pathways are necessary in order to develop expertise in urban planning?

The book *Cosmopolitan Habitat* is built on cooperation between the Institute of Urban Design and Planning at Leibniz University Hannover (Prof. Jörg Schröder) and the Department of Architecture at the University of Palermo (Prof. Maurizio Carta). We are grateful to the DAAD German Academic Exchange Service, which funded *Cosmopolitan Habitat* as a dialogue between universities in Germany and Southern Europe. The book is also founded on the impact of Covid-19 pandemic on cities and on academic work, which led to the establishment of a blended model of dialogue between cosmopolitan universities. The publication of *Cosmopolitan Habitat* is possible thanks to all the participants who worked together to develop this topic over the past two years, to all the students and PhD candidates involved, to all the urban stakeholders and members of city administrations and active urban society who took part in the discussions, and especially to all the international experts who extended the dialogue to become truly cosmopolitan in scope.

01
VISION

COSMOPOLITAN DESIGN

PLANNING THE
NEOCOSMOPOLITAN HABITAT

COSMOPOLITAN POSTCARDS

10–51

Figure 1
Cosmopolitan Postcards cover image
Graphic by Julia Hermanns
for the Chair of Territorial Design and Urban Planning LUH

COSMOPOLITAN DESIGN

JÖRG SCHRÖDER

The initiative *Cosmopolitan Habitat* first came into existence in 2019 as a joint research on the future of cities and the role of urbanism in society. The initial intention of the project is best illustrated by its title, which combines *Cosmopolitan* (from the classical Greek *kosmos*: world and *politai*: citizens) with *Habitat* (from Latin *habitare*: to dwell). It aims to construct an international dialogue that focuses on the city as a laboratory in which civilisation can tackle global challenges. *Cosmopolitan Habitat* calls for research and debate aimed at the development of a cosmopolitan paradigm in urbanism, including conceptual models, urban strategies, and spatial practices for the Open City.

The Covid-19 pandemic joined the list of global challenges threatening cities—climate change, migration, and inequalities—and added a new global dimension and urgency to the question of health. As such, the pandemic crisis that occurred during work on *Cosmopolitan Habitat* can be seen as having provided an opportunity to think about, discuss, and design for change. Among other things, this might mean trying to lay out visions for the future in the face of uncertainty, and helping to accelerate existing positive processes while opposing negative ones—particularly the social frictions and spatial-territorial segregation that have been magnified by the impact of Covid-19. It may be said that the pandemic has cast light on already pre-existing failures to shape cities as liveable spaces, such as inadequate housing, precarious work, a lack of economic prospects, and insufficient public spaces and social infrastructures.

Cosmopolitan Habitat raises the question of the role of the city in society, in everyday practices and as common and public space. Cities—and with them the urbanistic disciplines and interdisciplinary work on urban phenomena—can be seen as a component of irreversible changes currently occurring globally. In between practice, research, and governance—and linked to culture and creativity—urbanism needs to define objectives to reach for, adapt our understanding of situations, and draft novel ways of acting and involving ourselves and others. This outline calls for a courageous vision in research and innovation—for urbanism in the theatres of academia and in society, but also for cities as laboratories for resilience, as frontiers at which to grasp the complexities of the present and to open pathways for the future.

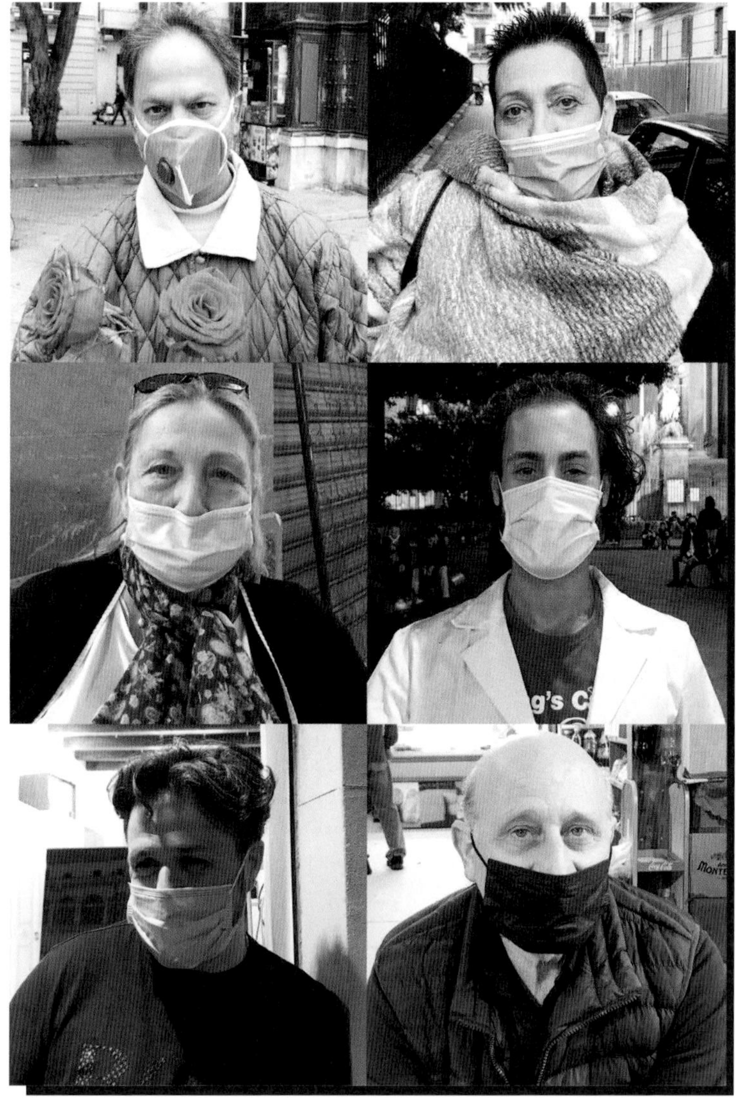

Figure 2
Urban Portraits, 2020
Photos by Leandra Leipold

Cities: laboratories for cosmopolitan innovation

As a framework for the *Cosmopolitan Habitat* initiative, we can refer to the Sustainable Development Goals set by UN for 2030. Specifically, we seek to address the actual and foreseeable conflicts between Goal 10, reducing inequalities, and Goal 13, taking measures to combat climate change. A similar point is made in the policy agenda of the European Green Deal, which not only views decarbonisation and green economy as an economic opportunity to de-couple economic success from finite resource consumption but also highlights the objective of social inclusion in this process. As such, there is a double challenge for cities to act as both stages and active agents in the implementation of policies. We understand this challenge as a call for more precise answers about how cities can orient themselves more radically to sustainability and resilience (Goal 11 of UNSDG) and how they can contribute in a larger, global sense. As a recent catalyst for this approach, the New European Bauhaus initiative sets the aim "to bring the European Green Deal to life in an attractive, and innovative and human-centered way. It will be a movement based on sustainability, accessibility, and aesthetics..." (von der Leyen 2020). A crucial element will be to focus on the life of citizens and on cities as places where a multitude of phenomena occur at the same time, interacting with people, spaces, and functions.

Over the past years, cities have already started to understand themselves, and to act, as an avant-garde developing innovative concepts for transforming climate change measures into opportunities for a new quality of life and comprehensive visions for urban futures (Carta 2017). This approach not only regards metropolises as poles of innovation, such as those organised in the C40 Alliance Cities Climate Leadership Group (including, for example, the concept of the 15-Minutes-City in Paris), but also identifies poles and networks of innovation in peripheries (Schröder, Carta, Ferretti, Lino 2018; Lino 2020). Nevertheless, a broad and focused scientific—and political—debate about the role of cities as active agents in terms of place-based and place-sensitive strategies cannot yet be made manifest; especially not one targeting their role as comprehensive drivers of innovation and questioning their one-directional mission to implement sectoral place-blind policies.

With regard to climate change, a strengthened focus on cities appears increasingly crucial. As Bruno Latour (2014) states, the Anthropocene leads all agents to share the same shape-changing destiny, which cannot be represented by older concepts building on subjectivity or objectivity—and can neither be reconciled or recombined as nature and society. He urges us "to distribute agency as far and in as differentiated a way as possible." Richard Sennett (2018) points out—as one main characteristic of the concept of the Open City—that, over time, an open system is necessarily non-linear, "and within that frame range[s] from path-dependency to the patterns of chance" in interaction between the material creation and social behaviour that together form "agency" in the city.

Hence, *Cosmopolitan Habitat's* starting point postulates that urban futures in and after the Covid-19 pandemic require a shift towards resilience in cities and territories. It asks how cities can become creative and vibrant places to invent, explore, experiment, and live as an open community, able to face global challenges and at the same time to enhance urban inclusiveness and urban economies. Cities that—to suggest just some working fields—use open data and digital technologies, recycle spaces and infrastructures, stimulate urban productivity, offer opportunities, reshape neighbourhoods and urban spaces, and reconnect to a territorial dimension and to nature;

Figure 3
Urban Scenes, 2019
Photos by Federica Scaffidi (1, 3), Riccarda Cappeller (2)

and particularly, cities that extend and invigorate multiple ideas of the Open Habitat (Schröder 2018) towards a civilisatory spirit that proposes to understand cities as internationally connected laboratories for cosmopolitan innovation.

A cosmopolitan paradigm

Ideas about cosmopolitanism can be found from the very origins of the democratic model of the city: Athens in the 5th century BC. It could be said that the roots of the democratic vision of cities as *Habitat* are tinged with an interest in and a larger vision of *kosmos* in cultural and economic terms, as well as the view of civilisation as a mission. In modern philosophy, cosmopolitanism involves a global political dimension, that—following Immanuel Kant or Jürgen Habermas—can be assigned to an elite and enforced from above or fostered from below through civil society movements. While cosmopolitanism can be understood as a normative issue, Ulrich Beck (2011) points out that cosmopolitanisation is concerned with social facts, in everyday life and in events, that are linked with the erosion of the clear boundaries that once separated markets, states, cultures, and people. In terms of globalisation and climate change, cosmopolitanisation refers to the existential, global entanglements and confrontations that are linked to these processes of erosion. Beck views the cosmopolitan implications of global climate change as a paradigm shift for sociological analysis based on the concepts of second modernity and risk society in conjunction with reflexive sociology. His understanding of cosmopolitanism and cosmopolitanisation is articulated in three components: an empirical research perspective, a social reality, and a normative theory (2006).

One of the critiques of Beck's *Cosmopolitan Vision* seems indeed to have been confirmed by the current pandemic: the lack of empirics regarding the actors that drive cosmopolitanism. This may be ascribed to as-yet unconsidered processes of re-nationalisation that have been virulent for a number of years, but could also be extended to the role of cities, which is not yet included in the discussion. A crucial interface for cosmopolitan agency—one which has also been exposed by the pandemic—is that between research and action. According to Beck's definition of the risk society (1992), "we become radically dependent on specialised scientific knowledge to define what is and what is not dangerous in advance of encountering the dangers themselves." It becomes clear that knowledge does not arrive in the form of clearly recognisable truth but in "mixtures" and "amalgams" transported by "agents of knowledge in their combination and opposition, their foundations, their claims, their mistakes, their irrationalities." Beck pointed out that this is "a development of great ambivalence. It contains the opportunity to emancipate social practice from science through science" (ibid.).

Nevertheless, the constant new insights into the dialogue between science and politics during the Covid-19 crisis are being discussed by media and society with an—at least for Germany—novel intensity. A clearer and more differentiated awareness of the role of scientific knowledge and the need for political decision-making seems to be evolving as a result. Questions are being raised not only about the reliability of scientific statements based on or at least informed by scientific evidence for political purposes, but also about what forms of statements scientists can and should make, and about how these statements can be used. An interest in understanding the process of knowledge production can be noted: evolving every day, in a cosmopolitanised manner, and examining previous understandings and precising (or falsifying) explanatory approaches. This can be seen as quite a change for the common image of the apparently 'solid' natural sciences that are in the limelight these

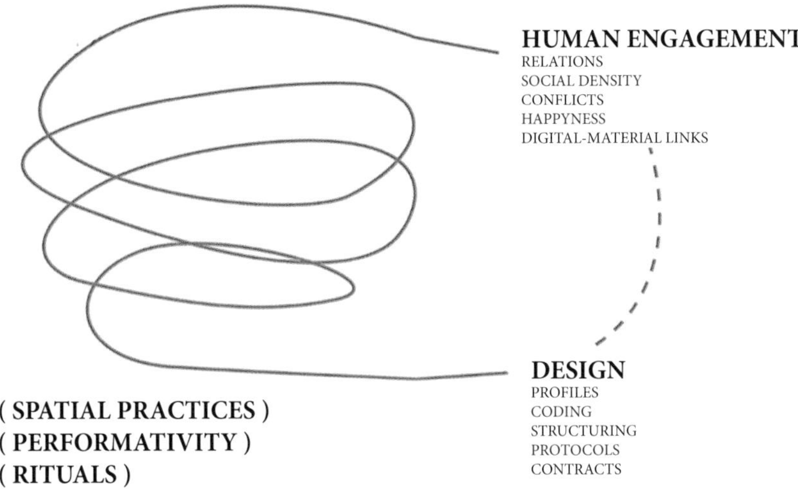

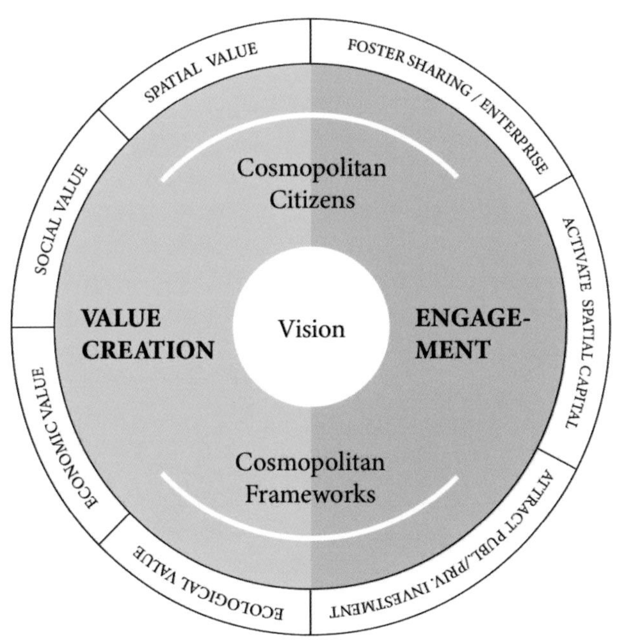

Figures 4 and 5
Cosmopolitan Design feedback loop /
Cosmopolitan engagement and value scheme
Graphic by Chair of Territorial Design and Urban Planning LUH

days. Economic, social, and cultural sciences have also been included in these recent debates, and the nature of more qualitative responses is also discussed. Surprisingly, however, there has only been a very fragmented discussion of the role of cities and urbanism in this context.

Towards a "cosmopolitan turn" in urbanism

It is surprising not only because of the situation's relevance to the future Habitat, but also because the relevance of urbanistic research might be appreciated more today than it has been in the past. Urbanism, called a "science of action" (Handlungswissenschaft) by Gerd Albers, underlies global challenges—especially regarding climate change—and is called to bring local potentials in the game like all forms of science a "gravitational pull of the world" (Beck 2016) that transforms our concept and vision. Taking inspiration from Beck's aim—to "reinvent the social sciences for the age of cosmopolitanisation"—urbanism could understand climate change as a "laboratory for methodological cosmopolitanism". Its field of research would be as much the effects and mechanisms of cosmopolitanisation with regard to cities as the activities taken up by society—in interaction with space—to shape *Cosmopolitan Habitats*. Comprehensively, three main methodological areas can be identified:

- **Providing a fresh start for empirics**—between actors and spatial dynamics/potentialities, including design/research models, creative exploration, and transformation processes;
- **Fostering multi-actor research** where innovation is created through collaboration by academic institutions, private actors, and public administration bodies (in accordance with the multi-innovation paradigm of the architectural disciplines, which is also based on the exchange of roles and figures)
- **Enhancing agency-oriented research** through contextual and transdisciplinary access.

Now, Max Weber's position—science is not able to tell anybody what should be done, but only what could be done—is a methodological principle built on the difference between descriptive and normative statements that certainly applies to research in urbanism—in its own multidisciplinary setup of urban design, urban planning, and urban studies. Nevertheless, urbanism as a "science of action" must not only provide transparency through a larger awareness of research phases, but must also engage with the interdependencies between the phases in order to make them more explicit:

- **The context of discovery**—locating and defining issues or problems;
- **The context of justification (or analysis),** which encompasses scientific reasoning and the methodological as well as methodical steps needed to set up hypotheses based on models and theories and to validate them (the core of Weber's statement);
- **The context of impact,** which considers both the expansion of knowledge and theory and their societal relevance and practical uses.

In this regard, Mittelstraß (2018) distinguishes between orientation knowledge and instrumental knowledge, with both methodological and normative intent. In a transdisciplinary rationality, hermeneutics and construction—as he calls it—would coincide. A further reference for the positioning of innovation and research in urbanism is mentioned in the New European Bauhaus initiative, which aims to become "a bridge between science and technology and the world of arts and culture"—pointing towards a double nature and overall creative orientation in urbanism today that helps to overcome

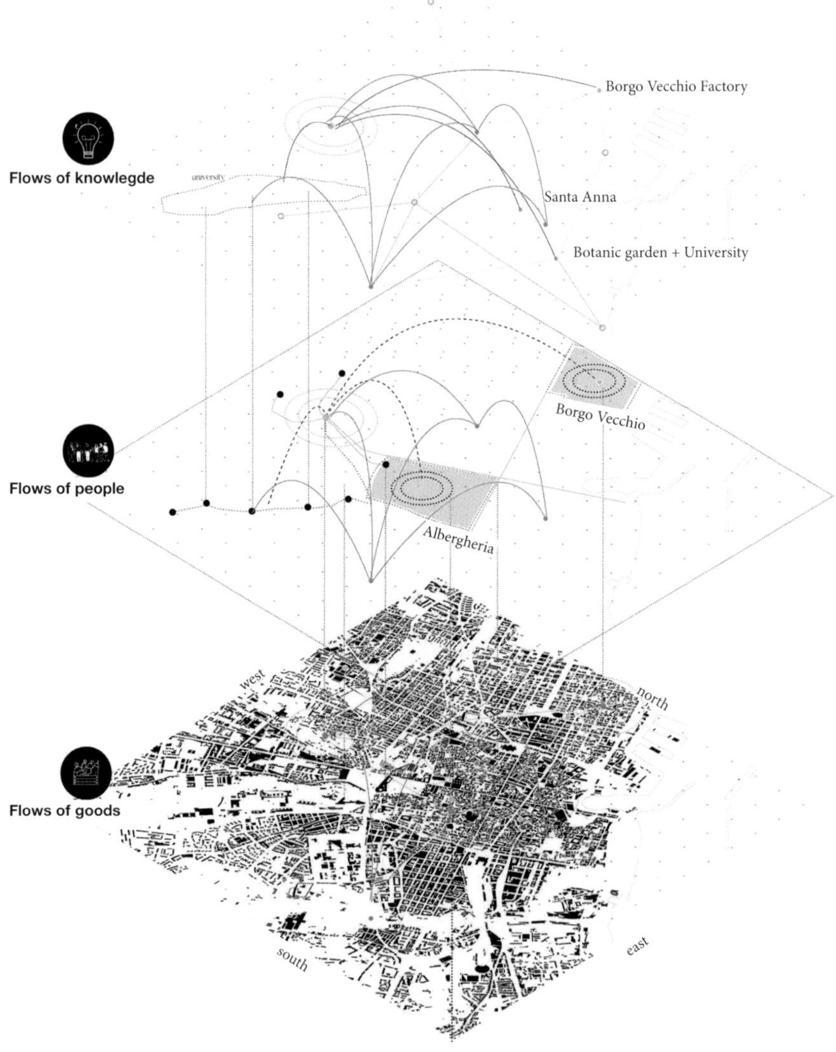

Figure 6
Palermo cosmopolitan dynamics
Elaboration using data from www.openstreetmap.org
Graphic by Mara Piel, Marie-Sophie Waldminghaus,
for the master's design studio at the Chair of Territorial Design and Urban Planning LUH

obsolete borders between urban design, urban planning, and urban studies, as well as their linkages with other disciplines. This also implies the questioning of the borders between analysis and synthesis on a new methodological basis.

Design research in urbanism

In opening up pathways for new theoretical access and for methodological and empirical tools in urbanism, the orientation towards *Cosmopolitan Habitat* provokes the extrapolation of two fields that promise higher methodological precision:

- **a specific concentration on space,** the way it changes, and its relation to context in the form of complex, evolving constellations and processes, pointing to a better understanding of interactions between space, culture, economy, and society as well as of material/digital interrelations, and
- **a performative perspective on space,** provoking multiple forms of evidence in material, formal, functional, perceptive, and imaginative senses; setting experience, movement, and action in space as part of empirical inquiry.

In the first instance, however, it is clear that certain questions need to be delineated more clearly. This is particularly the case with regard to the dazzling role and concept of design as it is linked to the fundamental influence of cognition in urbanism. In this sense, the traditional understanding of design as spatial creativity deployed to a certain use, or the current prominence of "design-thinking", needs to be transformed in order to redefine the concept of design in urbanism. At the moment, design is seen as appealing due to its promise of easily measurable "products", and theoretical definitions so far have concentrated on systematisation in assessing problems and developing solutions (Archer 1964), as well as in identifying cognitive and practical skills underlying design thinking and expertise in design (Cross 1982). In a response to this, Frayling (1993) discussed possible ways of including design in research, among them the use of design as empiric tool. A further step needs to be taken for a "cosmopolitan turn": developing a methodology for the use of cognitive, strategic, and projectual aspects (Visser 2006) in a processual concept of design in interaction with social feedback loops of circular design (Schröder 2020). In this sense, cognition in urbanism gains a deeply interactive character and becomes—intrinsically linked to design—an interface between orientation knowledge and instrumental knowledge.

Urban narratives

Several experimental case studies in *Cosmopolitan Habitat* explore how the challenge of climate change can provide a much-needed opportunity for methodological innovation. Due to the need for a new cultural and communicative approach to the fundamental change in ways of initiating, shaping and governing urban transformation, one of the recurring topics concerns narratives in urbanism. Narratives can be a particularly effective tool for integrating voices form a diversified society and multiple migratory backgrounds, both with regard to involving cultural resources (Jullien 2016) and in terms of constructing shared urban visions. There has been an ongoing discussion about storytelling as prescriptive or descriptive tool in urbanism since the 1990s (Ferretti 2018), which one could see as an opening-up of the discipline to cultural practices, cultural sciences, and the arts. On one hand, it has led to the drawing of functional typologies of "planning narratives" (Ameel 2020), but on the

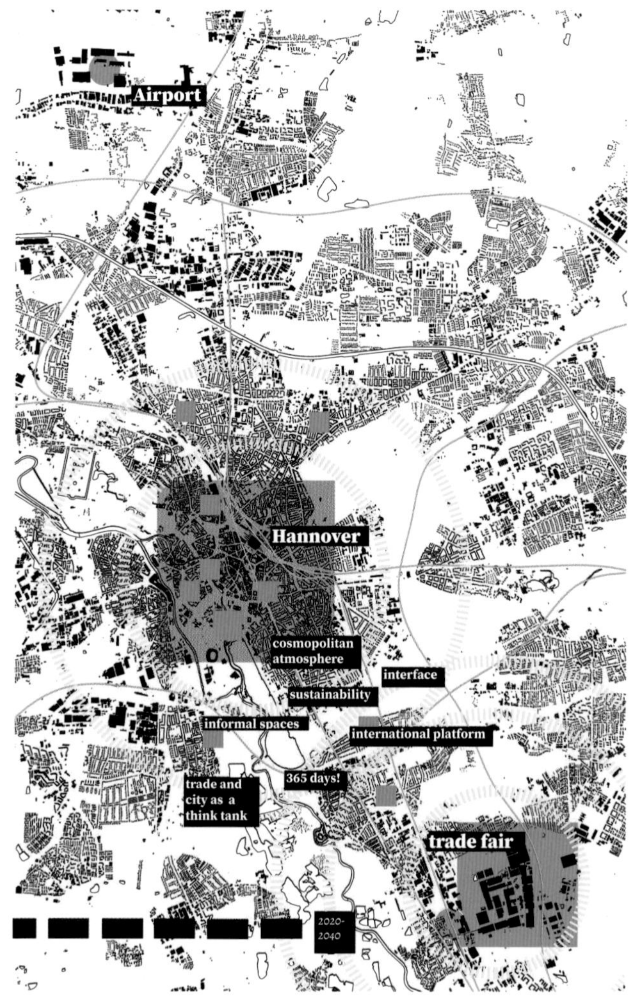

Figure 7
Hanover, the city and the trade fair: Cosmopolitan interface perspective
Graphic by Julia Hermanns for the Chair of Territorial Design and Urban Planning LUH

other hand it has also garnered criticism concerning a lack of transparency with regard to the role of narratives in urban projects and strategies, as well as about the way stories are generated and used in different narrative approaches (van Hulst 2012). In a further step, a more accurate look at possible transfer but also differences in regard to corporate design and branding has been discussed (Schröder, Ferretti 2018). In order to provide more transparency while also enhancing creativity and effectiveness, a closer examination of the interaction between different narrative approaches and of the linkages between scales (the city, certain places, urban spaces or buildings, or everyday activities and events) is necessary. This may be overlaid with the examination (and creation) of formats that include a diverse set of independent stories rather than master narratives (Childs 2008). As such, narratives can become also an effective tool for bridging top-down and bottom-up approaches in order to construct a common ground for shared visions. The ambiguous nature of narratives between analytical-interpretative and strategic-projectual, subjective and objective dimensions offers a promising field of research with regard to the genesis and impact of narratives in different constellations of context and process (Schröder, Cappeller 2020). Examining the hidden aspects of narratives as urbanistic know-how, critical reflection, and artistic exploration can lead to new insights into mechanisms for scaling up and co-creating structural change in cities. In this context, narratives also need to be set into discussions about design/research interfaces: to ask not only about creative and designerly components in the individual parts of processes of urban transformation—from analysis to strategy-building, implementation, adaption, and evaluation, with special attention to communication, participation, and engagement—but also to question their role in the overall process and its methodology. In the (deliberate and transparent) blending of performative analysis and projective visioning, a clearer methodological approach can support us in understanding and learning how a city—as a territorial system of interconnected layers, dynamics, and actors—is accessible in a diachronic and trans-scalar perspective (Solà-Morales 2002).

Thus, narratives support the recognition of potentials and limitations of fields and spaces of change. In a larger sense, they contribute to sharpening the tools of qualitative research in urbanism based on concepts of space not (only) as a separated "material imprint" of social-economic change, but as a hybrid construction of figurative, material, functional, and imaginative flows (Castells 1996) that is fundamental to urban agency. In this sense, urban space can become a medium and tool for sharing narratives as a form of cognition and knowledge production (Cappeller 2020). The work on urban narratives, therefore, aims to develop new concepts and tools in urbanism: through a performative and creative analysis that links multiple avenues of research, including texts and movies, references and innovative forms of mapping, diagramming and information interaction, as well as through a strategic and inter-scalar projectual and structural approach that combines spatial activators and connectors, urban patterns and networks, and urban practices. Several case studies on narratives and their influence on overall methodology are included in this book:

- **Cosmopolitan Postcards**: shifting between subject and object referentiality, the postcards were curated with the intention of comprehensively organising field research, photography, drawing, and interviews as well as direct contributions and statements by students, experts, and citizens. The use of Instagram offered a further examination of the influence of digital tools in the organisation of narratives.
- **Cosmopolitan Videoworks:** the videoworks occupy a position in-between description

and projection, questioning what role boundaries, limits, and borders can play in opening up the potentials not only of a city but of its inscribed energies, concepts, and practices in shaping urban space, that are directed towards more interactive, more material, and more emotional qualities of space.

- **Projects: Open City** (Schröder, Scaffidi 2020) and **Projects: Urban Narratives** (Schröder, Cappeller 2020) represent urban analysis and design projects directed towards inventive exploration as a basis for strategies that not only deal with, but actively foster positive spatial change and dynamics; they combines spatial activators and connectors, urban patterns and networks, and urban practices. On a conceptual level, the move from staying fixed to oppositions towards the consideration of dynamic factors and polarities—crossing the inherent limits of systems—implies extending the notion of city towards more complex spatial relationality.

If urbanism is called on to contribute a novel and relevant perspective for the role of cities in climate change, this perspective cannot be intended only to foster existing practice and to evaluate good practices. The current and coming challenges demand a wave of research and innovation in urbanism. It needs to explicitly derive its contribution to societal questions and its positioning in academia from a new focus on design and creativity.

BIBLIOGRAPHY

Albers G. (1997) *Zur Entwicklung der Stadtplanung in Europa*. Wiesbaden, Vieweg.

Ameel L. (2020) *The Narrative Turn in Urban Planning*. London, Routledge.

Archer B. (1964) *Systematic method for designers*. London, Council of Industrial Design.

Beck U. (1992) *Risk Society: Towards a New Modernity*. London, Sage. Originally published in German in 1986 as *Die Risikogesellschaft* by Suhrkamp, Frankfurt.

Beck U. (2006) *The Cosmopolitan Vision*. Cambridge and Malden, Polity Press.

Beck U. (2011) "Cosmopolitan Sociology: Outline of a Paradigm Shift". In: Rovisco M., Nowicka M. eds. (2011) *The Ashgate Research Companion to Cosmopolitanism*. Farnham, Ashgate.

Beck U. (2016) *The Metamorphosis of the World: How Climate Change Is Transforming Our Concept of the World*. Cambridge, Polity Press.

Cappeller R. (2020) "Cooperative Architecture. Urban Space as Medium and Tool to share Narratives". In: *FAM Magazine* 52–53, pp. 142–147.

Carta M. (2017) *Augmented City. A Paradigm Shift*. Trento and Barcelona, ListLab.

Castells M. (1996) *The Rise of the Network Society, The Information Age: Economy, Society and Culture Vol. I*. Cambridge, Blackwell.

Childs M. C. (2008) "Storytelling and urban design". In: *Journal of Urbanism* 1(2), pp. 173–186.

Cross N. (1982) "Designerly Ways of Knowing". In: *Design Studies* 3(4), pp. 221–227.

Ferretti M. (2018) "Narrative: stories from the periphery". In: Schröder J., Carta M., Ferretti M., Lino B. eds. (2018) *Dynamics of Periphery. Atlas of Emerging Creative and Resilient Habitats*. Berlin, Jovis, pp. 104–108.

Frayling C. (1993) "Research in Art and Design". In: *Royal College of Art Research Papers* Vol. 1(1). London, Royal College of Art.

Jullien F. (2016) *Il n'y a pas d'identité culturelle*. Paris, Éd. del'Herne.

Latour B. (2014) "Agency at the Time of the Anthropocene". In: *New Literary History* 45(1). Johns Hopkins University Press, pp. 1–18.

Lino B. (2020) "Branding as a Lever for Resilient Transformation". In: *Topos Magazine* (2020) Special issue: urbanes.land. Available online at: https://urbanesland.toposmagazine.com/client_articles/branding-as-a-lever-for-rresilient-transformation-the-sicani-mountains-in-sicily/ (20.12.2020).

Mittelstraß J. (2018) *Theoria. Chapters in the philosophy of science*. Berlin, de Gruyter.

Schröder J., Carta M., Ferretti M., Lino B. eds. (2018) *Dynamics of Periphery. Atlas of Emerging Creative and Resilient Habitats*. Berlin, Jovis, pp. 10–29.

Schröder J. (2018) "Open Habitat". In: Schröder J., Carta M., Ferretti M., Lino B. eds. (2018) *Dynamics of Periphery. Atlas of Emerging Creative and Resilient Habitats*. Berlin, Jovis, pp. 10–29.

Schröder J., Ferretti M. (2018) *Scenarios and Patterns for Regiobranding*. Berlin, Jovis.

Schröder J. (2020) "Circular Design for the Regenerative City: A Spatial-digital Paradigm". In: Schröder J., Sommariva E., Sposito S. (2020) *Creative Food Cycles - Book 1*. Hannover, Regionales Bauen und Siedlungsplanung, Leibniz Universität Hannover.

Schröder J., Scaffidi F. eds. (2020) *Palermo Open City*. Hannover, Regionales Bauen und Siedlungsplanung Leibniz Universität Hannover.

Schröder J., Cappeller R. eds. (2020) *Cosmopolitan Habitat: Urban Narratives*. Hannover, Regionales Bauen und Siedlungsplanung, Leibniz Universität Hannover.

Sennett R. (2018) *Building and Dwelling: Ethics for the City*. New York, Farrar, Straus and Giroux.

Solà-Morales I. (2002) *Territorios*. Barcelona, Gustavo Gili.

Van Hulst M. (2012) "Storytelling, a model of and a model for planning". In: *Planning Theory* 11(3), pp. 299–318.

Visser W. (2006) *The cognitive artifacts of designing*. Mahwah, Lawrence Erlbaum Associates.

von der Leyen U. (2020) "A New European Bauhaus". Op-ed article by Ursula von der Leyen, President of the European Commission. Available online at: http://ec.europa.eu/commission/presscorner/detail/en/AC_20_1916 (15.10.2020).

Weber M. (1919) *Wissenschaft als Beruf*. München, Duncker & Humblot.

Figure 8
Urban Portraits, 2021
Photo by Leandra Leipold

“Denique caelesti sumus omnes semine oriundi; / omnibus ille idem pater est, unde alma liquentis / umoris guttas mater cum terra recepit, / feta parit nitidas fruges arbustaque laeta / et genus humanum, parit omnia saecla ferarum, / pabula cum praebet, quibus omnes corpora pascunt / et dulcem ducunt vitam prolemque propagant; / qua propter merito maternum nomen adepta est.

Once more, we all from seed celestial spring, / To all is that same father, from whom earth / The fostering mother, as she takes the drops / Of liquid moisture, pregnant bears her broods, / The shining grains, and gladsome shrubs and trees / And bears the human race and of the wild / The generations all, the while she yields / The foods wherewith all feed their frames and lead / The genial life and propagate their kind; / Wherefore she owneth that maternal name.

Lucretius, “De rerum natura”, 1st century BC
translated by William Ellery Leonard

PLANNING THE NEOCOSMOPOLITAN HABITAT

MAURIZIO CARTA

Living the new complexity: rethinking the cosmic city

Reflecting on cosmopolitanism is a philosophical activity before it is a political, social or—as far as we are concerned—urban planning action. It requires a deep reflection on the meaning of being connected to a place *and also* to the whole world, of being individuals *and also* related to a planetary community and to the consequences of our inhabitation of the Earth (and the Cosmos). Nature, like us humans, is not made up of things in and of themselves, but of an entanglement of relationships and events, of evolutionary processes that take place in time and space (Rovelli, 2016). And even our cities do not escape this universal law: everything is correlation, flow, openness, vibration. In short, cosmopolitanism calls us to answer a cognitive challenge rather than a practical one. The current scenario at a global scale is characterised by a health, economic, social, and cultural crisis in which the rethinking of the mobility of people and the reduction of interactions is answered by the materialisation of borders, barriers, and confinements. Humanity is in a cognitive crisis that concerns the relationship it has with itself, with others, and with reality. We live in an increasingly complex world: one in which everything is connected, but also one within which dramatic disruptions are produced. Often, however, a paradigm of simplification dominates, which illusorily separates humanity from nature, locks us up within national borders, fragments knowledge, and stiffens identities. The spread of this model increases regressive tendencies and the risk of future catastrophes. Changing the paradigm in order to live the new complexity is the challenge of the twenty-first century. Accepting this challenge means rethinking fundamental human activities from the position of a new urban thinking. In a fearful society that withdraws into the confines of "small homelands", the concept of the open society itself—as discussed by Karl Popper (1945)—is challenged by new protectionisms and sovereignties.

To the already-complex management of the presence, at both local and global scales, of multi-ethnic and multicultural societies with an influence on traditions and local identity is added the difficulty of managing a coronavirus pandemic that runs along the infrastructures of cosmopolitanism. To this it should be added that the proliferation of inequalities, social conflicts, and situations of personal distress makes the issue of social inclusion even more relevant through the renewed experience

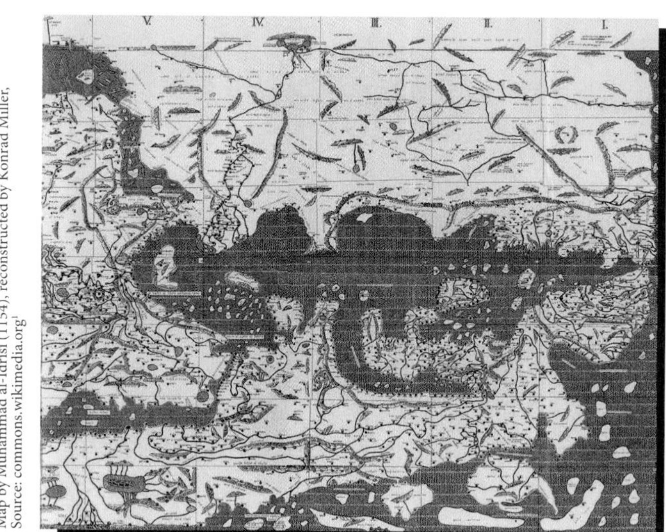

Figure 1a
Mediterranean in the Tabula Rogeriana
Map by Muhammad al-Idrisi (1154), reconstructed by Konrad Miller,
Source: commons.wikimedia.org[1]

Figure 1b
Atles català (Catalan Atlas)
Map by Abraham and Jehuda Cresques (1375), reproduction of the 20th century
Source: commons.wikimedia.org[2]

of the planetary dimension of our humanity. The scenario of metamorphosis we are experiencing pushes us even further to review paradigms and rethink—without abandoning—the real meaning of the Western cosmopolitan political tradition (Beck, 2006). The cosmopolitan political tradition in European thought begins with the Greek philosopher Diogenes, who, when asked where he came from, responded that he was a "citizen of the world", connected to both the *polis* (the city and its political dimension) and the *kosmos* (the world and its cultural dimension). Rather than declaring his lineage, city, social class, or gender, he defined himself as a human being, implicitly asserting the equal worth of all human beings. This was the philosophical and political basis for a human network of culture in the Mediterranean (figs. 1a, 1b); a true "civilisation factory", in the words of Paul Valéry (1931). Following centuries of philosophical and political definitions, the American philosopher Martha Nussbaum (2019) today proposes a "noble but flawed" vision of world citizenship. Given the global prevalence of material want, the lesser social opportunities of people with physical and cognitive disabilities, the conflicting beliefs of a pluralistic society, the challenges of mass migration and asylum-seeking, and the spread of an epidemic of disease, what political principles should we endorse? Nussbaum takes on the challenge of reconnecting humanity, nonhumans, and the natural world. And beyond this she argues for an even more thrilling vision: the whole biosphere conceived of and treated as a "cosmic city" in which humans carefully do their part to ensure that the capabilities of all creatures can be activated as much as possible. In her aspirational community, the commons afford each individual the resources she or he needs to flourish.

In this vision, cosmopolitanism takes on a novel dimension: the importance of not only being connected with the world of humans, but of needing to review our role as citizens of the planet entangled with the natural world and with the multiple identities of the cultures that enrich the cities we inhabit. A renewed, and broader, vision of cosmopolitanism brings us back, therefore, to the original meaning of the term as used by Diogenes. Being citizens of the world means being connected to all worlds—the worlds of other humans, animals, and plants, as well as those of data, ideas, research, rights, and so on. The *Cosmopolitan Habitat* is, therefore, the connection of all the components of the planet; the material and the immaterial ones. All these correlations precipitate in the physical space of our lives, enriching it and asking for adequate forms that allow them to be expressed: the world is our home and we are at home in the world, but we must redesign this "common habitat". Particularly in the times we live in, when the SARS-CoV-2 virus has raced across the planet, infecting more than 100 million people, killing more than 2 million, and forcing almost half of the world's population into lockdown, the pandemic has revealed humanity as an "imperfect species" (Pievani, 2019): arrogant, but fragile when disconnected from the world. A radical metamorphosis that profoundly changes the way we inhabit the planet (Beck, 2016) is needed to contain the pandemic's effect effects, overcome it, and rebuild the strong relationship between humans and nature.

As such, the concept of cosmopolitanism is not univocal: rather, it has some extremely varied and occasionally contrasting facets, making the word "cosmopolitanism" a permeable and pneumatic container that only the new project of a "cosmic city" can fill with renewed meaning. The new *cosmopolis* must be configured as an urban paradigm capable of shaping new forms of interconnected living. On the one hand, the *cosmopolis* is almost synonymous with a global city, capable of opening itself to the *kosmos* or to the different species living on the planet, and manifesting relationships, functions, meanings, and the added values that only a plural city is capable of manifesting.

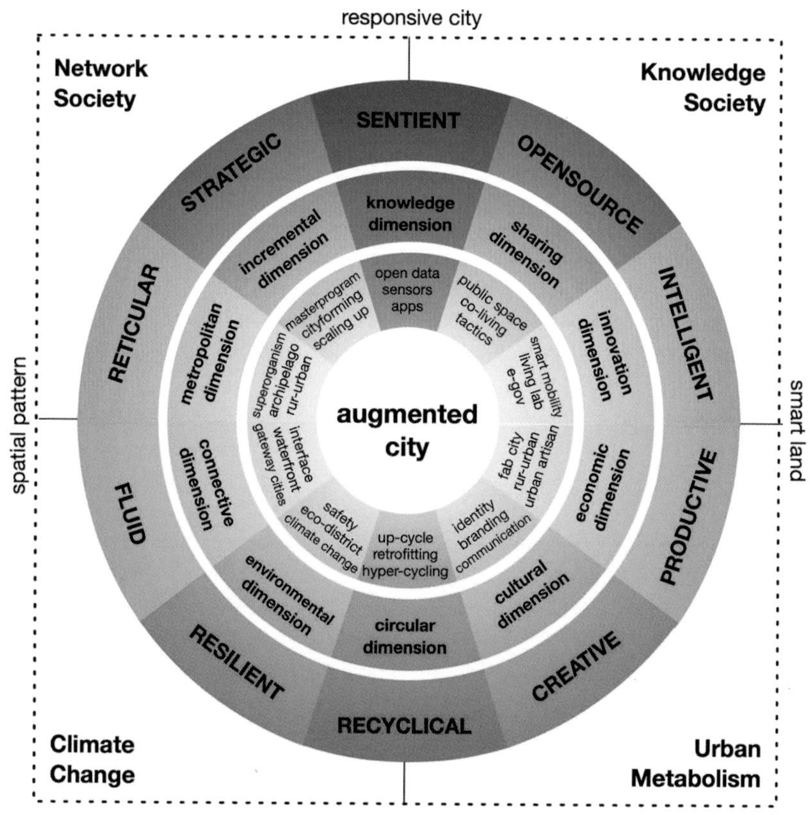

Figure 2
The Augmented City Circle:
ten dimensions for fighting against the four main challenges
Graphic by Maurizio Carta

Cosmopolis, however, is also a city in which the meaning of everything is enclosed within the system of relations between communities (multi-species) and the spaces (multi-level) they build and inhabit. The *cosmopolis* is a city in which the individual parts are appropriate to the citizens who live there, guaranteeing their fundamental rights to well-being and happiness. In the new *cosmopolis* we find the triple correspondence between cities, nature, and citizens; it manifests within itself the perfect form of this pact of interests. The spatial order of the cosmopolitan city is a mirror of the health—in its broader sense—of the inhabitants (human and nonhuman) who live there. As urban planners, we cannot stop at the level of philosophical and political thinking, but have the obligation to expand to the operative level: to understand what the structural places, functions, and relationships are in the new *cosmopolis*, and what elements characterise it. How does a cosmopolitan city operate in an age of rethinking connections and of the suspension of predatory globalisation? According to Jon Binnie (2006), we must face and overcome the limits of traditional "cosmopolitan urbanism".

A cosmopolitan city is inhabited by multicultural and multi-species communities that are open to the possibility of meeting each other and the possibility of mutual cooperation, as well as willing to face the plurality and hybridisation of public space and new places of living. The new cosmopolitan atmosphere enhances and shapes urban planning and design frameworks, providing the city with new places that are the result of complex relationships. Some of these places are those of the contemporary city, but frequently animated by new meanings: the streets, the squares and the courtyards, the city gates and places that generate flows (ports, airports, stations, etc.), the places of culture strengthened by a new distributed localisation of services (theatres that extend into the streets, museums that meets the suburbs, schools that extend their activities to the outdoors, etc.), as well as gardens and parks that are connected through an urban ecological network and enter buildings or climb onto roofs, becoming places for free time, culture, and education. These spaces characterise the quality and the reputation of the cosmopolitan city. Thus, we must explore a new cosmopolitanism—a Neocosmopolitan habitat—based on digital connections and local safety, on openness to the world and the empowerment of local communities, on hybrid spaces and new citizens. The Neocosmopolitan cities must be able to span the different scales of different worlds: the large scale of global relations and the small scale of the different worlds of proximity to which cities must open up, shaping their spaces both to enable correlations and to guarantee "cosmopolitanism from below" (Appadurai 2013)—which opposes class, neighbourhood and language conflicts. The Neocosmopolitan habitat is composed of heterotopic spaces "because they break up and entangle commonplaces" (Foucault, 1966); it is based on building global connections and local solidarity among humans and non-humans. It is a true "multi-specific city" (Coccia 2020). Therefore, it doesn't merely call for maintenance or minor updates: it calls for "futuredesign" (Carta 2019), a radical attitude of being proactive towards the future, designing it instead of forecasting it. In face of this radicality, we must adopt a new paradigm, more dynamic, plural and open, but we need a shift!

The Neoanthropocene turn

We are in a syndemic: a perverse alliance between different pathologies of unsustainable development (Singer 2009). While most analysts have been searching for the "black swan" (Taleb 2007), waiting fearfully for the arrival of an unexpected event to generate the next crisis, nobody has wanted to see the "grey rhino"—a well-known risk that we would like to ignore—running furiously towards us, announcing the latest leap in the severity of the environmental crisis; the umpteenth consequence of

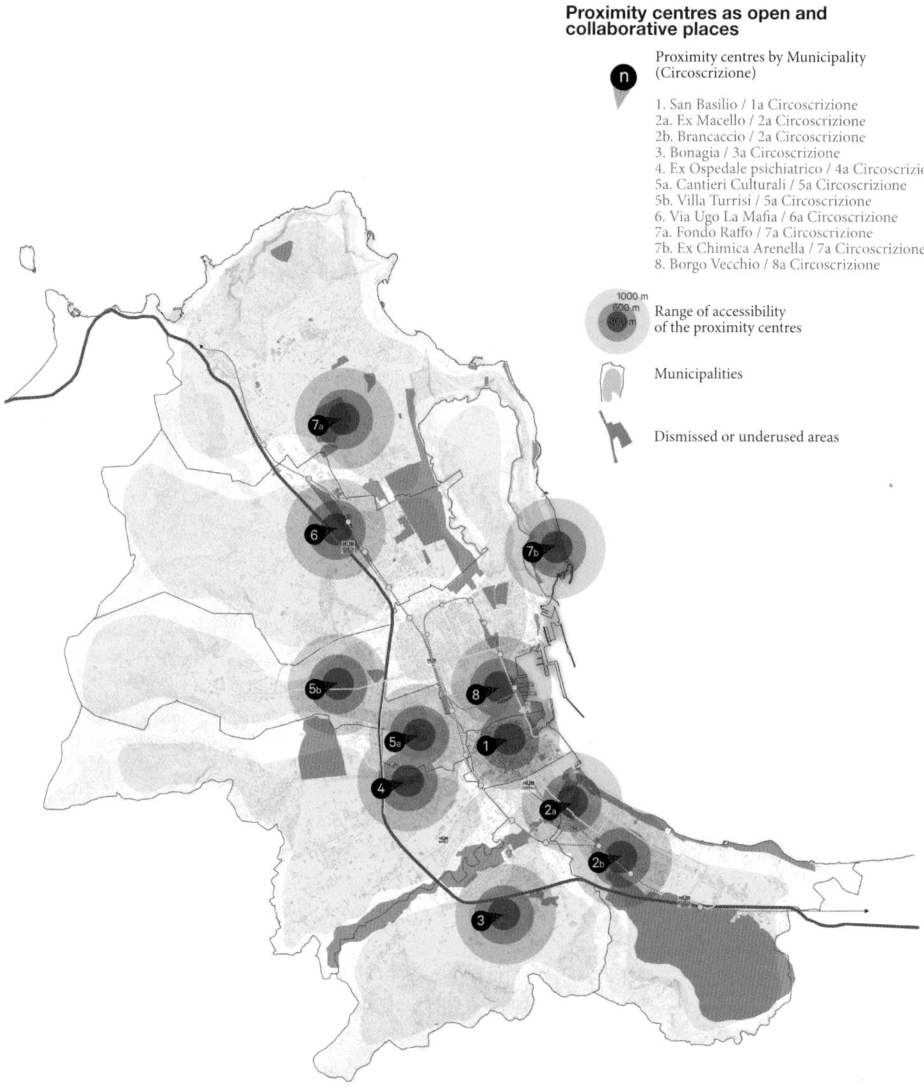

Figure 3
The archipelago of proximity centres as open and collaborative places in Palermo
Graphic by DARCH, Unipa, 2020

climate change on our lives. After numerous unheard alarms (Meadows et al. 1972; Rockström et al. 2009), the Covid-19 epidemic was, in fact, a signal sent by the planet to our species to warn us to change: 98% of the Earth (nature) rebelled against the enormous environmental impact produced by the voracity of the remaining 2% (cities). The virus, indeed, has torn apart humanity's illusion that it has emancipated itself from ecosystem dynamics and is independent of nature, dominating it with arrogance. Humanity must return to living in balance with other living species and with the planet itself, because we have entered the "new climate regime" (Latour 2017); we must abandon the presumed superiorities behind which we hid the real fragility of our urban systems throughout their predatory expansion. We are not, in fact, facing yet another normal crisis, but are instead in the apical phase of an "ecological pandemic" produced by the territorial, social, economic, and climatic changes generated by the Anthropocene (Stoermer, Crutzen 2000). Responsible for expansive urbanisation that has ravenously devoured natural soil, cultural palimpsests, vegetable plots, coasts and mountains, forests and beaches and generated huge social injustice, the Anthropocene is the "super-spreader" of the syndemics that affect our lives and our world. So, we must broaden our vision of the health-critical, adopting the syndemics model of health for our world. This model focuses on the biosocial complex, which consists of interacting, co-present, or sequential diseases and the social and environmental factors that promote and enhance the negative effects of disease interaction. Specifically, the syndemics approach examines the ways in which social environments, especially conditions of social inequality and injustice, contribute to disease clustering and interaction as well as to vulnerability (Horton 2020). We need a competent and systematic reflection in order to learn from the crisis, to understand how to revolutionise our behaviours once the pandemic has been defeated, and to avoid—or mitigate—the next crisis (which is inevitable if we do not change our development model).

How can cities become a safer place to invent, explore, experiment, and live as open community in the dramatic times of Covid-19? What are our strategies for facing global challenges while simultaneously enhancing urban inclusiveness and urban economies? How can cities act as open and interconnected places and, at the same time, guarantee the right to health? The Covid-proof city should both increase its safety measures and provide appropriate solutions to climate change. But more than this, a Covid-proof city should renew its cosmopolitan dimension, working around more complex dimensions of urban life. Today, as we overcome the epidemic, we must learn from the crisis and use the innovative force of "emancipatory catastrophism" (Beck 2015) to effect a restart that involves greater awareness and incorporates rules and actions that accelerate a reconsideration of our way of living on this planet. We need a changed development model based on a new alliance with nature; one based on the adoption of a proactive attitude that allows us to act today, planning a for future that is not dystopian but that produces a different present; a present founded on a renewed alliance between all living species, on a new relationship between cities and territories, and on rethinking the identity of places and their interconnections. In the face of this crisis, active planners and city makers must experiment to achieve effective, sustainable development that is visionary and pragmatic at the same time (Carta 2019), convinced that we can live in a "good Anthropocene" where humanity assumes the responsibility of solving the problems it has created (Rockström, Klum 2015). We must manage the transition from the consumption-based Paleoanthropocene to an emerging generative and responsible "Neoanthropocene" (Carta 2017; Carta, Ronsivalle 2020), reactivating the traditional alliance between human and natural components as co-acting forces; we must be guided by an

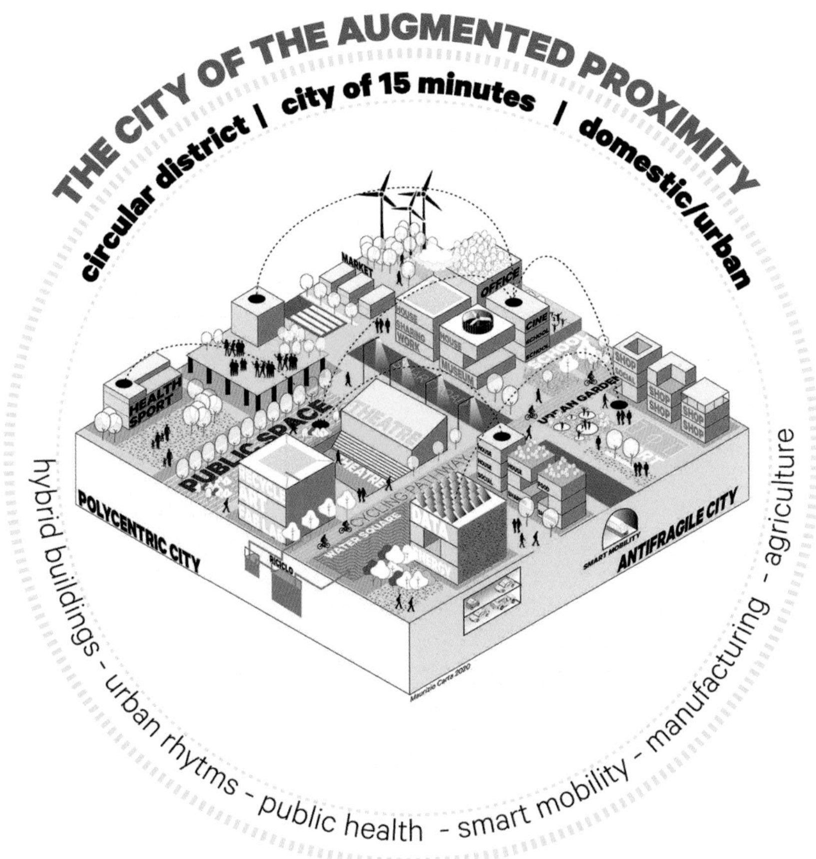

Figure 4
Conceptual diagram of the city of the augmented proximity
Graphic by Maurizio Carta, 2020

ethic of integration between humanity and nature and between cities and the environment in order to take collective responsibility for acting against climate change.

Designing the Neocosmopolitan augmented city

As researchers, educators and planners, the Neoanthropocene challenges us to adopt a responsible and militant approach and to have the courage to enact a metamorphosis that not only reduces the ecological footprint of human activity, but which uses the collective intelligence resulting from new ideas and sensitivity to the environment, landscapes, and cultural heritage, spreading across the globe as a renewed, integral ecology that is turned into planning protocols and tools, urban devices and spaces, and new life cycles. The commitment of decision-makers, planners, architects, citizens, and enterprises will be needed to work on urban settlements characterised by surplus and overproduction derived from changing urban patterns, on dismissed settlement fabrics, rural areas in transition, and infrastructure networks in transformation. These places will need to be addressed through actions of modification, removal, or re-invention that reboot the components— without destroying them—in order to reactivate some functions for pursuing generative perspectives and increasing their generative resilience. At the end, we need a new species of cities and communities, which I call "augmented cities" (Carta 2017), as the habitat for humans and nonhumans in the Neoanthropocene. The augmented city is a new paradigm that generates a spatial, social, cultural, and economic device capable of providing new and urgent answers to the metamorphosis we are going through. It is the answer to the four main challenges of contemporary society: improving the knowledge society, rethinking the network society, fighting climate change, and implementing the urban metabolism (Fig. 2). The effects of the Anthropocene are mainly urban, because the expansion of cities has devoured the natural soil, the identity structures of the cultural palimpsests, and the vegetable plots of the cities; it has invaded delicate natural ecosystems, awakening and expanding diseases previously confined to wild environments. How can we extricate ourselves from the planetary environmental crisis, which is above all a crisis of urban habitats? The answer can only be urban, and based on a rethinking of cities as places for living in balance with other living species, in homeostasis with the planet. Especially in Europe, we must update the idea of cities as privileged places of creativity, public health, and social justice. This means returning to designing cities that are compact but porous to nature and polycentric with differentiated identities; that have a more adequate circular metabolism of water, food, energy, nature, waste; and that place people in greater proximity to services, places of production, and public health networks. The pandemic teaches us that we must redesign in order to regenerate, as the ecological degradation produced by the Anthropocene proved to be untreatable with growth—which ultimately was an outrageous predator of the planet's vital resources, a generator of recursive crises (Morin 2020), and an accelerator of inequalities.

The regeneration of human habitats after the climate, health, and economic crisis will require changing our ways of living in domestic and collective spaces and workspaces, as well as learning from the new practices that we are currently experiencing as a result of social distancing (new, mature digital relationships, modalities of sustainable mobility, cooperative solidarity, etc.). The objectives of Neocosmopolitan Augmented City must be to:

- amplify the short radius of proximity, extending and enriching the functions of living in a polycentric pattern;

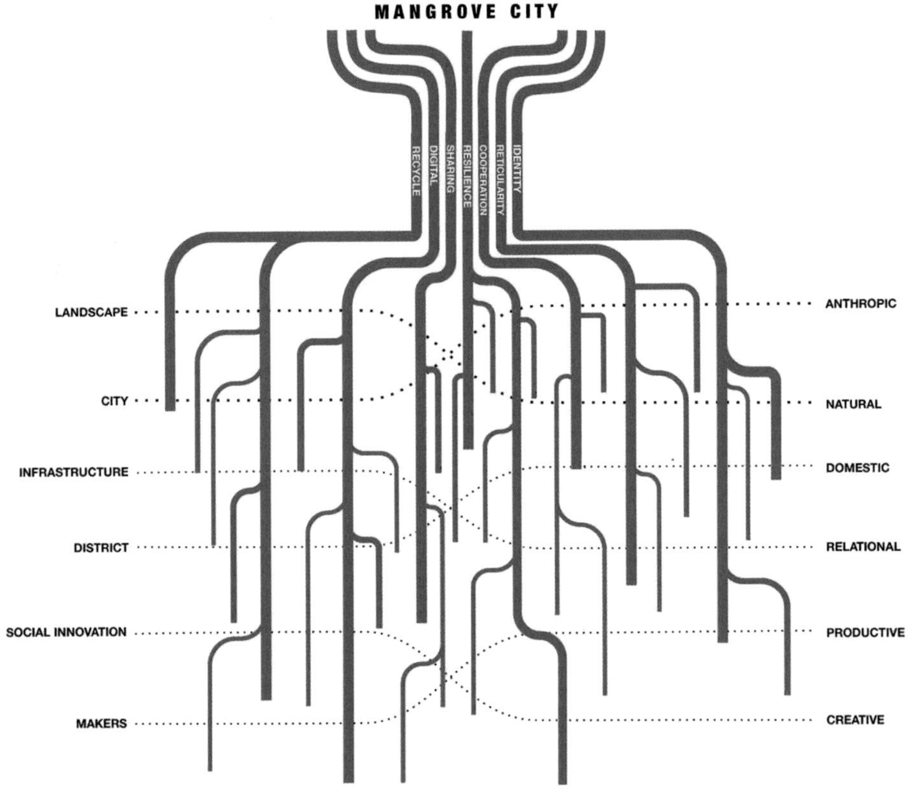

Figure 5
Conceptual diagram of the mangrove city as a Neocosmopolitan habitat
Graphic by Maurizio Carta, 2020

"Mangrove cities as Neocosmopolitan habitats: metamorphic spaces that generate interscaling, hybrid, and inter-specific places for human, natural, and spatial regeneration."

- strengthen the spatialisation of activities and flows, verifying their effects on urban space;
- rethink the density / intensity of urban functions in more flexible and less rigidly abstract forms;
- insert nature into public and collective spaces to reconnect the human habitat to the natural world.

In concrete terms, we must replace the rigid separation of our places for living, working, leisure, and producing, which currently require unsustainable physical mobility, with an urban and architectural project of circular places that do not produce waste and which, amplified by technological and digital innovation, can accommodate temporary and multiple functions within a cycle that takes into account the whole day or year in the distribution of functions, in its collaboration with nature, in attracting temporary uses, in the reception of functions with high level of innovation, in the refuge of citizens in difficulty. Places that are no longer rigid and fragmented, with an inertia that deters them from hosting new functions, but are instead flexible, transforming quickly to adapt to the increasingly elastic needs of post-pandemic cities. Pneumatic places that expand and contract as needed, both in the course of the normal transformation of cities and even more so in the event of an emergency. Houses, schools, hospitals, and offices will change after discovering new functions that they may contain, eliminate, or exchange with other places.

Above all, we will no longer have to plan the traditional distribution of houses, schools, offices, squares, roads, gardens, parks, hospitals, and theatres, but will instead have to facilitate a fertile bricolage of places which, when needed, together act as houses, schools, offices, squares, parks, orchards, theatres, bookstores, museums, and places that provide care, with all spaces taking on multiple roles in the life cycle of cosmopolitan communities. We must activate new spaces and networks in the Neocosmopolitan habitat, using the accelerating capacity of openness, connections, and transcalarity to lead us towards attractive places, new mixed uses for abandoned spaces, and new distributed urban networks. Rethinking crisis-proof urban space means reasserting—innovating—the open society as a matrix of cosmopolitanism in order to reactivate cities as powerful generators of freedom, rights, equality, culture and places of plurality and relationship: a system of individual social issues that leave their tribe and relate (with new and more adequate prevention and health responses) to the rich tumult of the community, returning to exercise a fruitful proxemics of urban spaces (Hall 1966). The challenge for Neocosmopolitan augmented cities will be to recover their natural polycentrism: the diversity of their neighbourhoods which, ceasing to be fragile suburbs, will return to being places for lives and not just for homes; bridging the educational, working, cultural, natural and digital divides, acquiring micro-places of public health and becoming self-sufficient energy communities, providing facilities for women, children, and young people, and bringing nature back into our homes. I imagine cities with renewed and richer urban proxemics, made up of an archipelago of communities (Fig. 3) that reduce their frantic centripetal mobility and that facilitate a more measured mobility, thereby guaranteeing the answer to many—though not all—needs within fifteen minutes of the home. Paris, Barcelona, and Milan are among a number of cities currently experimenting with this model. It will therefore be necessary to extend the domestic space by expanding those intermediate spaces that enable a life of safe relationships: widening sidewalks and providing temporary pedestrianisation to expand playgrounds for children and for adult activity, creating new tactical urbanism interventions for bar and restaurant seating that guarantees necessary social

DIMENSIONS OF COSMOPOLITANISM

1. CULTURAL

in terms of the integration of cultures and the breadth of cultural relations

OBJECTIVES / FACTORS	INDICATORS
1.1 Syncretism of urban space	• Multifunctional spaces (equipment, accessibility, facilitation) • Flexible spaces (equipment, increase, accessibility) • Spaces for empowerment and leadership from below, spaces for dialogue and cultural mediation, places for deliberative assemblies (equipment, ease of use, initiatives)
1.2 Places of internationalisation	• Major cultural attractors of global significance, e.g., theatres. museums, foundations, monumental sites, etc. (equipment, eputation, accessibility, openness, connection)
1.3 Places of cultures, narratives and religions	• Cultural centres, institutes for the promotion of foreign cultures, places of prayer, neighbourhood libraries, narrative shows, social theatres (equipment, programming,accessibility, users, attendance)
1.4 Places of creativity and innovation	• Fablab, co-working, atelier, creative companies (equipment, users, accessibility)
1.5 Image of the place	• Street art and other visual and performing arts devices in non-dedicated spaces, audio, video, artistic installations, film locations and film commission activities (diffusion, involvement, frequency)

2. SOCIAL

in terms of cohesion and well-being of people and the pursuit of aspirations

OBJECTIVES / FACTORS	INDICATORS
2.1 Social dynamism	• Spaces for formal and informal education (equipment, users, accessibility, ease of use) • Spaces for the protection of rights and legal assistance (equipment, users, accessibility, ease of use, number of initiatives) • Support for starting work, active job policies, social incubators, patronages, places of cultural mediation, community associations, international collaboration networks (equipment, users, accessibility, ease of use, capillarity)
2.2 Living	• Co-housing, social housing (equipment, mixité, accessibility, type of in habitants)
2.3 Sustainable mobility	• Local public transport, car / bike-sharing, carpooling (equipment, frequency, ease of use, capillarity)
2.4 Personal services	• Social, health and welfare services, night shelter centres, family communities, socio-educational communities for minors, nursing homes for the elderly, reception centres for immigrants, recreational services for children and young people, playground (equipment, users, capillarity, openness, ease of access)

* **INDICATORS**
Indicative and non-exhaustive examples of architectural, urban, political, functional, and organizational response devices capable of configuring the cosmopolitan city (the possible units of measurement of the impacts in brackets)

3. ECONOMIC
in terms of widespread productivity and community development

OBJECTIVES / FACTORS	INDICATORS
3.1 Economic growth	• Spaces for production and micro-production, traditional and innovative manufacturing (equipment, users, accessibility, ease of use, affordability)
3.2 Differentiated offer of internal trade	• Multi-ethnic markets, international gastronomic districts (equipment, users, openness, variety of offer)
3.3 Internationalization of trade and the economy	• Facilitation of foreign investments, attraction of companies from abroad, strengthening of ports and airports also with exchange and exhibition services connected to the international level, location of the headquarters of large companies, consulates and offices for international exchange, congress centre, fair (number initiatives, equipment, users, accessibility, ease of use, administrative simplifications, support infrastructures, incentives and tax breaks)
3.4 Reduction of construction costs and building regeneration and property management	• Energy efficiency of buildings, new eco-sustainable construction techniques, refurbishment of abandoned buildings, Smart buildings (equipment, innovation, ease of access, inhabitants involved)

4. ECOLOGICAL
in terms of fight against climate change and mitigation of effects

OBJECTIVES / FACTORS	INDICATORS
4.1 Reduction of carbon emission and of other polluting substances	• Carbon neutral building, zero soil consumption, closure of the water and waste cycles, energy efficiency, environmental education (surface, volume, reduction of consumption, number of initiatives, users involved, extension, effectiveness)
4.2 Enhancement of soil permeability	• Greenways, urban agriculture, urban forestry, depaving, water squares and lamination areas, blue infrastructures (surface, extension, permeability rate)
4.3 Promotion of the biodiversity and the relation nature-city	• Urban horticulture and farms, botanical gardens, greenhouses, community gardens, landscape design, vegetal walls and roofs (extension, surface, agricultural and farm production, biodiversity)
4.4 Spaces for the coexistence among species	• Educational farms, spaces for pets, beehives, aviaries, greenhouses for butterflies, biospheres, land art, urban foraging activities (diffusion, surface, variety of species, people involved)

Figure 6
Cosmopolitan Impact Chart
Source: DARCH, Unipa, 2020

distancing, re-naturalising spaces, bringing theatres and cinemas into public spaces, reusing abandoned buildings to accommodate shared functions. This is my proposal for the "city of augmented proximity": a sort of pneumatic, osmotic belt that enriches our domestic spaces, becoming a city project that fills our neighbourhoods with vegetable gardens, productive activities, and spaces for a safe and distributed relational life (Fig. 4). A domesticity augmented by public space and defined by a proximity perimeter that allows residents to take advantage of activities that are not only individual, but also collective—cosmopolitan in the sense previously explained—within the limits of safety and capable of being isolated in case of danger. An open habitat generated by the people who live there and who move in and through it in a permanent urban entanglement. And, finally, to boost this correlation between spaces, we need to design a large and effective network of greenways: real arteries for human and natural mobility. A pathway for slow mobility that safely connects neighbourhoods, liberating space from parasitic car parks, ensuring safety; a pathway that uses and reuses parks and gardens, disused railways, and courtyards and alleys.

Measuring cosmopolitan impact to augment capabilities

The urban habitat can achieve this new cosmopolitanism only if it rethinks the impacts of openness and identity as well as those of the relationship between the global (to be rethought) and the local (to be reactivated). It is time to ask whether the urban metabolism can also assume the characteristics of the *Cosmopolitan Habitat* that are aimed at generating the happiness of its inhabitants through choices and behaviour that improve the circularity of the city in a new alliance with different communities and species. The heterotopic *Cosmopolitan Habitat* is alive, and comes alive, with outside elements that contribute to its nature as a city open to the world and inside elements that offer open urban experiences. New scenarios of action and fields of experimentation for urban planning are opening up in the oscillation between local place and world. The main challenges to which the cosmopolitan city refers are gathered around three issues: a) the resolution of the social conflict and spatial tensions resulting from migration, alongside the identification of urban practices that are able to empower plural coexistence and integration (places of hospitality and sharing, informal urban planning and associations' activities in support of coexistence and integration); b) the generation of world-places as local nodes of global networks to support a cosmopolitan culture (places of internationalisation, multicultural centres, spaces for creativity and innovation); c) the reconnection of human, animal and vegetal ecosystems as a common platform for coexistence. The new cosmopolitan spatial/social structure of the city demands an evaluation of the impact of cosmopolitan makers in co-creating urban change. Decision makers and urban planners must face the challenge of evaluating and conceptualising the impacts of the new cosmopolitanism using an appropriate set of indicators and measures. In order to lead our design activity and responsibilities, the Augmented City Lab of the University of Palermo therefore proposes (as an open-source research agenda) a first set or beta version of cosmopolitan impact parameters based on four dimensions of cosmopolitanism (the cultural, social, economic, and ecological dimensions) as well as on relative objectives and factors (as shown in Fig. 6) measured by a number of indicators. This set of parameters can be considered a checklist for planning the Neocosmopolitan Habitat.

Conclusions

In order to not squander the evolutionary force of the crisis we are living through, we must not merely be satisfied with a different way of thinking: we must implement concrete actions. Therefore, the transformation towards syndemics-proof *Cosmopolitan Habitats* will have to be based on four challenges:

- improving tools and measures for representing new, inter-specific urban phenomena,using the greatest number of different sources (human and natural, social and technological, formal and informal) and new parameters in order to integrate them into a cosmopolitan governance (are the decision-makers cosmopolitan enough?);
- facilitating civic and natural hacking and the collaborative reshaping of habitats;
- stimulating ecological, gender, ethnic, and cultural policies; acting by time planning in order to rethink urban multi-rhythms;
- rethinking, including through the use of new rules and design tools, the location of natural/urban functions and the configuration of fabrics according to a polycentric, reticular, and open vision of the city.

After we humans have defeated our microscopic but powerful antagonist, and after we have learned to change the way we live on the planet, the anti-syndemic Neocosmopolitan city will be both safer and more open thanks to the resilience, creativity, and new hybridisation that we will have introduced into its spatial fabrics. The city of the Anthropocene was the trigger for the viral pandemic; the crisis-proof city must be an antidote and antibody for it. But the time has come for the 'tipping point' from the fragile, rigid, and fragmented city of the twentieth century to the flexible, porous, and cosmopolitan city of the twenty-first century; from the predatory city to the open and generative city of the Neoanthropocene.

FOOTNOTES

1_http://commons.wikimedia.org/wiki/File:Tabula_Rogeriana_1929_copy_by_Konrad_Miller.jpg

2_http://commons.wikimedia.org/wiki/File:Europe_Mediterranean_Catalan_Atlas.jpeg

BIBLIOGRAPHY

Appadurai A. (2013) *The Future as Cultural Fact. Essays on the Global Condition.* New York, Verso Books.

Beck U. (2006) *The Cosmopolitan Vision.* Cambridge, Polity Press.

Beck U. (2015) "Emancipatory Catastrophism: What does it Mean to Climate Change and Risk Society?". In: *Current Sociology* 63(1).

Beck U. (2016) *The Metamorphosis of the World.* Cambridge, Polity Press.

Binnie J., Holloway J., Millington S., Young C., eds. (2006) *Cosmopolitan Urbanism.* Routledge, London.

Carta M. (2017) *Augmented City. A Paradigm Shift.* Trento, ListLab.

Carta M. (2019) *Futuro. Politiche per un diverso presente.* Soveria Mannelli, Rubbettino.

Carta M., Ronsivalle D. (2020) "Neoanthropocene Raising and Protection of Natural and Cultural Heritage: A Case Study in Southern Italy". In: *Sustainability* 12(10). p. 4186.

Coccia E. (2020) *Métamorphoses.* Paris, Payot & Rivages.

Crutzen P. J., Stoermer E. F. (2000) "The Anthropocene". In: *Global Change Newsletter* 41, pp. 17–18.

Foucault M. (1966) *Les Mots et les Choses. Une archéologie des sciences humaines.* Paris, Gallimard.

Hall E. (1966) *The Hidden Dimension.* Garden City, N.Y., Doubleday.

Horton R. (2020) *The COVID-19 Catastrophe: What's Gone Wrong and How to Stop It Happening Again.* Cambridge, Polity Press.

Latour B. (2017) *Facing Gaia: Eight Lectures on the New Climatic Regime.* London, Polity Press.

Lovelock J. (1972) "Gaia as seen through the atmosphere". In: *Atmospheric Environment* 6(8), pp 579–580.

Meadows D.H., Meadows, D.L., Randers J., Behrens III W.W. (1972) *The Limits to Growth.* New York, Universe Book.

Morin E. (2020) *Sur la crise: Pour une crisologie suivi de Où va le monde?* Paris, Flammarion.

Nussbaum M. (2019) *The Cosmopolitan Tradition: A Noble But Flawed Ideal.* Cambridge (MA), Belknap Press.

Pievani T. (2019) *Imperfezione. Una storia naturale.* Milano, Cortina.

Popper K. (1945) *The Open Society and Its Enemies.* London, Routledge.

Raworth K. (2018) *Doughnut Economics: Seven Ways to Think Like a 21st-Century Economist.* London, Random House.

Rockström J., et al. (2009) "Planetary Boundaries: Exploring the Safe Operating Space for Humanity". In: *Ecology and Society*, 14(2).

Rockström J., Klum M. eds. (2015) *Big World, Small Planet: Abundance within Planetary Boundaries.* Yale, Yale University Press.

Rovelli C. (2016) *Seven Brief Lessons on Physics.* London, Penguin.

Schroeder J., Carta M., Ferretti M., Lino B. eds. (2018) *Dynamics of Periphery. Atlas of Emerging Creative Resilient Habitats.* Berlin, Jovis.

Singer M. (2009) *Introduction to Syndemics: A Critical Systems Approach to Public and Community Health.* New York, Wiley.

Taleb N. C. (2007) *The Black Swan: The Impact of the Highly Improbable.* New York, Random House.

Valéry P. (1931) "La méditerranée est une fabrique de civilisation". In: *Regards sur le monde actuel.* Paris, Librarie Stock.

World Health Organisation (2007) *A Safer Future: Global Public Health Security in the 21st century.* Geneva, WHO Press. Available online at: http://www.who.int/whr/2007/en/ (17.03.2020).

"A visual collection that continuously grows as an urban study, inviting to explore the cosmopolitan."

COSMOPOLITAN POSTCARDS

RICCARDA CAPPELLER, JULIA HERMANNS

The *Cosmopolitan Postcards* are a first approach to narratives in the context of *Cosmopolitan Habitat*: they represent a visual and collective brainstorming, realised through postcards produced in a digital format and collected on Instagram. As investigators and as interpreters of voices collected in interviews and of observed activities, students condense micro-narratives into the form of quotations, images, and drawings. This curatorial approach facilitates discussions about subjective views, the ways they interact, and polyphony. The investigation addressed the cities of the universities involved—Palermo and Hanover—and the locations of the case studies. The structured and directed approach of collecting these visual narratives is methodologically articulated through exploration, the selection of narratives, representation, and reflection in a constant process of laying out questions and findings: gathering and transmitting ideas, thoughts, associations, and "found footage" from different places. The main idea was to start a visual collection able to grow continuously throughout the research project and contribute to a translation of the conceptual idea into a real-life study, encouraging different participants to think about cosmopolitanism and communicate it as postcards to send away, collect digitally, and bring together in a later exhibition. The visual translations, metaphors, and associations make the topic easier to grasp and understand; they provide examples and illustrate atmospheres, places, or situations that might already transmit cosmopolitan aspects and ideas without intending to do so, supplying hints that provoke deeper examination. The design of the postcards is based on the idea of mixing first impressions, tourist sights, and symbols relating to the cities under examination; to convey them as a new cosmos to look at, to question, and to share ideas about. The shiny colours attract the viewer and, in particular, capture new, serendipitous visitors through Instagram, to which the postcards were uploaded during the coronavirus pandemic. A further level of examination is introduced by sorting the postcards according to their topics or fields—ranging from humorous comics, images of spatial phenomena, and situations to quotations, (group) portraits, activities in the university areas, urban streets, and everyday places—for subjective discussion as well as to question shared narratives.

Postcards by participants
of the *Cosmopolitan Postcards* action

Postcards by participants
of the *Cosmopolitan Postcards* action

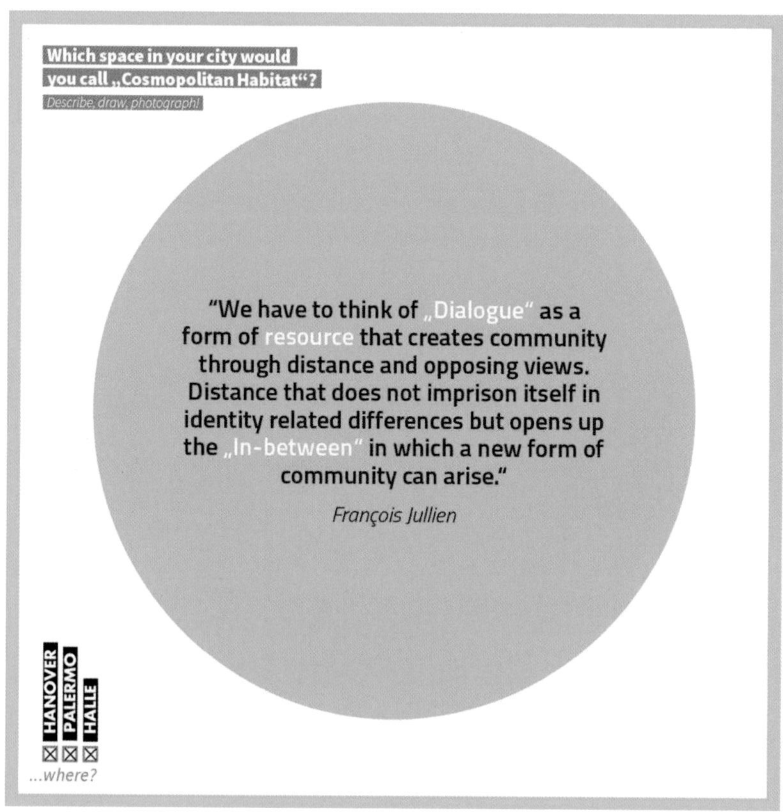

Postcard by Enno Alting

Postcard by Federica Scaffidi

Postcard by Federica Scaffidi

Postcard by Elizaveta Misyuryaeva

Postcard by Lara Aussel

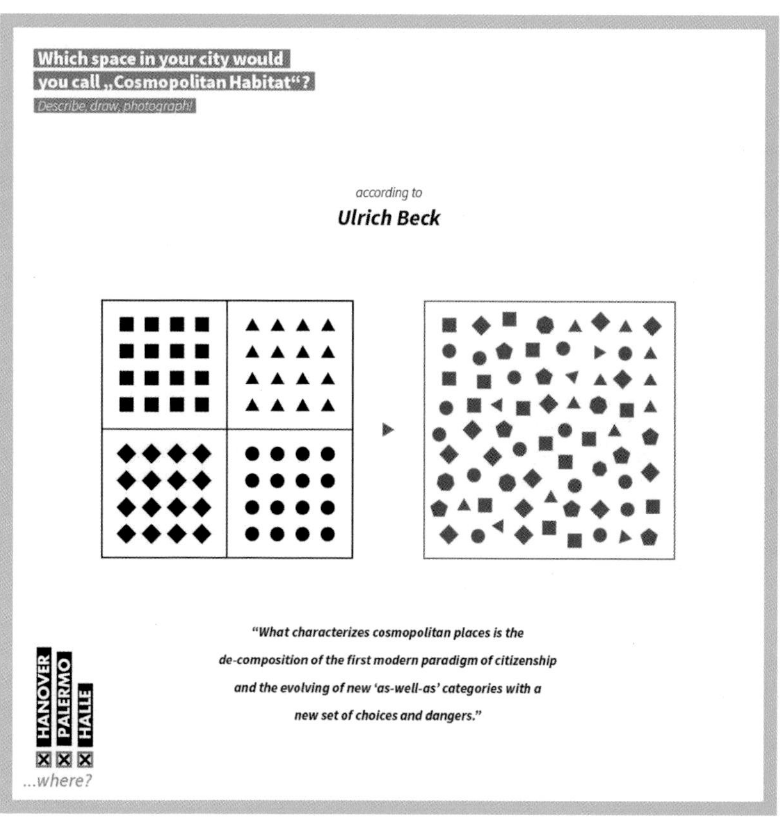

Postcard by Matthias Tippe

02
ACTIONS

PALERMO

HANOVER

HALLE

FLENSBURG

52–119

video works palermo 19

THE COSMOPOLITAN CITY

RICCARDA CAPPELLER, FEDERICA SCAFFIDI, BARBARA LINO

One could propose that a cosmopolitan city is inhabited by a multifaced and multiple community, open to the possibility of meeting the other and willing to face the sociality of public spaces as well as open to new places intended for meeting others. As such, a cosmopolitan city would be characterised by a community that is often global in origin, with strong multicultural connotations, and a city that meets the highest level of urban provision in terms of services, places, and opportunities—both of which contribute to increasing and multiplying positive tensions. The cosmopolitan city and cosmopolitan citizenship together give life to the *Cosmopolitan Habitat.* The workshop *Videoworks Palermo* focuses on the performance and perception of urban spaces in the highly global yet extremely specific and instantaneous city of Palermo. It combines urban exploration skills and activities, spatial thinking, arts, interactive communication, and urban design in order to enhance new approaches to urbanism. Referring to Richard Sennett's multiple ideas of the Open City, and to Maurizio Carta's Augmented City framework as a spatial, cultural, social, and economic platform for enhancing our contemporary life, it looks at spaces of urban change and innovation, focusing on processes in transition, the potentialities of places, and narratives. Creative storytelling addresses the spatial dynamics of change in relation to new networks and territories. We want to think of narratives that describe social, economic, and ecological phenomena within a temporal and spatial frame, making sense of the hybrid character of today's spaces. Narrative approaches such as those first realised in the 1960s and 1970s by the Smithsons, Kevin Lynch, Edmund Bacon, and others are still part of the academic discourse (Havik et al. 2017). The workshop was organised by the Institute of Urban Design and Planning of Leibniz University Hannover in collaboration with the Department of Architecture at the University of Palermo. It conceives of the city as a laboratory, which requires the understanding and mapping of existing social and built relations, mobilities, flows, connecting elements, intertwining layers, and atmospheres; an active creation and projection of ideas as well as their communication. Bringing these elements together in a conceptual idea of space and what Jane Jacobs (1961) calls the "choreography of daily life" nearly automatically leads us to the medium of film, which, like architecture, uses movement and time to enable perception. In experiencing architecture and space through filmmaking, fieldwork, and observation, the city is approached from a different perspective and creates a new format for architectural knowledge and design interventions that is artistically manifested. "Experimentalism is ... constantly taking apart, putting together, contradicting, provoking languages and syntaxes that are nevertheless accepted as such" (Tafuri 1976).

BIBLIOGRAPHY

Havik K., Notteboom B., de Wit S. eds. (2017) *OASE 98 Narrating Urban Landscapes.* Rotterdam, NAI010.

Jacobs J. (1961) *The Death and Life of Great American Cities.* New York, Random House.

Tafuri M. (1976) *Architecture and Utopia. Design and Capitalist Development. Cambridge*, MIT Press. Originally published in Italian in 1973 as *Progetto e utopia* by Laterza, Rome and Bari.

DISCOVERING DANISINNI

MARA PIEL, LEA FRENZ
EMILIA ABATE, ALESSIA ALVICH, GIOVANNI DAVID, PAOLO NEGLIA
TEXT BY FEDERICA SCAFFIDI

Palermo is a mixture of layers, shapes, colours, and sensations. How can one explore the city? The video suggests observing the socio-cultural scene of Palermo by walking around the city. In the first instance, the video shows its viewers an image of the city built from stunning views, beautiful architecture, and vivid atmospheres. However, what the authors really want to reveal are the hidden treasures of the city: urban spaces that are unknown to tourists and even to many local inhabitants. The authors use the image of a clown discovering the city, in order to provoke interest and make people curious about what is happening around them. This is the main objective of the video: finding a way of attracting people's attention and shifting the visual weight in the urban space, in the beauty of the architecture, in the urban-agricultural context behind the object being observed. The rhythmic and cheerful notes hide a provocative and ironic streak. What you looking at? Are you looking at the finger or the moon? You, people, look at the beauty of the city! Do not be shocked by my appearing as a clown, but look around my city with the same wonder with which my eyes look. Discover Danisinni, a sociocultural and natural oasis in the condensed urban context, where creativity, community involvement, and social cohesion make this place a real space of innovation. Enjoy the city, its spaces, its vivacity and vibrancy, its different layers and levels; appreciate it, and playfully discover your surroundings.

ZISA: WHERE IS THE WATER?

LEONA SCHUBERT, SEVILAY AKYÜREK
VITA LUCIDO, ANTONELLA MARCHESE, ROSARIA OCCHIPINTI, MARIA PIA PAPIA
TEXT BY FEDERICA SCAFFIDI

The opening slogan of this video is "Palermo città d'acqua / Palermo water city". The video is conceived as an investigative report that uses irony to reveal the real water conditions in the city of Palermo. The music and the first images of the Zisa, a UNESCO-listed Arab-Norman castle, where a lush and fruitful oasis should remind viewers of an Arabic paradise, demonstrate the lack of water. So, where *is* the water? From this starting point, the video and its authors conduct a treasure hunt through the street of Palermo. Palermo is a city of water; over the past few years, its connection to the sea has been rebuilt through the regeneration of the city's waterfront, first with the reactivation of the Foro Italico and later with the urban regeneration of the city's leisure harbour and the renovation of the Porticciolo, the small harbour of Sant'Erasmo. The video shows how people live in these spaces: running, walking, fishing, and enjoying this part of the city. Water is hidden in many of the city's urban spaces. You can find water in the city markets, in the many drinking fountains, in the urban parks, in the historical fountains of the city centre; behind beauty, architecture, and folklore. The video's authors illustrate the city's cultural and social capital, as well as the link between Palermo, its inhabitants, and the water system. They metaphorically imagine pouring water from other locations in the city onto the Zisa gardens, creating a new liveable place for Palermo.

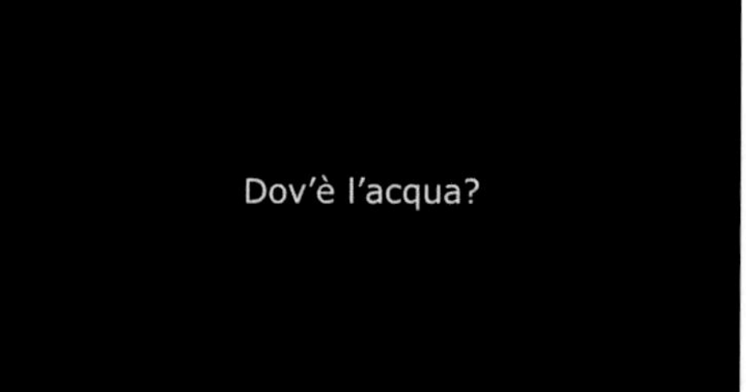

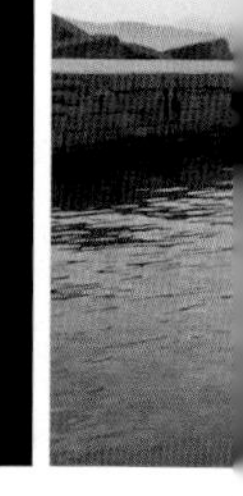

CAPO: BREAK DOWN THE WALL

EDUARD MICA, JULIA THEIS
ALBERTO CANNIZZARO, BEATRIZ MORINHO E SOARES, ALFREDO PENSABENE, FANECA RIBEIRO
TEXT BY FEDERICA SCAFFIDI

"Break down the wall" shows an important aspect of the city of Palermo, starting with the nightlife on the city's main pedestrian street, Via Maqueda. In this part of the city, shops, restaurants, and traditional food coexist and share the urban space with the many tourists who come to Palermo to visit the city and taste its delicious food. The video shows one of the most attractive places in the historical centre, with its picturesque yellow lights and the Teatro Massimo (the city opera). Here, both local inhabitants and tourists mingle in a common and cultural space. However, the other side of this touristic development is the Capo neighbourhood, the underdeveloped part of the city behind Via Maqueda. By shooting this area, the authors emphasise the ambiguity and double aspect of most contemporary cities. On one side, you can happily eat your panini and tasty Sicilian food—and on the other, you will find a different world, characterised by neglect and messiness. However, the most important message that the video's authors want to convey is to discover your own city; to visit the places that are not positively affected by tourism and the urban agenda and to reflect on them. *Stop*, they say; the video aims to interrupt this way of living and invites people to discover the real city, walk around its hidden spaces, and think about how to reactivate and regenerate them.

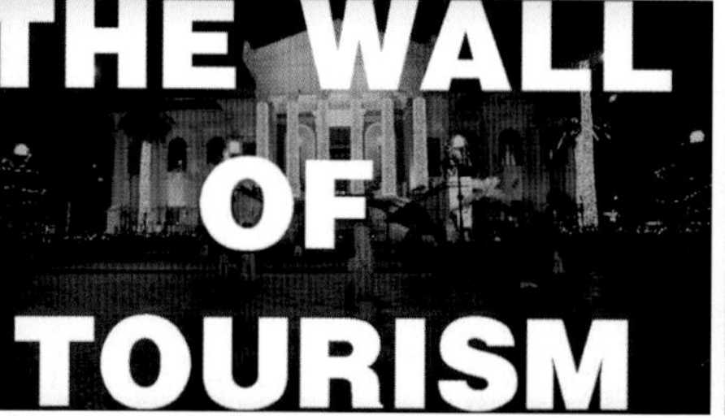

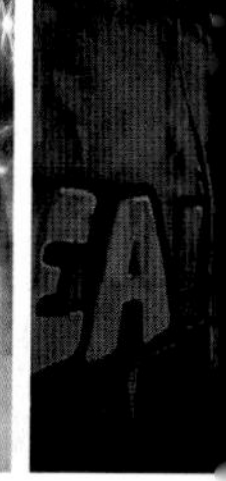

OP

LIVE

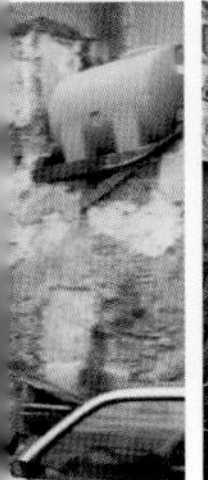

BREAK

WALL

work shop palermo 20

COSMOPOLITAN HABITAT WORKSHOP

ANNALISA CONTATO, FEDERICA SCAFFIDI

The *Cosmopolitan Habitat* workshop invites international PhD candidates, students, young scientists, academics, and urban planning and design professionals to discuss and reflect on the spatial dimensions of migration, the different human cultures that increasingly characterise European cities, and new living spaces in the project area, the historic centre of Palermo. The students, together with young urban planning and design scientists, are asked to discover potentialities for *Cosmopolitan Habitat* in Palermo and design new future scenarios. The projects in each area of the historic centre must emphasise the three characteristics of *Cosmopolitan Habitat* (Cosmopolitan Atmospheres, Cosmopolitan Accelerators, Cosmopolitan Makers) through innovative and creative design solutions. The workshop explores the four *mandamenti* (quarters) of the historic centre of Palermo: Palazzo Reale, Monte di Pietà, Castellammare, and Tribunali. For each mandamento, a student group (composed of students from UNIPA and LUH) works together to develop concepts and spatial visions for urban design interventions in the urban focus areas.

1. Mandamento Tribunali

The area lies in the north-east of Palermo, close to the waterfront. It is the former Arab settlement of Balarm, historically known as Al-Khalesa. It includes a mix of cultures and architectures and hosts some of the city's most important, such as the Palazzo Chiaramonte and the Palazzo Abatellis.
Urban focus areas: Piazza Magione, Teatro Garibaldi, Palazzo Butera, and Piazza Kalsa.

2. Mandamento Palazzo Reale

The area is a space of multiculturalism and social fermentation. It is a place of encounters, changes, and flows. It hosts new entrepreneurial ventures, participatory processes, the Ballarò market, and two UNESCO sites: the Church of San Giovanni degli Eremiti and the Royal Palace.
Urban focus areas: Piazza Mediterraneo, Complesso Santa Chiara, Ballarò market, Piazza Carmine

3. Mandamento Monte di Pietà

The area is characterised by the many circular Arabic alleys that uniquely define its urban fabric. The picturesque Capo market makes it a colourful place, full of contradictions and potentialities. Its urban stratifications are also visible in the cathedral, where the tomb of Federico II is located.
Urban focus areas: Piazza Beati Paoli, Piazza Sant'Anna al Capo, the courthouse, Palazzo Riso, Piazza del Gran Cancelliere, Piazza Sant'Onofrio, empty space (informal parking area).

4. Mandamento Castellammare

The area is named after the Castello a Mare, a former prison fortress that was demolished in 1923. The neighbourhood includes important cultural places, such as the regional archaeological museum, the Fondazione Sicilia, the Teatro Biondo, and an area of archaeological investigation.
Urban focus areas: Piazza Fonderia, Vucciria market, the archaeological area of Castel San Pietro.

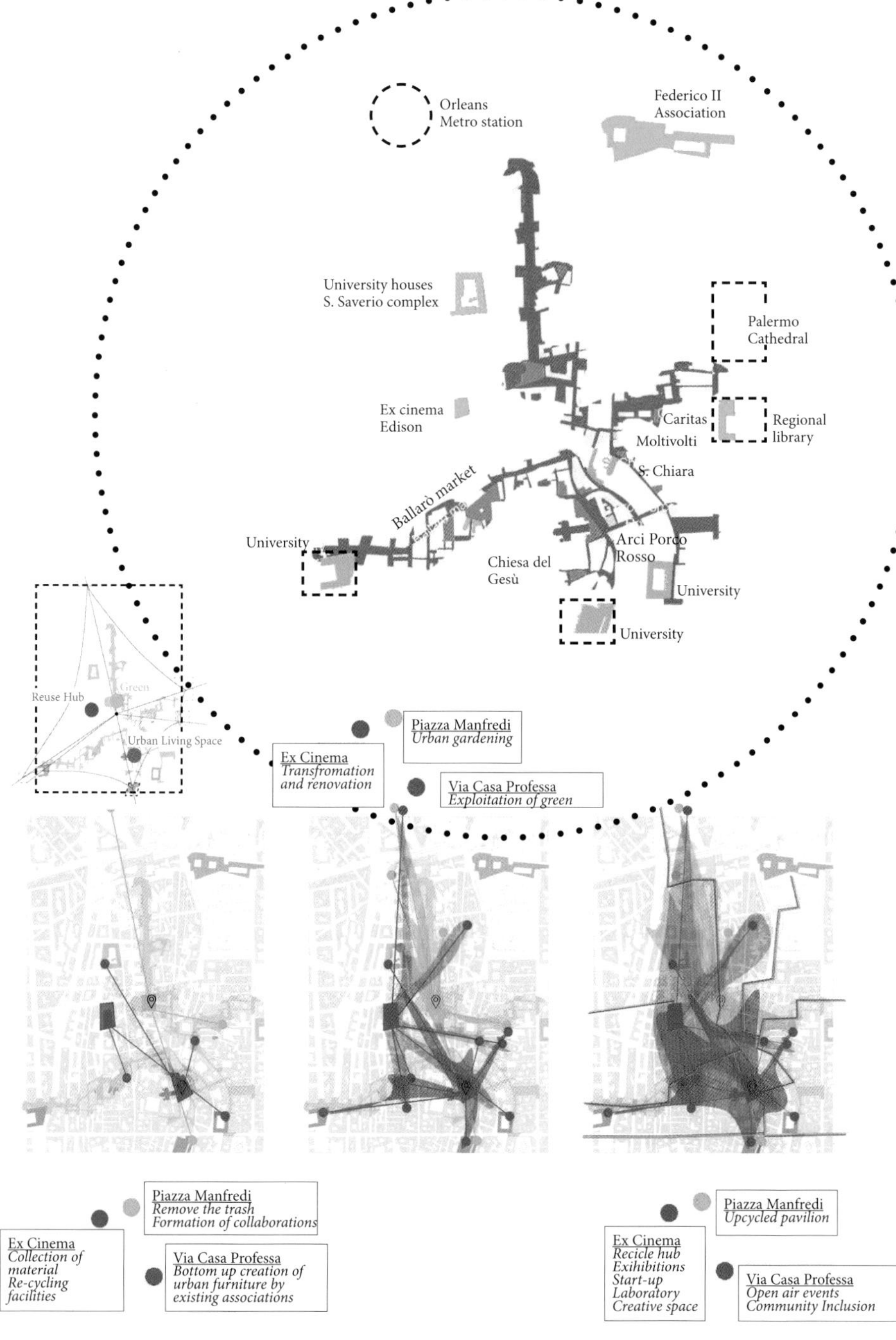
Orleans
Metro station
Federico II
Association
University houses
S. Saverio complex
Palermo
Cathedral
Ex cinema
Edison
Caritas
Moltivolti
Regional
library
S. Chiara
Ballarò market
University
Arci Porco
Rosso
Chiesa del
Gesù
University
University
Reuse Hub
Green
Urban Living Space
Piazza Manfredi
Urban gardening
Ex Cinema
Transfromation
and renovation
Via Casa Professa
Exploitation of green
Piazza Manfredi
Remove the trash
Formation of collaborations
Ex Cinema
Collection of
material
Re-cycling
facilities
Via Casa Professa
Bottom up creation of
urban furniture by
existing associations
Piazza Manfredi
Upcycled pavilion
Ex Cinema
Recicle hub
Exihibitions
Start-up
Laboratory
Creative space
Via Casa Professa
Open air events
Community Inclusion

BALLARÒ GOES CIRCULAR

SERGIO BISULCA, MARIA CALDERONE, ILARIA INFANTOLINO
TILL CONNOR, SARENA LIESER, ANGELA GAINI, FAYA YOUSSEF

Palermo is a special city for a number of reasons. Among these are its location in the centre of the Mediterranean, which has played an important role in the history of the city, and the multi-layered cultures that make its architecture and heritage so unique. On the other hand, this city rich in values and history must also deal with challenges such as migration, social and spatial fragmentation, and mobility and economic problems. After a preparatory investigation into some of the different scales of Palermo, we chose to analyse the historical *mandamento* known as Palazzo Reale. Taking into account the most interesting findings of the analysis, including green spaces, vacant spaces with potential, infrastructures, and the presence of local associations and historical activities, we proposed a programme of actions and interventions in line with the *cityforming protocol*—a method that has the ability to activate new scenarios, create community in fragmented social scenarios, and deal with global and local challenges. Palazzo Reale is the oldest neighbourhood in Palermo. This district changes its face every time you turn a corner; nowhere else is the juxtaposition of dilapidated housing and exquisite historic buildings quite so jarring. The district is populated by a community mad up of different ethnic groups, and visiting almost feels like taking a trip to another continent. The presence of universities, student housing, and social associations us relevant, as they make the district very lively. The core of the district is the historic Ballarò street market.

What if applying the *cityforming protocol* to the *mandamento* Palazzo Reale could lead to Palermo being the capital of recycling? Starting from this ambitious dream, the group worked to define the concept for "Ballarò goes circular". After identifying the most relevant elements and activities in the project area, three strategic spaces with potential were selected: the former cinema Edison, Piazza B. Manfredi, and Via Casa Professa. The general strategy can be represented as a spiderweb connecting all the important spots and activities with particular and interrelated goals and involving a variety of actors (such as universities, migrants, citizens, and associations) within the three redevelopment areas. The former cinema could be transformed into a Reuse Hub aiming to create awareness of trash, waste, and recycling and to trigger creativity and wasteless production using the collected non-organic materials. The informal parking spaces in Manfredi Square could be transformed into an urban garden where activities related to food-sharing and production take place using organic waste from the market. Through a bottom-up urban furniture development, the poor-quality urban spaces along Via Casa Professa could be transformed into an gathering urban space for existing associations and for the hosting of open-air events. The idea takes into account existing challenges, open spaces, buildings with potential, and people, using a "what if" approach that proposes programmes and steps to generate resources able to trigger the development of a *Cosmopolitan Habitat.*

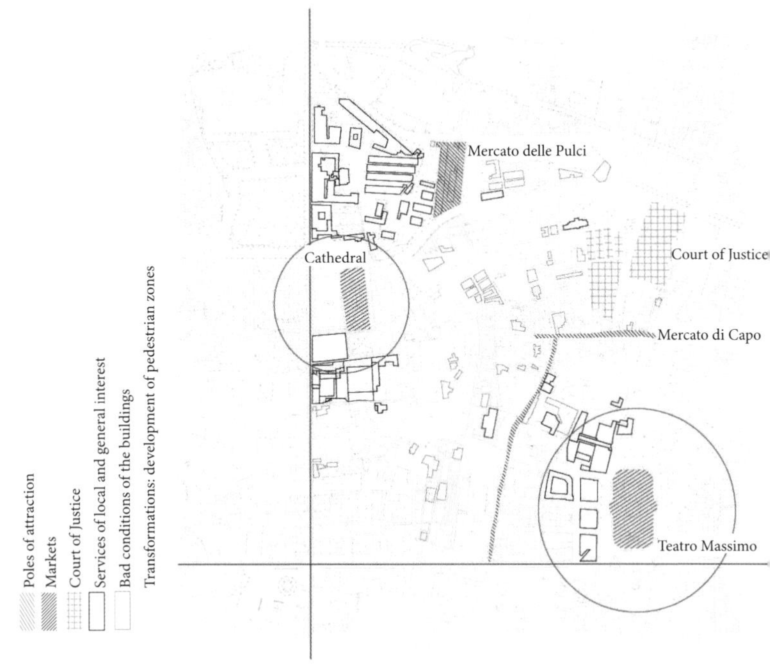
Mercato delle Pulci
Cathedral
Court of Justice
Mercato di Capo
Teatro Massimo
Poles of attraction
Markets
Court of Justice
Services of local and general interest
Bad conditions of the buildings
Transformations: development of pedestrian zones

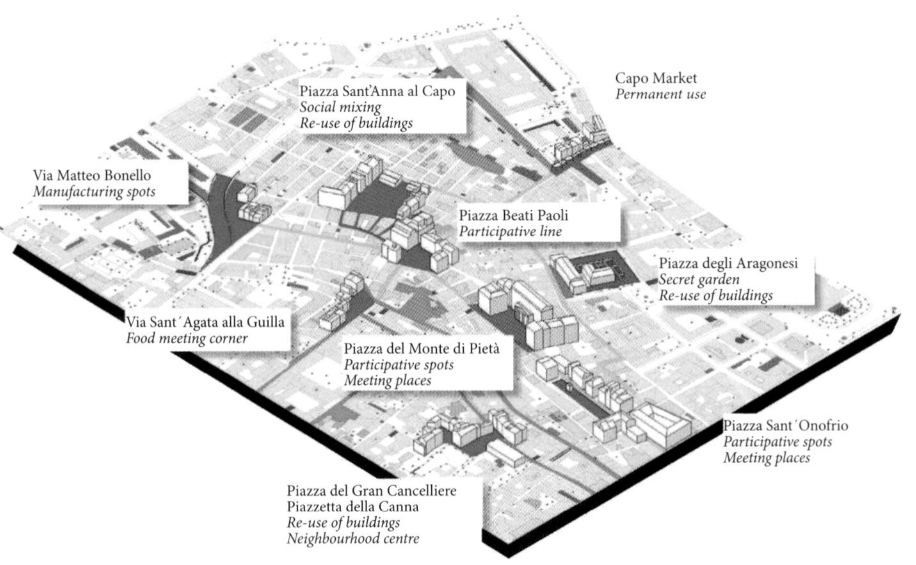
Piazza Sant'Anna al Capo
Social mixing
Re-use of buildings
Capo Market
Permanent use
Via Matteo Bonello
Manufacturing spots
Piazza Beati Paoli
Participative line
Piazza degli Aragonesi
Secret garden
Re-use of buildings
Via Sant´Agata alla Guilla
Food meeting corner
Piazza del Monte di Pietà
Participative spots
Meeting places
Piazza Sant´Onofrio
Participative spots
Meeting places
Piazza del Gran Cancelliere
Piazzetta della Canna
Re-use of buildings
Neighbourhood centre

C-OPEN LAB

LAURA AIELLO, PAOLA LATTUCA, ALFREDO PENSABENE
ALESSANDRA GULLOTTO, ANNA-SOPHIE HEIMES, LEANDRA LEIPOLD,
KAYA-SOPHIE LIFFLER, PAULA SCHEIBKE, JAN ZÜLCHNER

Monte di Pietà is one of the four historic districts of Palermo. Founded in the Arabic period, it is also known as "Il Capo" in reference to the historic market of the same name. Our analysis focused on the urban fabric of the *mandamento* Capo. The internal area of Monte di Pietà appears to be more neglected than the rest of the district on several fronts. The built structures are in a critical condition, especially in the centre of Capo away from the touristic places and buildings. Social life takes place around the big buildings in the area, such as the cathedral or the Teatro Massimo, which are also highly touristic places. Green, open spaces are rare and only to be found in the northern part of the district; the public transport network forms a circle around the area. The project aims to reactivate the central area of the *mandamento*, starting with the reuse of degraded and abandoned places with unexploited potential. To this end, a network of interconnected functions will be created to support the cosmopolitan community, ensuring greater proximity to places of social life, production, and services, with the primary objective of reactivating everyday life within the *mandamento*. In addition to reactivating the centre, the community of residents will be supported by a new range of participation and meeting points.

The cityforming protocol is divided into three phases: creative colonisation, collaborative consolidation, and sustainable development. The protocol describes a process that is able to reactivate the stationary metabolism of an area step by step, starting from its latent regenerative components, enabling multiple cycles, and increasing intensity in order to create a new urban sustainable ecosystem over time. Through these sequential steps, the protocol produces the "urban oxygen" necessary to form an appropriate ecosystem; one able to generate a new active metabolism that reactivates inactive cycles, reconnects broken ones, or activates new ones that are more adapted to the city's new character as a place of transition. In the first step, activating different sites to develop a public space in the area is the most important part. This is done by establishing the three specific aspects: 1) the green line, representing biotope spaces such as small green areas with plants and trees or flexible urban structures; 2) the purple line, representing specific entertainment areas that incorporate videoscreens or other artistic elements; 3) the orange line, which represents the planning and reactivation of buildings in order to trigger social interaction. In the consolidation phase, inhabitants also need to be activated in order to connect the areas between the spots and create a fluid, continuous line within the Capo district. During the third step, the network can be expanded to other parts of Palermo in order to create social connectivity. Most of the places we want to focus on, such as Piazza Sant'Anna al Capo and Piazza del Gran Cancelliere, are now underused, for example as parking spots, and we want to reactivate them by creating common places. The project proposes adding components that are currently missing in order to create these community spots: participation points, secret gardens, co-working spaces, and entertainment areas.

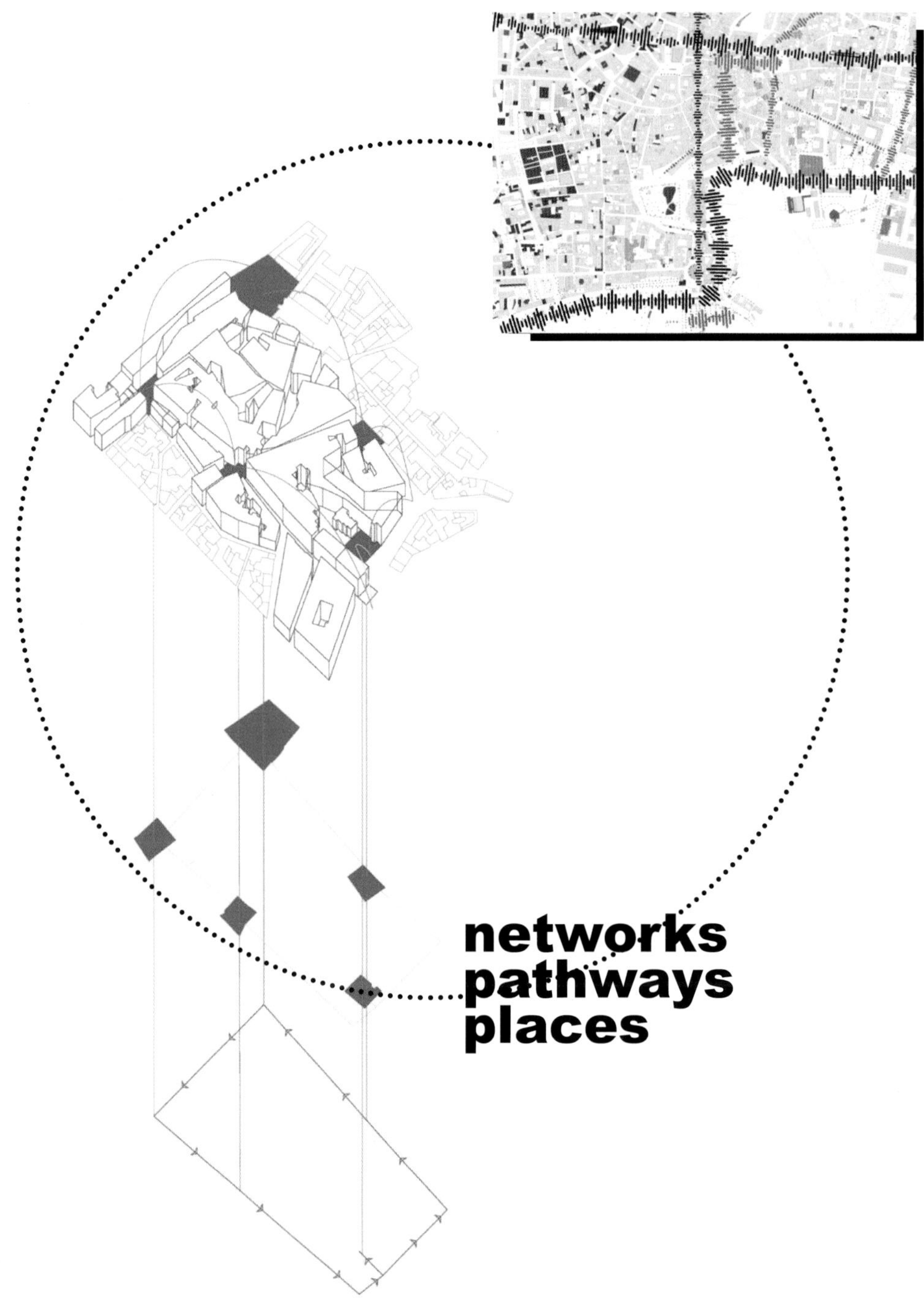

networks pathways places

ART-SENAL

ANTONIO CAPUTO, ROSANNA CLEMENTE, SARAH LO BUGLIO
HANNAH VETTE, ALA HALLASY, LENA BEETZ

Palermo was founded in the seventh century BC by the Phoenicians. They named it Zys, the name of a flower, referring to the shape of the city. Between 258 BC and 491 AD, the Romans took over the city and changed its name to Panormus, meaning “all ports”. In 535, the Byzantines laid the foundation for the city’s famous architectural typology. After it was conquered by the Arabs in 827, Palermo became part of the Emirate of Sicily. This prosperity continued under Norman rule, which started in 1072. Today, the Arab-Norman architecture is still present. Later, strong Spanish influence characterised the urban life and architecture of the city. At the time of the Italian unification in the nineteenth century, Palermo was one of the wealthiest cities in Italy. One of the first Arab planned cities in Europe was the Kalsa district, now known as *mandamento* Tribunali. The name originates from the Arabic name Al-Khalsa, which means “the Chosen”. In ancient times, a large part of what is now Kalsa was under water. The district was heavily bombed during World War II and remained abandoned for some time afterwards. Since then, the area that was destroyed has been revived and has become home to many street artists and galleries. One of the most famous contemporary art galleries is the Palazzo Butera. Many facades in Kalsa are covered in graffiti and murals financed and supported by the local government. Another district in Palermo rich in street art is the *mandamento* Castellammare. For this reason, we wanted to create a concept with artists at its forefront.

Starting with our analysis, we located all of the street-art murals in Castellammare and its surroundings. Moreover, we located the neighbourhoods, open spaces, and streets with potentiality and analysed their accessibility and liveability. We also noticed that the sounds and noises of the city create different atmospheres at different times of day, which we also wanted to incorporate in our concept. Art-senal is a concept that aims to connect creators from different backgrounds in Palermo with art lovers. Our concept foresees two main cornerstones intended to activate the quarter. The first cornerstone consists of temporary installations, such as small pavilions, street galleries, and open-air cinemas where creative people and craftspeople can showcase their work and talent. These instalments have the potential to revive Castellammare at different times of the day, strengthening the existing character of the mandamento, but could also be installed in different public spaces to help transmit a new atmosphere and create a new urban character. The second cornerstone are the permanent installations. Once artists and creators come to Palermo to showcase their work, they’ll need places to stay and work. As such, our concept offers them dwelling and co-working spaces, as well as permanent ateliers in which to display their work. To give these spaces an individual identity, the permanent installations should develop a certain character that enables people to recognise the connection between these buildings.

connection underground street roof

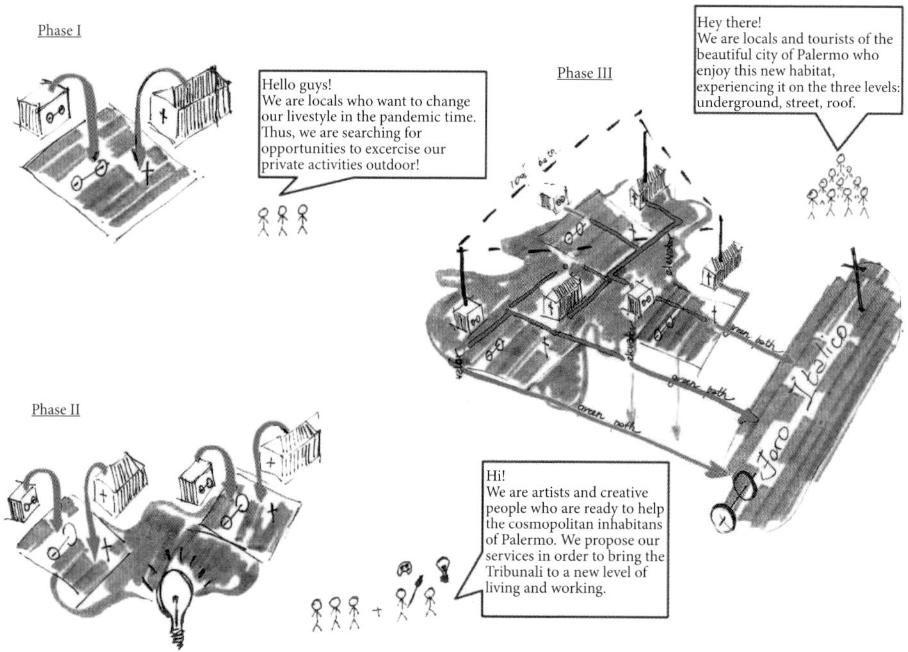

COMMUNITY FLOW

ROBERTA CARUSO, ROSSELLA CUSUMANNO, SABRINA OLIVO
LAURA-JULIA PETER, ANNA KOZACHKOVA

Both the density of the city of Palermo and the height of its buildings decrease from the historical core to the periphery in two directions—from sea to mountain and from south to north—resulting in more green space in the suburban areas. The historic centre, once surrounded by the city walls, is a highly dense area with a capillary system of narrow streets and lanes that were partly shaped by the drained Papireto and Kemonia rivers. The main axes, Via Vittorio Emanuele (the first road axis connecting the Roman Paleopolis and Neapolis), Via Maqueda (which divides the historic centre into four districts), and Via Roma (which connects the central railway station with the port) are the exception. Mandamento Tribunali is a historical quarter in the city of Palermo built in the ninth century as an Arab settlement. It originally served as an administrative centre, but became an Arab neighbourhood under the Normans. During World War II, the district was heavily bombed and remained destroyed for decades. For this reason, it was considered an "Arab quarter" where poverty and high crime rates prevailed. Today, Tribunali has been revitalised, but still retains a lot of residential buildings in poor condition. One of the measures introduced by the municipality to improve the quality of these marginalised areas is graffiti art. The district still has a network of narrow, winding streets—just as it did in the eleventh century—and is home to many cultural and religious places. An example is the Catholic church Santa Maria dello Spasimo in the late Gothic style. The absence of the roof makes it perfect for various open air events. An arts festival, Kals'art, takes place in the streets of the district in summer. This festival is followed by the Winter Kals'art. Last but not least, our exploration included the large, multi-functional Foro Italico public park, which gives the district access to the sea.

We planned our concept based on our analysis and in accordance with the cityforming protocol. In the first phase of the plan, we adjust the religious and cultural functions of the district to our pandemic and post-pandemic times. Buildings with these functions that also possess some surrounding outdoor areas are in focus here. We propose to use these spaces for church services, exhibitions, and other open-air events. This transformation supports the ongoing work of these cultural and religious institutions as well as creating an additional function for the outdoor spaces nearby. In the next step, we revitalise the transformed outdoor spaces, installing creative hubs where different activities, organised by local craftspeople, can take place. In the final step of the project, Palermo's little-known underground routes, which can be accessed via the old Arabian bastions, could be activated. Additionally, it will be possible to access the roofs of some buildings from the selected outdoor spaces via elevator. Thus, the concept aims to increase the reputation of the area for the locals as well as creating points of interest for tourists on three levels.

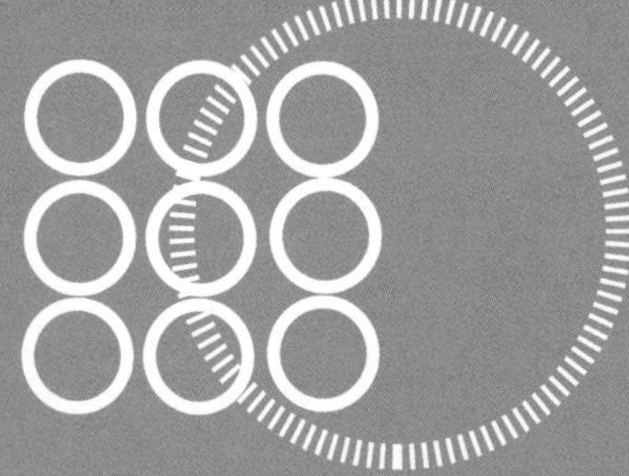

palermo atlas projects

THE SEEDS AND POINTS OF VIEW OF COSMOPOLITAN PALERMO

MAURIZIO CARTA, ANGELA ALESSANDRA BADAMI, DANIELE RONSIVALLE

The current global scenario is marked by an economic, social, and cultural situation in which the intensified flows of intangible assets and interactions contrast with border-based approaches to growth. Furthermore, multi-ethnic and multicultural societies positively influence local urban identities, but inequalities, social conflicts, and personal hardship continue to make the theme of social inclusion a challenge in urban welfare policies. Following the economic crisis that has characterised the last decades—increasingly so during the Covid-19 pandemic polycrisis—collaborative practices that rethink the relations between citizens, public bodies, and private entities have become more widespread. The process of self-collaboration entails a paradigm shift with regard to both social organisation and collaborative economy, as these are necessary for intercepting new, widespread needs. The sharing economy should also be included in considerations of this perspective.

Cosmopolis as ideal city: on the term and its use

As *cosmos* refers to the "order of things" and *polis* refers to the city (as well as to its collective citizenry, as in the Latin civitas) we will find that the word *cosmopolis* presents a double meaning. The first, and probably most commonly used, meaning of *cosmopolis* is almost synonymous with a global city that is able to open itself to the *cosmos*—or, in other words, to the universe—through the relationships, functions, meanings, and added values that only a large "global city" is able to offer. A *cosmopolis,* therefore, is not an unchanging city, but feeds on "liquidity" (as in Baumann) and generates the undetermined shape of the contemporary city. The *cosmopolis*, however, is also a city in which everything is contained within an ordered system of relations between the citizens and the spaces they build and live in. The *cosmopolis* is a city with an ideal shape in which each part makes sense when considered in relation to the citizens who live there, guaranteeing their fundamental right to happiness (as the Constitution of the United States of America does). In the ideal *cosmopolis*, we find the perfect correspondence between city and citizenry and the perfect example of a pact of association among people as citizens.

Can human habitat be cosmopolitan?

The city is not a merely an artificial mechanism, but is sustained by the relationship between the natural and the man-made, between the artificial and nature, just as habitats in nature are; this is reflected in our contemporary vision of metabolism-based urbanism. As such, a *Cosmopolitan Habitat* would be based on "biological" vitality: life in a cosmopolitan city means living the urban identity "in the making", with the goal of pursuing the happiness of its inhabitants. Migratory flows often proceed through territories, generating temporary occupation of urban spaces—but, in addition to this, migration phenomena also produce longer-lasting transformations with the potential to take root within urban tissues and produce new urban tissues, or modify them. Both dynamics impact the policies for a melting-pot society by affecting the selection of new new governance and participatory styles, new approaches to conflict mediation and new urban facilities.

The challenge of the cosmopolis involves a long-term shift from a single place to the world, and—conversely—from global flows to local identity, and requires ongoing work on:

- the resolution of spatial conflict resulting from migration and the identification of practices and devices that act as accelerators of "plural coexistence" and integration, which should be encouraged by designing places of hospitality, sharing and exchange, implementing informal urban planning and funding social movements and associations in support of coexistence and integration, etc.;
- fostering "world-places" that act as the local nodes of global networks in order to support a cosmopolitan culture: places of internationalisation, multi-cultures, creativity, and innovation.

Palermo is already meeting this challenge in both points of view. The city is proud of its high level of "plural coexistence", and the concept of plural cultures has been widespread for the last ten years. Really, Palermo is enriched by place of hospitality, sharing and exchange and the local community is almost integrated with the new incoming communities. The challenge of Neocosmopolitanism (see Carta pp. 26) is taken up by many communities from Asia, Africa, and Europe who share their traditions, cultures, and ways of life, and are proud to exhibit their identity. For example, people are not ashamed to hold festivals or parades celebrating their deity across the city, and are able to buy their traditional foodstuffs into the local street markets.

Neocosmopolitanism requires world-places that act as local nodes of a global network: this function is embodied, for example, by universities and musical and artistic colleges. They support internationalisation, multi-cultures, creativity, and innovation because they transfer knowledge and technology from a worldwide context to a local one. This is even truer in the age of Covid-19, as humankind is globally engaged in overcoming the crisis and the world's research network is focused on this common goal. More generally, the humanities, music, and performing arts play an important role, as culture and performance demonstrate: UNESCO sites, festivals, movie sets, and other cultural expressions produce a cosmopolitan kaleidoscope. When communities (not just a single community) inhabit *Palermo-Cosmopolis*, they recognise its *Cosmopolitan Habitat*. The evidence for its existence is a strong syncretism that produces hybridisation and integration. The new "contaminated" social structure of the city, as well as the delineation of the urban habitat (living spaces, urban spaces, work spaces, etc.), can provide opportunities for the syncretic development of the *Cosmopolitan Habitat*, and it is in front of the sectoral specialisation of the urban fabric and the gentrification processes.

How do people live in and move through Palermo-Cosmopolis?
A cosmopolitan city is inhabited by a multicultural community open to meeting other people and willing to meet the challenge of sociality in public spaces. The inhabitants of the cosmopolitan city do so in the places that result from this new integrated (syncretic and ultimately mixed) sociality. Some of these places lie within the contemporary fabric of the city, often animated by new meanings: squares and urban facilities, urban gateways (stations, ports, airports), and cultural activities that are further integrated in the urban fabric by the addition of hybrid and itinerant activities, as well as of places for recreation, business, and research. We live in a cosmopolitan city because it has a cosmopolitan identity. Beyond this, urban planning helps us to improve and empower these places through a new design that is more integrated with community needs: our project has the potential to impact and reshape the city's current status, increasing or decreasing its cosmopolitan attitude. We can measure and assess this impact: the Urban Planning Studio has developed a set of design hypotheses in order to evaluate the cosmopolitan atmosphere, design strategies, functions, and places of *Palermo-Cosmopolis*. The following maps, figures, and pictures illustrate two aspects of Palermo in detail. The example maps from the *Cosmopolitan Atlas* show the seeds of potential that Palermo contains in terms of places, activities, and communities, as well as the role the city is playing in improving its cosmopolitanism.

The following example projects by the students of the three Urban Planning Studios envisage and imagine how Palermo could develop as a cosmopolis by designing syncretic spaces aimed at sharing and integrating cultural identities, living spaces, and challenges.

NOTE

The Urban Planning Studio discussed here formed part of the Master's Degree in Architecture 2019–20 taught at the Department of Architecture of the University of Palermo by professors Maurizio Carta, Angela Alessandra Badami, and Daniele Ronsivalle. The *Cosmopolitan Atlas* is an unconventional atlas made up of twenty-two maps in which students have discovered, evaluated, and assessed new points of views concerning the cosmopolitan condition of Palermo. The *Cosmopolitan Habitat* projects are a set of experimental urban design solutions that apply regeneration, refurbishment, new development, and the proposed solutions to the challenge of improving the cosmopolitanism of Palermo, identifying and highlighting their strengths and opportunities and paring down their weaknesses.

BIBLIOGRAPHY

Baumann Z. (2000) *Liquid Modernity*. Cambridge, Polity.

EUROMEDITERRANEAN NETWORKS

LIDIA BADAGLIACCA, GIORGIA CALANDRA, ALESSANDRO CARDULLO, FRANCESCA LA MATTINA

The Mediterranean is a crossroads of flows: flows of people, goods, cultures, and information that constitute potentials and challenges, requiring improved logistics as well as the management of complex international relations. The maps represent the city of Palermo as a node of these flows—from the Euro-Mediterranean scale to the provincial and local scale—in order to understand its functions and its relationships, as well as the limits we are likely to face when planning the future city from a reticular and cosmopolitan perspective.

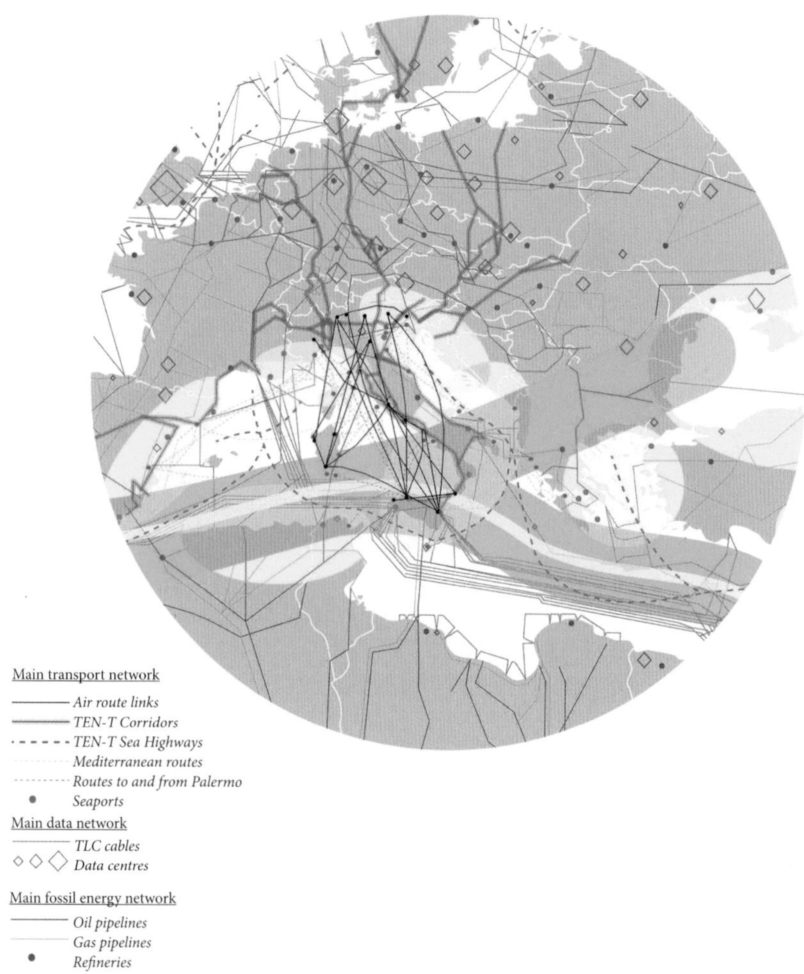

MIGRATION FLOWS

ELENA GROGER, FRANCESCA D'ANNA, GIOVANNI RAFFO, MARTINA NASCA, MIRIAM MANTEGNA

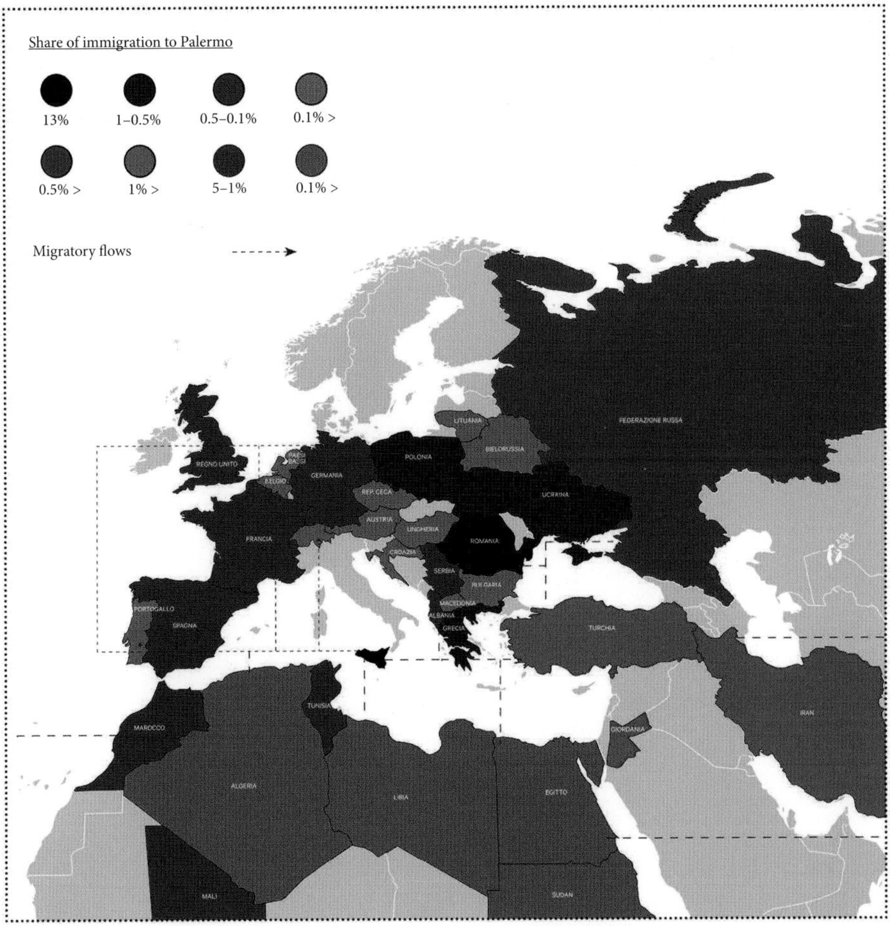

Share of immigration to Palermo

13% 1–0.5% 0.5–0.1% 0.1% >

0.5% > 1% > 5–1% 0.1% >

Migratory flows

REGNO UNITO
PAESI BASSI
BELGIO
GERMANIA
POLONIA
LITUANIA
BIELORUSSIA
FEDERAZIONE RUSSA
UCRAINA
REP. CECA
AUSTRIA
UNGHERIA
ROMANIA
FRANCIA
CROAZIA
SERBIA
BULGARIA
MACEDONIA
ALBANIA
GRECIA
PORTOGALLO
SPAGNA
TURCHIA
TUNISIA
MAROCCO
ALGERIA
LIBIA
EGITTO
GIORDANIA
IRAN
MALI
SUDAN

Nigeria 2.08%

Mauritius 3.50%

China 3.85%

Fliippines 6.92%

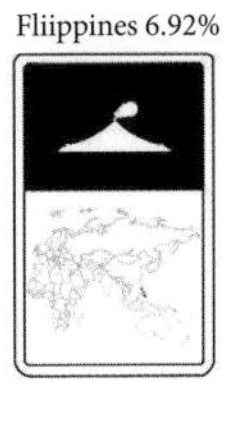

Ghana 10.41%

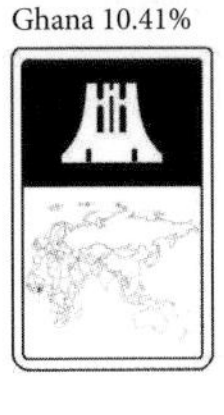

Sri Lanka 13.52%

Bangladesh 20.75%

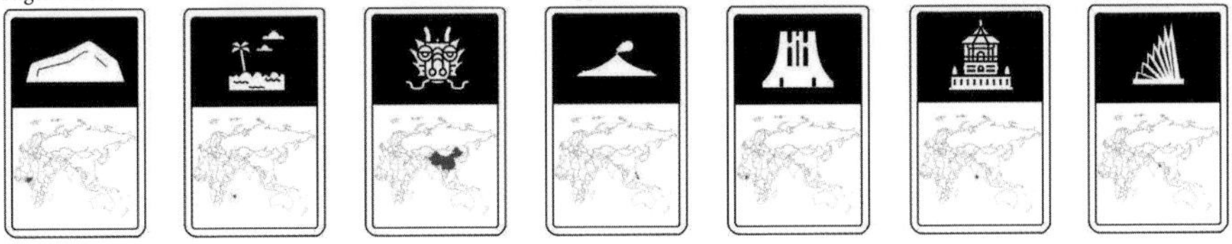

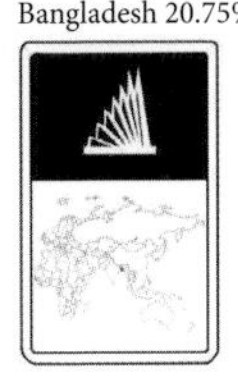

Percentage of foreign residents by country of origin

FOREIGN POPULATIONS IN CENSUS FIGURES

FRANCESCO CIMADOR, THADSAYINI JEYAKUMAR, ANGELA MONDELLO, LUANA PIZZUTO

While immigrant communities are now fully integrated, they continue to preserve and pass on their cultures. Foreign communities make up about 4% of the total resident population (Istat 2018), with some variation on an annual basis. With more than 5,000 members, the Bengali community is the largest of the foreign communities permanently settled in Palermo, followed by the Senegalese, Romanian, Ghanaian, Filipino, Moroccan, Tunisian, Chinese, Mauritian, and Ivorian communities. The map of the distribution of foreign citizens shows a concentration in the historic centre and its surrounding areas.

Africa
Ghana
Morocco
Tunisia
Asia
Bangladesh
Sri Lanka
Philippines
China
Europe
Romania

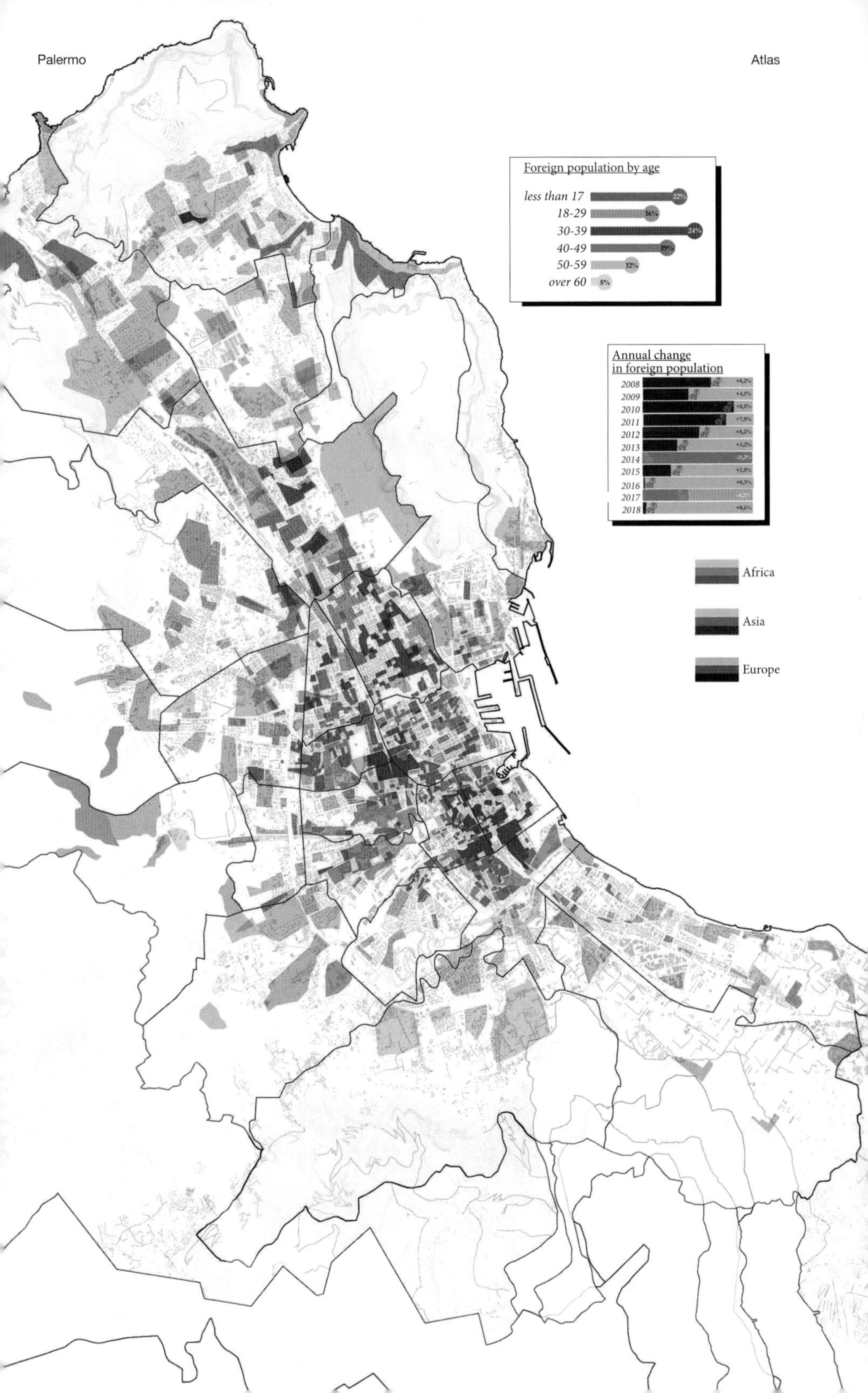
Foreign population by age
less than 17
22%
18-29
16%
30-39
24%
40-49
19%
50-59
12%
over 60
5%
Annual change
in foreign population
2008
+6,2%
2009
+4,1%
2010
2011
+7,5%
2012
2013
+3,2%
2014
2015
+2,5%
2016
+0,3%
2017
2018
+0,6%
Africa
Asia
Europe

CATHOLIC COMMUNITIES, PLACES, AND RITUALS

GAIA FAUCI, ROSA MARIA GELSI, MARIA CHIARA NASTRI, CHIARA VITABILE

Spread throughout the city of Palermo are many different types of places associated with the Christian Catholic community. Before the advent of Christianity, cults devoted to pagan deities expressed themselves through a series of ritual manifestations of a commemorative and festive character. You can still feel this ambience in Palermo. An recurring image is that of the atmosphere created on the occasion of the Festino, which is dedicated to Santa Rosalia, the patron saint of the city. The presence of ecclesiastical buildings in the city is remarkable: some of them maintain an active and direct relationship with the community while some are places of religious syncretism in which multiple faiths coexist.

- Churches
- Parish Churches
- Oratories
- Confraternities
- Catholic Schools and Institutions

Syncretism places

Murals with religious theme

Sanctuary

Informal place for ceremonies

"Acchianata" pathway

S. Benedetto's Pilgrimage pathway

COMMUNITIES, PLACES, AND RITUALS OF OTHER FAITHS

ALFREDO MICHELE AMICO, CHIARA CAPRIO, FRANCESCA CROCE, MASSIMO GAMBINO

The presence of many foreign communities has activated new places, some of them temporary, dedicated to the various religions present in Palermo. A process of the merging of ideological elements from different religious cultures, allowing adherents to share moments related to their liturgical traditions, is also present. An example of this process is present in the Church of San Nicolò all'Albergheria. Despite being a sacred place for Catholic Christians, it hosts a religious event on the first Sunday of every month in which Muslim, Tamil, and Christian worshippers share a moment of prayer and brotherhood. Another place where you can witness moments of religious and cultural integration is the Oratory of Santa Chiara. Activities that aim to aid the integration of the various faithful within the territory of Palermo take place here, providing play activities play for children and assistance for adults. Another example of the connection between the different religious communities is the devotion shown by the Tamil Hindus of Palermo to Santa Rosalia—the beloved "Santuzza"—whose sanctuary is located on top of Mount Pellegrino.

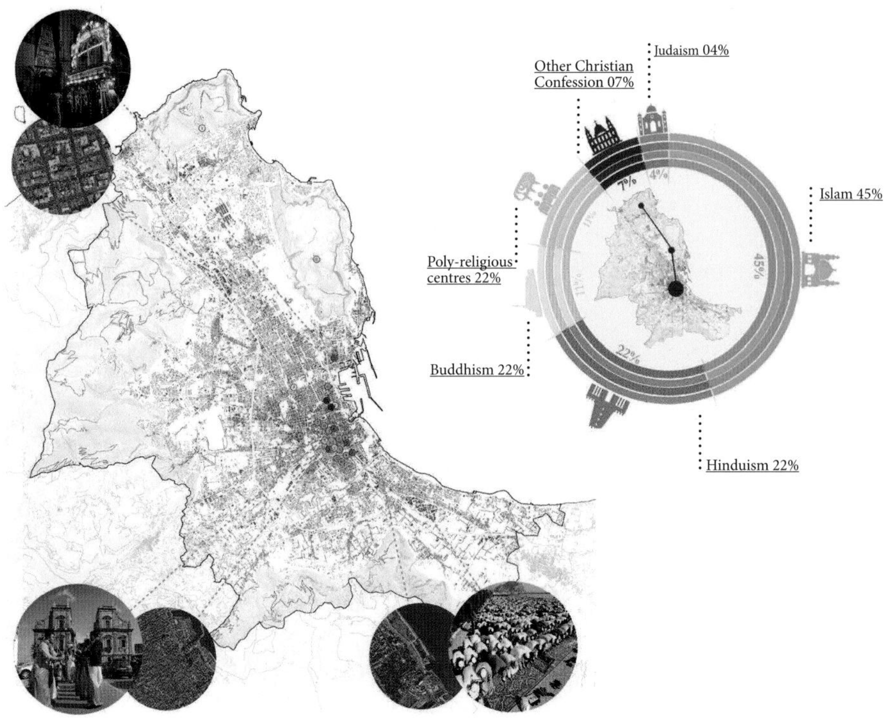

THE UNIVERSITY AND THE CITY

ALBERTO CANNIZZARO, PEDRO FANECA, ALFREDO PENSABENE, BEATRIZ SOARES

A more qualified, fair, and equitable cosmopolitan city arises from the spreading of culture and from involving citizens and their values of urban identity. Culture plays a pivotal role in the life of the city and its openness to the world. The university not only deals with education, but is also committed to the dissemination of culture through the presence of libraries, museums, and laboratories. In addition to UNIPA, Palermo hosts research centres (CNR and CdRn) and colleges for artistic and musical training. There are also private universities in the city that contribute to the dissemination of culture and international openness.

THE IMAGE OF THE CITY

EMANUELA BONURA, LAUSA CASTELLUCCIO, EDOARDO CICALA, NATALIA DI GANGI

The construction of the urban image and urban imagination of Palermo has been, and continues to be, a collective action of collaborative codification generated by and from both real images and fictions. In other words, the memory of the real city is replaced by a memory of the imaginary that becomes reality; the memory itself becomes the *topos*. Whether their scenery was real or imaginary, their reception critical or enthusiastic, the movies that have used Palermo as a film set always reflect, and sometimes encode, part of the image of the city. For this reason, the mapping of film locations in the atlas underlines and highlights the charm of the historic centre, where most of the films—comedies, dramas, thrillers, romances, biographies and historical stories—have been set.

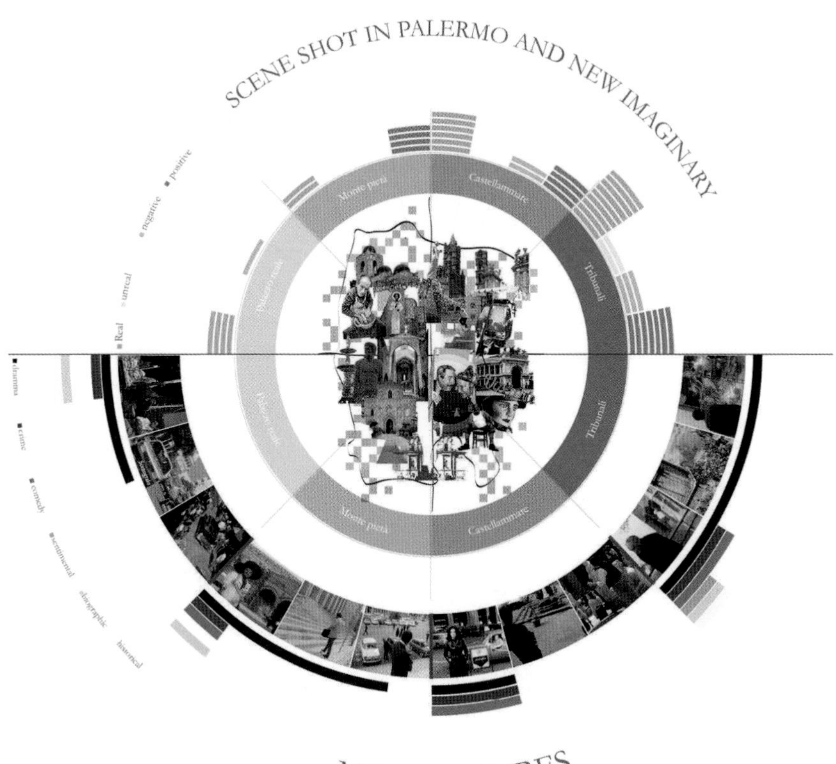

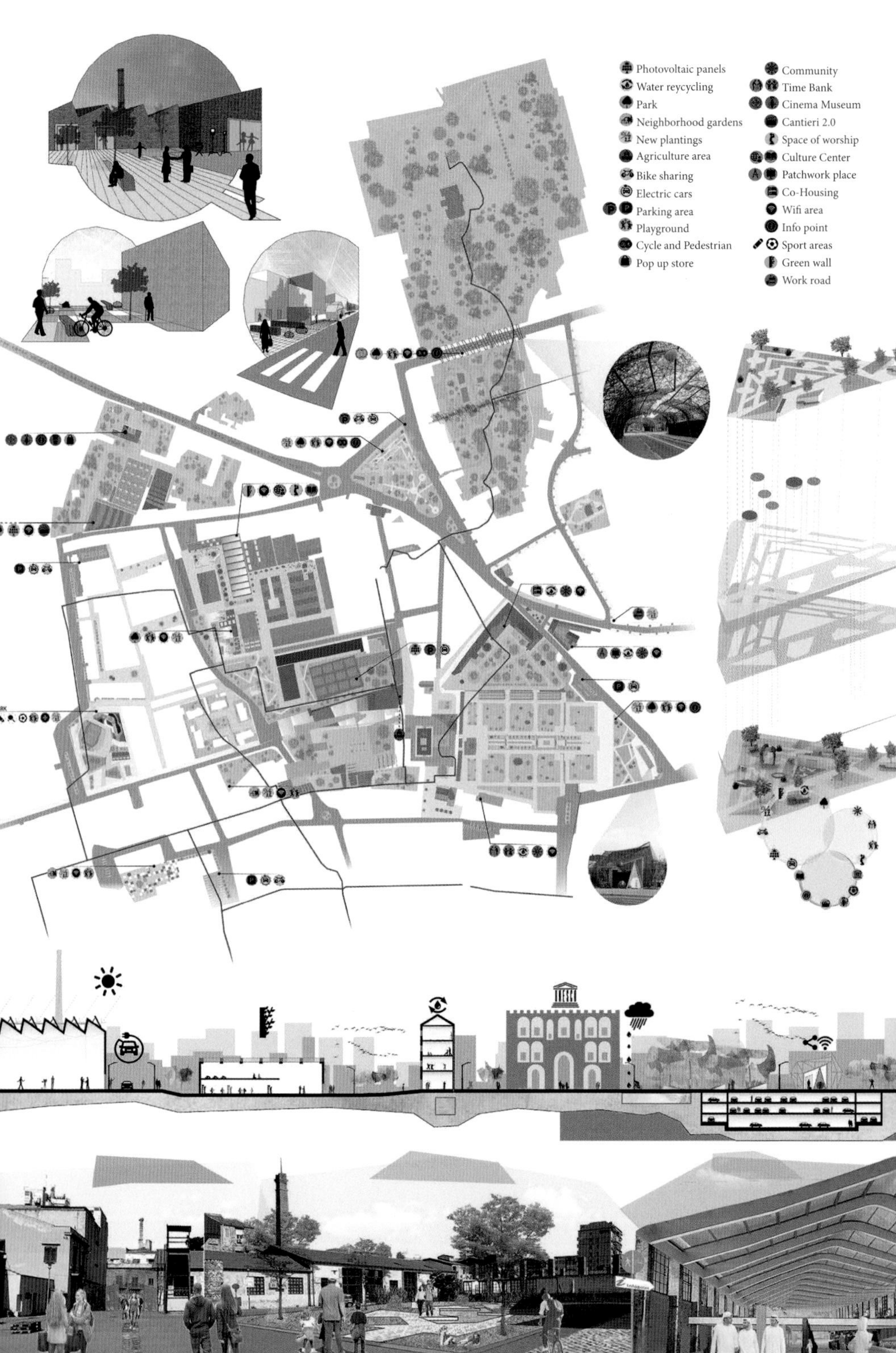
Photovoltaic panels
Water reycycling
Park
Neighborhood gardens
New plantings
Agriculture area
Bike sharing
Electric cars
Parking area
Playground
Cycle and Pedestrian
Pop up store
Community
Time Bank
Cinema Museum
Cantieri 2.0
Space of worship
Culture Center
Patchwork place
Co-Housing
Wifi area
Info point
Sport areas
Green wall
Work road

CITY OF CONNECTIONS

ALFREDO MICHELE AMICO, CHIARA CAPRIO, FRANCESCA CROCE, MASSIMO GAMBINO

In this project, the Zisa urban district, including the Cantieri Culturali cultural centre, is connected through a green network of historical gardens. In the first phase, colonisation, the project aims to connect these spaces through the simple but disruptive action of opening their gates. The consolidation phase covers the construction of a new pedestrian and cycle network and the improvement of the existing one, as well as the creation of co-housing for students and artists in the former Institute of the Sacred Heart. In the development phase, it will be possible to establish cultural attractors, for example in the former Educandato Whitaker residential school and the former Gulì factories.

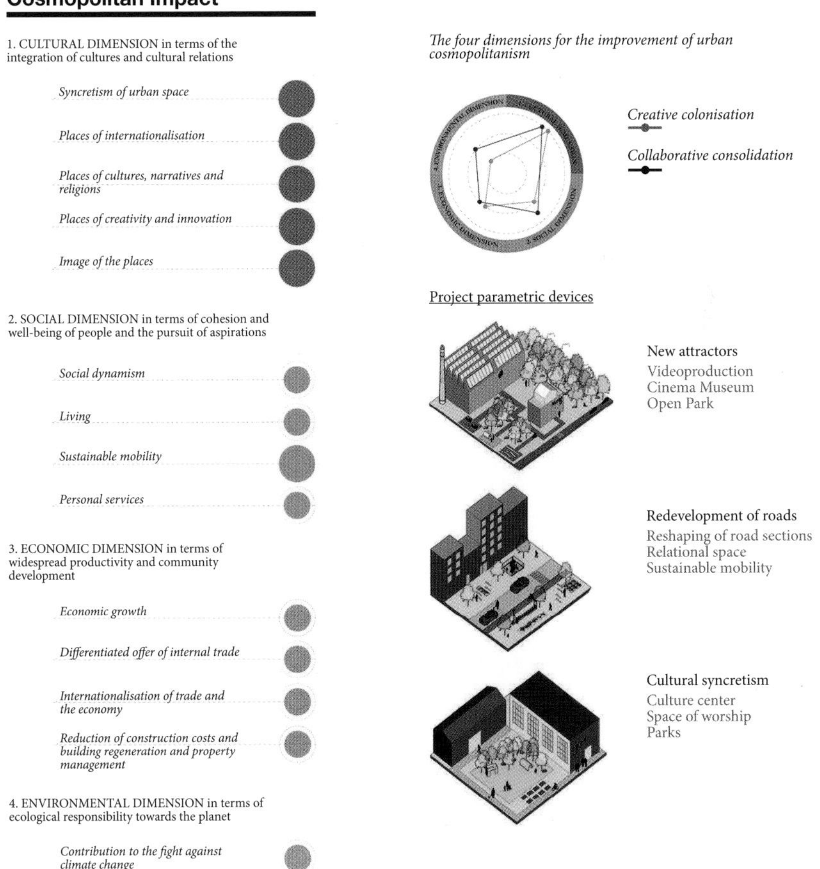

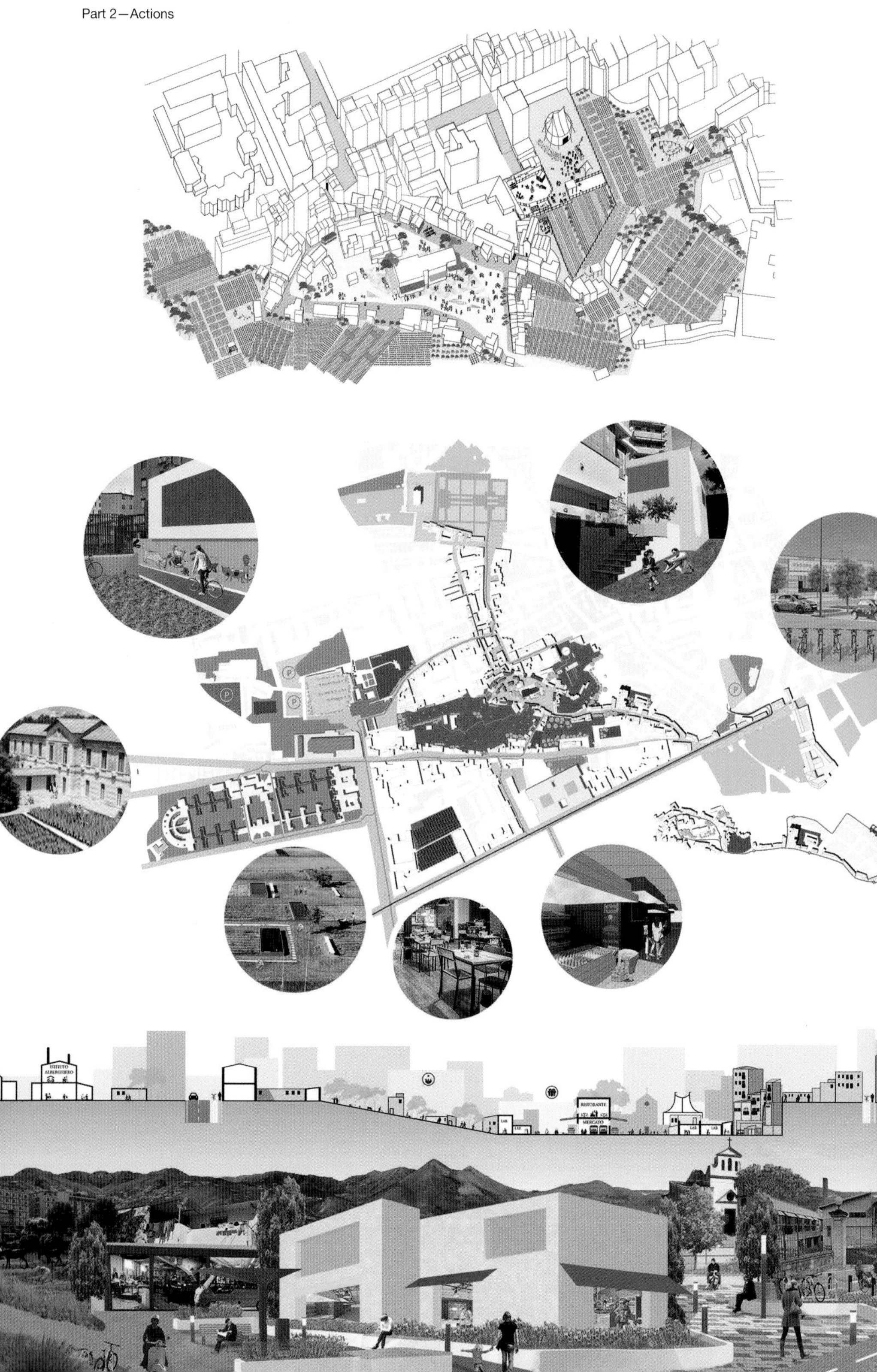
ISTITUTO ALBERGHIERO
RISTORANTE
MERCATO
LAB

THROUGH DANISINNI

EMILIA ABATE, ALESSIA ALVICH, GIOVANNI DAVID, PAOLO NEGLIA

The project focuses on the redevelopment of the Danisinni area, the creation of new training facilities and the reconnection of the area with the urban infrastructure—including the nearby district of Zisa, the former psychiatric hospital, and the Norman Palace. Among the main objectives are the recovery of the water cycle and the redevelopment of abandoned spaces in order to convert them to productive-agricultural and leisure uses, while at the same time creating the conditions for their irrigation. New spaces for study and research may also be created in some of the former hospital's pavilions. Ultimately, the redevelopment could provide spaces for co-housing and social housing, craft workshops, and a covered zero-kilometre fruit and vegetable market and catering facility.

Cosmopolitan Impact

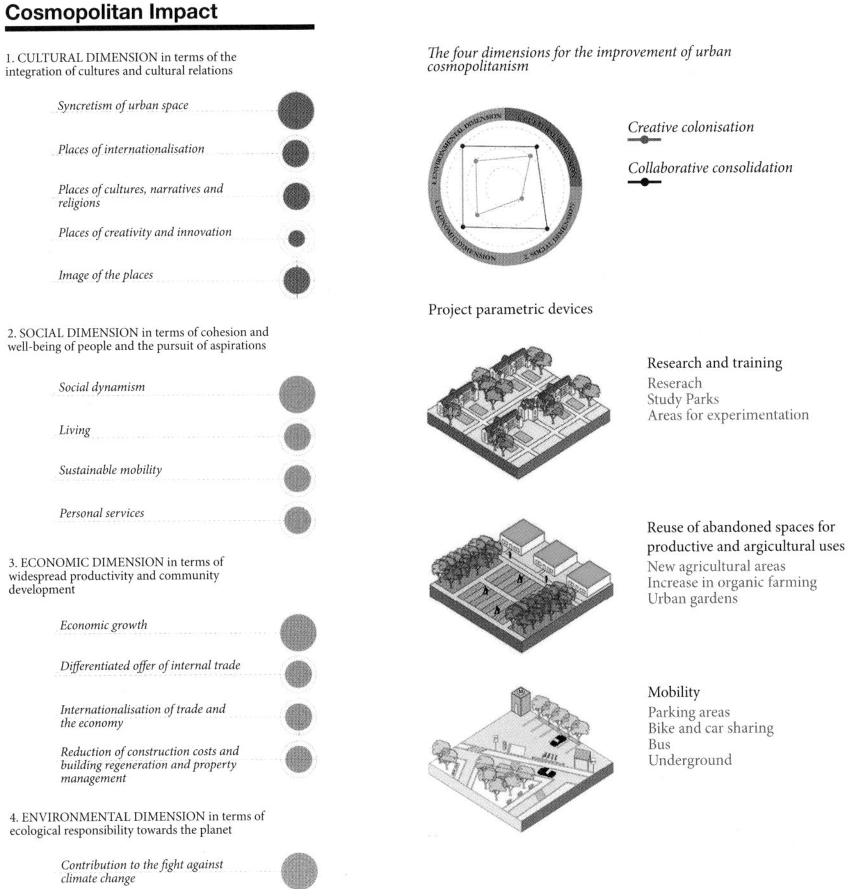

School of Urban Regeneration

CULTURE-AL HALISAH

LIDIA BADAGLIACCA, GIORGIA CALANDRA, ALESSANDRO CARDULLO, FRANCESCA LA MATTINA

This study for an urban regeneration project in the ancient district of Kalsa focuses on cultural activities and spaces that, through different levels of meaning, will reshape these places to become new urban attractors. One of the most significant interventions aims to connect Piazza Magione to other great places in which culture is generated—Palazzo Butera and Steri, Palazzo Abatellis, the Church of Spasimo, GAM, and the Pantaleone Gallery—with a cultural artistic path.

Cosmopolitan Impact

1. CULTURAL DIMENSION in terms of the integration of cultures and cultural relations

Syncretism of urban space

Places of internationalisation

Places of cultures, narratives and religions

Places of creativity and innovation

Image of the places

2. SOCIAL DIMENSION in terms of cohesion and well-being of people and the pursuit of aspirations

Social dynamism

Living

Sustainable mobility

Personal services

3. ECONOMIC DIMENSION in terms of widespread productivity and community development

Economic growth

Differentiated offer of internal trade

Internationalisation of trade and the economy

Reduction of construction costs and building regeneration and property management

4. ENVIRONMENTAL DIMENSION in terms of ecological responsibility towards the planet

Contribution to the fight against climate change

The four dimensions for the improvement of urban cosmopolitanism

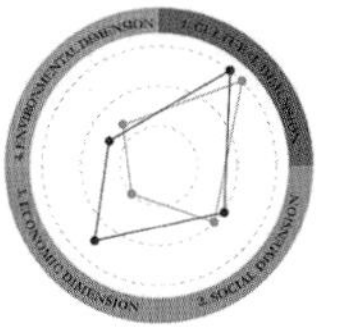

Creative colonisation

Collaborative consolidation

Project parametric devices

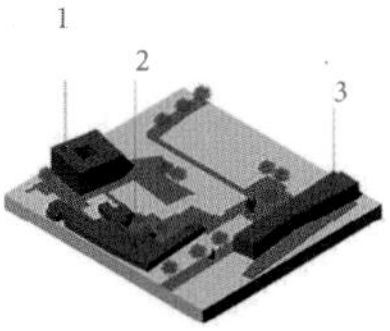

New cultural attractors
1 Steri Museum centre
2 Administrative centre widespread museum
3 Palazzo Butera

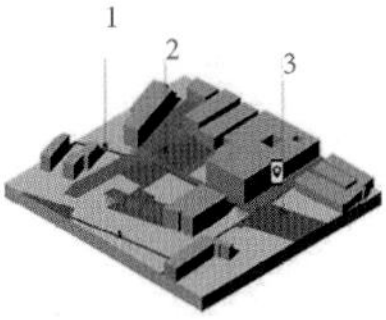

Slow mobilityimplementation
1 Cycle paths
2 Pedestrianisation
3 Bike-sharing

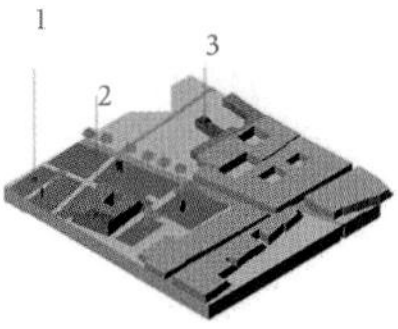

Energy production / New economy
1 Urban spaces for laboratory and commercial activities
2 Roof garden
3 Photovoltaic panels

PEDANA A SCOMPARSA
CONTENITORI PER RIFIUTI
ECOISOLA
VANO TECNICO
0 30 60

BALHARA

DAVIDE CRUPI, PIETRO IRACI, STEFANO MIRANTI, ALAIN SCHIMMENTI

This study project for the Ballarò area implements a network of public spaces implemented and adds a multifunctional centre and a hotel to the district. The existing urban roads are enhanced to invite city users into the new commercial fabric, which—in addition to providing spaces for selling products and recycling—is useful in communicating local identities. The physical space is also regenerated through social activities and through the implementation of policies and instruments that facilitate development based on public-private partnerships.

Cosmopolitan Impact

1. CULTURAL DIMENSION in terms of the integration of cultures and cultural relations

Syncretism of urban space

Places of internationalisation

Places of cultures, narratives and religions

Places of creativity and innovation

Image of the places

2. SOCIAL DIMENSION in terms of cohesion and well-being of people and the pursuit of aspirations

Social dynamism

Living

Sustainable mobility

Personal services

3. ECONOMIC DIMENSION in terms of widespread productivity and community development

Economic growth

Differentiated offer of internal trade

Internationalisation of trade and the economy

Reduction of construction costs and building regeneration and property management

4. ENVIRONMENTAL DIMENSION in terms of ecological responsibility towards the planet

Contribution to the fight against climate change

The four dimensions for the improvement of urban cosmopolitanism

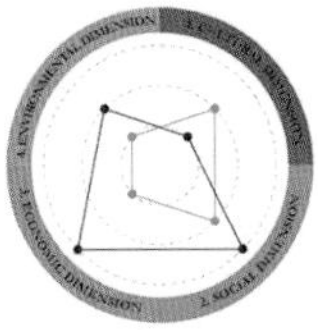

Creative colonisation

Collaborative consolidation

Project parametric devices

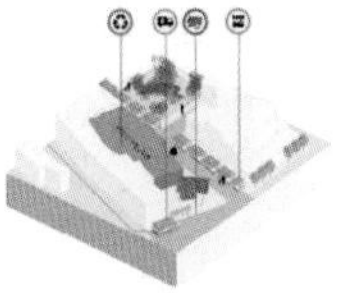

New attractors
Photovoltaic roof
Waste disposal route
Recy-Lab
Commercial space

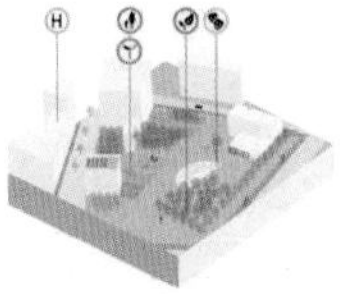

New urban gardens
Park
Hospital related services
Hospital
Theater
Sensory gardens

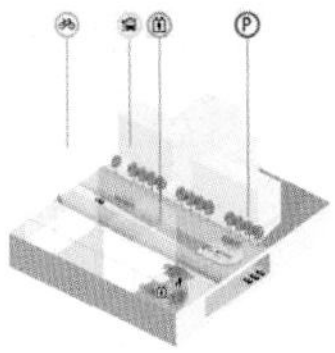

New eco-infrastructure
Underground parking
Ecological tram
Vertical connection
Bicycle lane

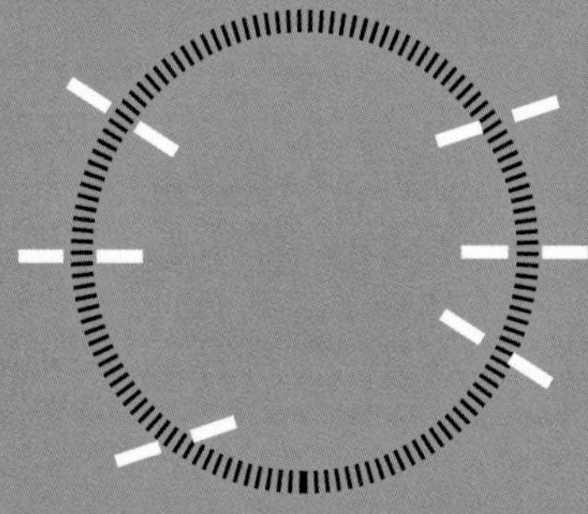

projects: open city

PALERMO OPEN CITY

FEDERICA SCAFFIDI, JÖRG SCHRÖDER

Located at the crossroads of the Mediterranean, Palermo recently received international attention with the *Manifesta* contemporary art event on the theme of "Cultivating Coexistence" and with the designation of its Arabic-Norman World Heritage sites. Both initiatives gave further strength to the city's cultural and social renaissance. The vision of Palermo as a laboratory for the humanities, arts, and culture necessitates a strong Mediterranean dimension: the city is a stage for the challenges of migration, climate change, and the very future of the south of Europe, especially for young people. How can the elements, energies, and networks of a collaborative city overcome spatial and social fragmentation? What role can boundaries, limits, borders, thresholds, and peripheries play in envisioning *Cosmopolitan Habitat*? The "Palermo Open City urban design studio" aims to develop new concepts and tools for architectural urbanism through a performative and creative analysis that links multiple research avenues—including texts and movies, location references and innovative forms of mapping, diagramming and information interaction—in a strategic and inter-scalar design approach that combines spatial activators and connectors, urban patterns and networks, and urban practices. Starting from the potentialities and resources of Palermo, the purpose of the urban design studio is to find innovative solutions for the location through the analysis of the following main topics:

- **OPENNESS** and **INTEGRATIVITY**—both towards migrants and as a general cultural, social, and economic idea—focus on the analysis of the diversity of Palermo's social realities, especially in emerging communities such as those in Danisinni. Thematic analysis on these topics, therefore, aims to observe local communities; to ask who is living in certain places, and how they are doing so.
- **FRAGMENTATION** focuses on built structures, infrastructures, and topography that on one hand offer the opportunity for novel boundaries and peripheries, and on the other hand express a cultural and social richness.
- **HERITAGE** may find expression in different ways—from World Heritage sites to recent or intangible heritage, existing in a diffuse and polycentric sense and driven by different initiatives. Interpreted as Creative Heritage, this theme can be seen as strongly referring to ideas of openness, migration, and internationality.
- **COLLABORATIVE CITY** concerns the activation of elements, energies, and networks. It involves the observation of processes of urban transformation that could be linked to a new material productivity, whether in terms of crafts, expertise, digital production, or intangible collaborations. In the design approach, the collaborative aspect of a city is emphasised by the use of new technological tools and by open, public, and sharing spaces. This links also to the UNESCO Network of Learning Cities, which Palermo has been part of since 2019.

MORE THAN FOOD

ISOLA DANISINNI

MARA PIEL, MARIE-SOPHIE WALDMINGHAUS

Food waste is a major global issue and a substantial driver of environmental degradation. In Palermo, this issue is very visible. A lot of food waste is left behind as a result of market leftovers, careless handling, and malfunctioning waste collection services and missing infrastructure. But at the root of the issue lies a superior problem: that of a non-sustainable economy accompanied by the unconscious consumption of goods. A primarily linear economy results in lots of waste. A sustainable transformation towards a circular economy and conscious consumption are necessary to tackle this cause. The circular economy does not end with the single use of a product. Further usage of leftovers and recycling enable a circular use of resources without waste or excess. The objective of this study project is to develop a strategy for an applied, closed food cycle in a specific area, which can then be expanded and transferred to other areas. In the urban fabric of Palermo, the neighbourhood of Danisinni stands out as a suitable place to realise this project. It is located quite centrally in the city and offers some private green spaces, but is isolated due to its topography and poor accessibility. As an island in the city, Danisinni offers the ideal conditions for a testing ground and starting point for further developments that aim to establish a self-sufficient community. Looking back at the area's history, people always have used the resources that were available to them. Today, the area is socially deprived and has an unemployment rate of 90%. Danisinni mainly consists of small residential buildings and open spaces. Some are used for farming or by the circus situated in the neighbourhood, but there is also a lot of unused space—for instance, a large area of wasteland and a closed site with a vacant school building at its centre. In line with the neighbourhood's traditional approach, our suggestion uses what is available and aims to work out and strengthen its potential.

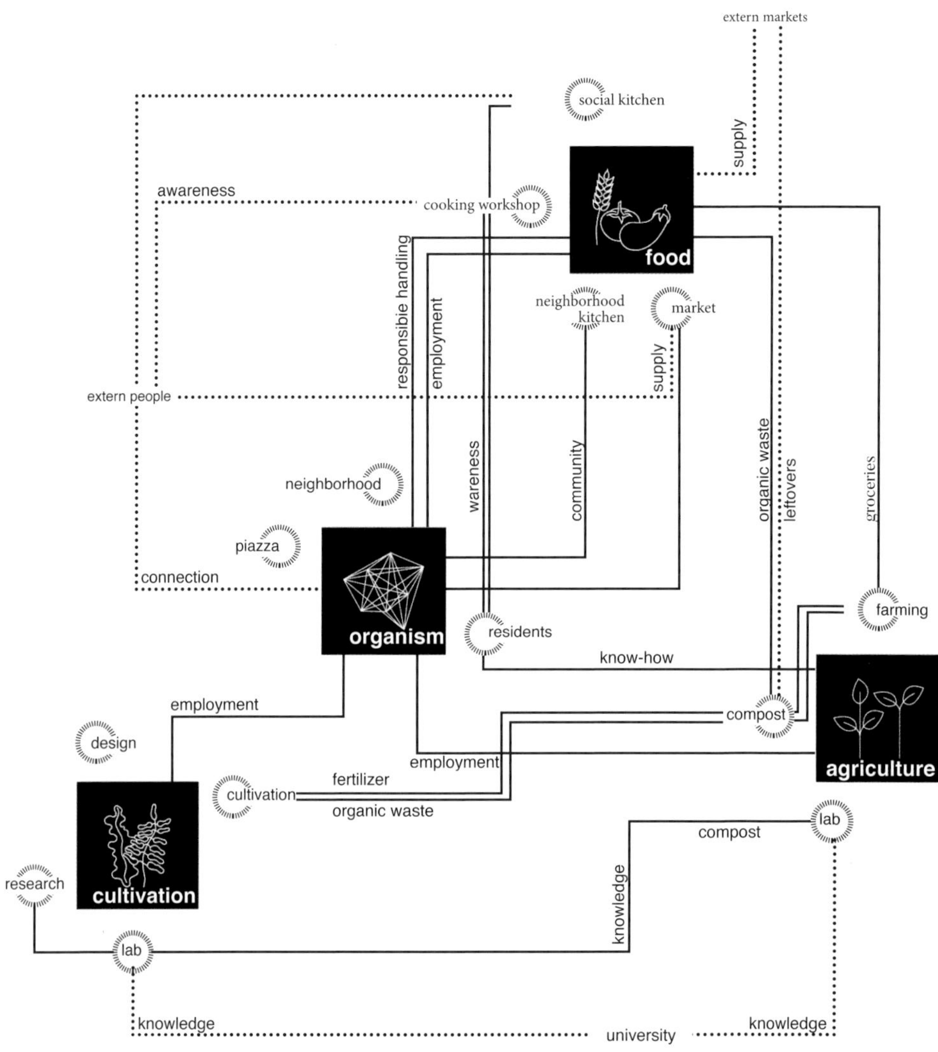

Figure 1
Issue #1 circular design - food
Graphic by the authors

The development proceeds in four phases, that build on each other and use given resources.

In phase one, the conventional food agriculture of the area is extended with experimental cultivation and associated research into innovative foods and products that sustainably complement the different production and use stages of the food already being produced. An example would be microalgaes, which can be cultivated in a resource-saving manner, would not compete with other food production, and can be used in multiple ways—as a superfood, to create sustainable packaging, or even to generate energy. In addition to this, the processing of the waste products of the food production would be an important field for research. A composting process would be developed for organic waste.

In phase two, the vacant school building is reactivated and labs are placed inside. These labs will work together with the farming and experimental cultivation operations to research innovative solutions and ways of improving food use and consumption and the handling of leftovers.

In phase three, the area around the school is shaped into a new piazza. This new piazza will act as both the spatial and thematic centre of the commune, as well as for the wider Danisinni area and its surroundings. The space will bring together and supplement the different food production steps from farming to consumption. To this end, new functions will be added: a market for distributing goods, a neighbourhood kitchen, and an outdoor dining area. These will act as communal areas that return a social element to preparing and consuming food. In addition, there will be space for art on the piazza, as well as for the existing community activities.

In phase four, further interventions are added. The "neighbourhood living room" will provide a community space for interaction, and cooking workshops will raise awareness of conscious food use, as well as imparting skills to prevent waste. Both interventions will be located in unused spaces on the border between the neighbourhood and the surrounding district and will form new spatial and programmatic connections. A recognisable design will be used to create an visible link between the cultivation fields and the piazza; the size and type of the design will be adjustable depending on available space and use.

Overall, this concept turns Danisinni into a functional organism. The different interventions interact with each other and operate together. The food use circle is closed, resulting in more than just the prevention of food waste: the effects extend across several ecological, social, and economic dimensions. Danisinni becomes integrated in its surrounding, community space is created, education and employment are enhanced, and income is generated. The "island" works as a node and is in exchange with its surroundings. The implementation of additional interventions in Palermo will lead to the formation of new nodes and extend the citywide network of flows of knowledge, goods, and people. The exchange and support provided through participation in a global network of pioneers in food production and zero waste will drive the cosmopolitan transition to sustainability.

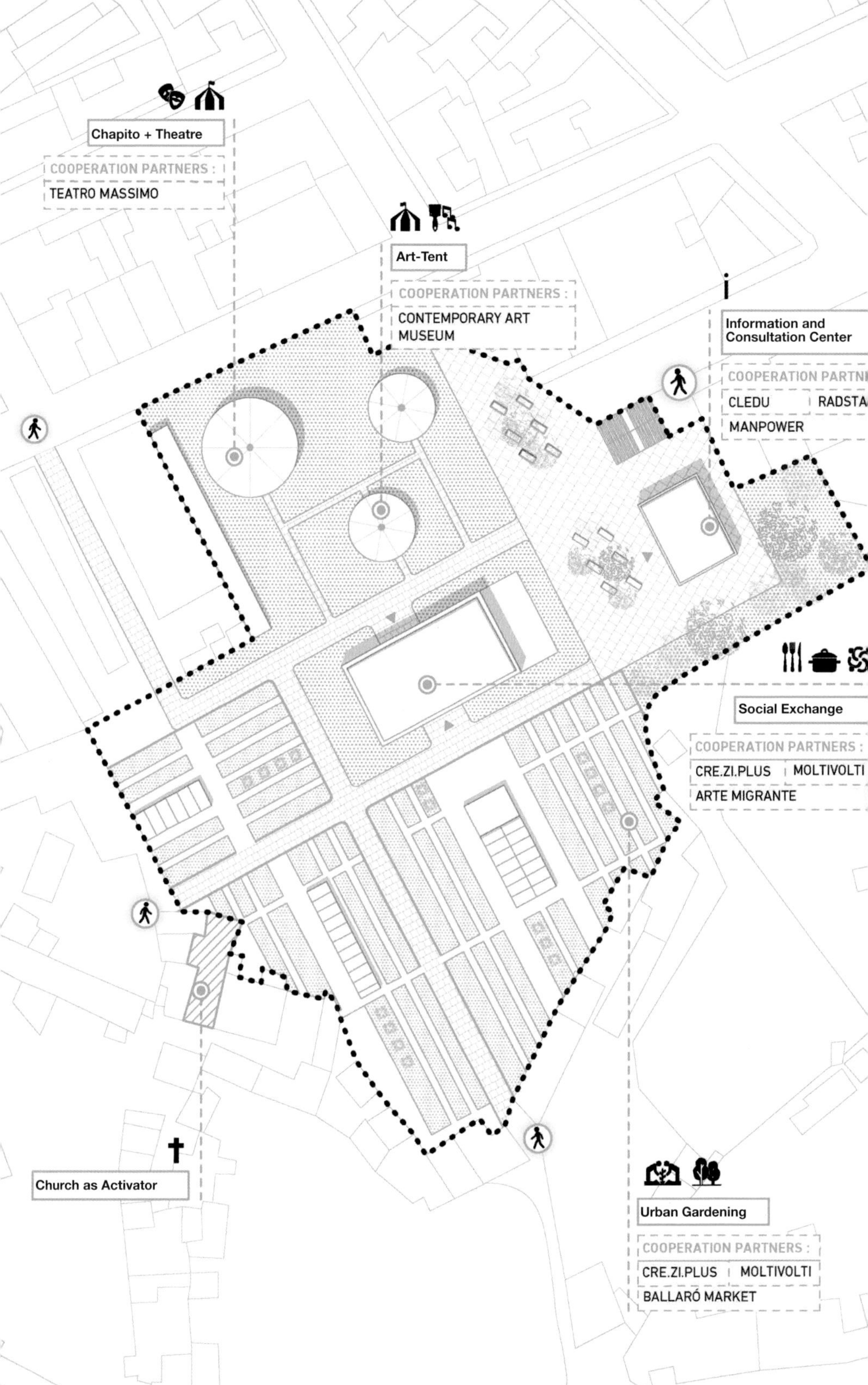

Chapito + Theatre
COOPERATION PARTNERS :
TEATRO MASSIMO
Art-Tent
COOPERATION PARTNERS :
CONTEMPORARY ART MUSEUM
Information and Consultation Center
COOPERATION PARTN
CLEDU
RADSTA
MANPOWER
Social Exchange
COOPERATION PARTNERS :
CRE.ZI.PLUS
MOLTIVOLTI
ARTE MIGRANTE
Church as Activator
Urban Gardening
COOPERATION PARTNERS :
CRE.ZI.PLUS
MOLTIVOLTI
BALLARÓ MARKET

CULTURE-UP! PALERMO

RANDA HARANI, LEONA SCHUBERT

The Sicilian capital Palermo, with its 663,401 inhabitants, is a city that can claim a unique cultural make-up. Due to its geographical position, the Mediterranean capital has been exposed to a wide range of influences from different civilisations since the very beginning of its historical record. In the past decades, this has been followed by ongoing immigration—which is itself reflected in a strong and captivating cultural richness and human diversity. The interculturality of Palermo is one of its greatest and most authentic characteristics. This individuality, which attracts a large number of visitors each year, has developed into one of the country's major economic pillars; tourism is one of the city's main sources of income. It is therefore all the more surprising to note that many cultural contact points in Palermo remain isolated and provide an insufficient amount of information to potential visitors—in many cases even lacking an individual website. It is sometimes almost impossible for tourists or even locals to take advantage of the entire cultural spectrum on offer and to discover which interests can be pursued in which specific places. It is also striking how limited the communication between many of these cultural anchor is, despite the wide range of similarities that they exhibit and despite the incredible potential this might open up. In this study project, this deficiency will be investigated and proposals for solutions to counteract this disadvantaged situation will be worked out. As a first step, the most significant cultural hotspots throughout Palermo are identified and examined. Taking this closer look makes it easier to determine which existing instances can be arranged thematically and which of those have the potential to achieve maximum mutual cooperation and opportunity. The aim is to create new platforms that will make it possible for the individual, segregated hotspots to come into more direct physical contact, enabling them to interact with and enrich each

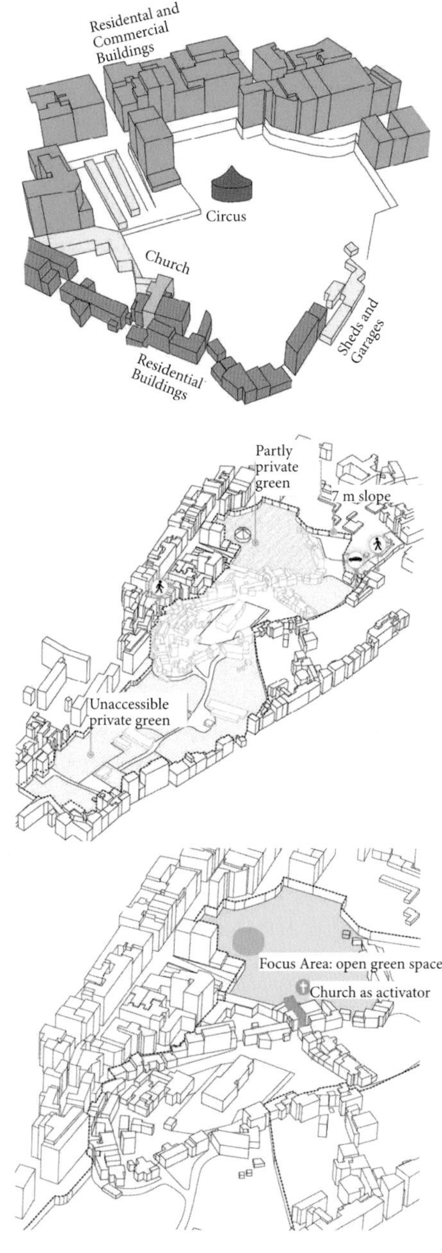

Figure 1
Danisinni Analysis
Concept design by the authors

other on a much stronger foundation. The selected hotspots should retain their primary location; the objective is to stretch their overall reach by expanding their territory. The hotspots are grouped together based on their points of interest, building a new platform for working towards an overarching subject matter. The most important criteria for the selection of the locations of the platforms were as follows: proximity to the city centre, urban planning dimensions sufficient to implement architectural design approaches, largely unused or vacant spaces, and existing cultural stimuli or impulses that the new project can build on. Various locations and themes were considered: Danisinni, with a focus on culture and social exchange; Parco Villa Filipina, with a focus on art and culture; and La Cuba, with a focus on language and culture.

The example of Danisinni illustrates what the functionality and real implementation of such a platform could look like and how it could work in the future. Danisinni is a small district in the southwest of Palermo characterised by a very high unemployment rate, poverty, and a lack of schooling among its residents, which does not make it a very popular place to live. Its building structure is largely flat and narrow, and it is situated on a plateau eight metres below the surrounding neighbourhood, which is composed of prefabricated apartment blocks. As a result, the district appears completely isolated from the wider city. Furthermore, while there are an enormous number of inaccessible and mostly private green spaces occupying a significant amount of space in the area, there are no places for social gathering and no existing social infrastructure other than the district's only church and the small "Chapito" circus in the eastern part of the neighbourhood.

The platform proposes a new intervention that attempts to counteract these unfavourable living conditions and to bring about changes that affect both Danisinni and the whole of Palermo simultaneously. Firstly, a new community garden where organic fruits and vegetables can be cultivated will be created. This will not only open up a new and solid source of income but can also develop into a place of social gathering. In addition to this, new architecture with the primary function of reinforcing social interaction within the area will be introduced: for example, as a co-working restaurant, a community kitchen where self-grown fruits and vegetables are processed free of charge, and a community living room where people can comfortably enjoy each other's company. To contribute to solving the unfavourable labour market situation, a new information centre will be created, where both locals and migrants can get legal help and advice aimed at improving their job opportunities. Finally, the circus tent theme will be expanded, and similar structures with additional temporary music and art installations will be set up to complete the picture. Various actors will be involved in this platform: Moltivolti, Arte Migrante, the Ballaró Market, Cledu, and many others will create a strong network of active collaboration. Not only will the quality of life in the Danisinni district be upgraded, but a profound networking sphere will be created through the incorporation of various parties. This partnership—both between the different hotspots of the platform and between different platforms—is to be supported by a new website that will make it possible to access all the necessary information on all related events and all participants involved. As an outcome of this intervention, the cultural hotspots initially identified will no longer be segregated, but will be connected both physically and virtually, extending a strong network across the city that makes it easier for locals, migrants, and visitors to have an overview of the whole range of cultural experiences that Palermo has to offer.

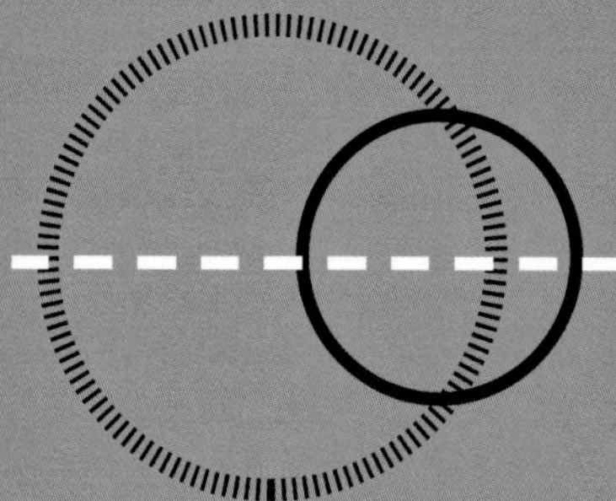

projects: urban narratives

URBAN NARRATIVES

RICCARDA CAPPELLER, JÖRG SCHRÖDER

In the search for *Cosmopolitan Habitats*, shared perspectives on multiple research avenues foster an open and ongoing dialogue about the creation and transformation of urban space. Three very different contextual situations—here in Hanover, the inner city of Halle, and the city and harbour of Flensburg—confront topics that address the cultural dimension of space, its role in extending existing resources, and the challenge of designing spaces for interaction that can serve as public spheres: creating opportunities for exchange, collaboration, and learning within an increasingly diverse and digitally connected society. The rethinking and rediscovery of neglected, under-used, and unused spaces and their qualities, as well as their various reinterpretations within the projects—which understand design as a *Re-cycle* practice (Ricci, Schröder 2016)—are linked to innovative ideas, locally relevant programmes, and strategies that include reflection on processual implementation and the consolidation of the cultural scene in place. Today, with the city characterised not only by multiplicity, coexistence, contradictions, social segregation, and spatial fragmentation, but also by complexity, it is important to identify common questions: how can urban structures aimed at interaction, community, and social use be thought of and reorganised in the context of the ongoing crisis and its future effects? What are the conditions and pathways for a heterogeneous and inclusive city that is built on the potentials of the city that already exists? What kinds of resources can we rely upon in urban transformation processes when we engage with heritage?

Aiming at performative and sustainable scenarios, the visions for each place are emphasised as narratives and understood as space-bound devices and mediators between analytical, projectual, personal, and collective approaches. They create stimulating relations between facts and emotions and provide means to make sense of and understand social phenomena and individual experiences (Bond, Thompson-Fawcett 2008). Situations "as found" can become starting points for urban actions and for creating catalysts—urban laboratories and experimental spaces—for imagined fundamental changes within each of the cities. Whether these situations represent sites of work and labour, cultural production, education, or performative interventions, they can provide institutions with new perspectives, as in the case the university campus and trade fair in Hanover; be bound to the idea of an inaugural event, as in the case of the Volkspark in Halle (a former cultural and political meeting place of a workmens' association); or propose long-lasting spatial solutions, such as those for re-activating Flensburg's eastern harbour area with a combination of new urban platforms, living spaces, cultural spots, and makerspaces in former silos. As "urban linkages", the multi-scalar design-research projects use creative aspects of cultural heritage and its capacities to achieve the "participation, inclusion and commitment of citizens" (Schröder, Carta, Hartmann 2018, p. 11).

BIBLIOGRAPHY

Ricci M., Schröder J. (2015) *Re-cycle Italy. Towards a proactive manifesto.* Roma, Aracne.

Bond S., Thompson-Fawcett M. (2008) "Multiplicities, Interwoven Threads, Holistic Paths: The Phronetic Long-Haul Approach". In: Maginn P. J., Thompson S. M., Tonts M. eds. (2008) *Qualitative Urban Analysis: An International Perspective. Studies in Qualitative Methodology, Volume* 9. Amsterdam, Emerald, pp. 51–78.

Schröder J., Carta M., Hartmann S. eds. (2018) *Creative Heritage.* Berlin, Jovis.

SINGER

VOLKSPARK RELOADED

ELIZAVETA MISYURYAEVA

In Halle, at the threshold between the respectable Giebichenstein residential district and the extensive Saale riverbank, the Burgstraße hosts the former cultural and political meeting space of the local workmens' association. The name "Volkspark"[1] translates to "people's park", but the site actually consists of a building erected in 1907 in the rather opulent shapes and dimensions of art nouveau and a large garden area. Its location overlooking the river has made it a famous example of a building with this function. Over time, however, meeting spaces like the ones it holds have become obsolete and are now having to be rethought. Despite its prestige, the Volkspark in Halle has not been spared this trend. It has been used for a variety of purposes throughout the years, though it is now once again left without a vision for its use. In the near future, the city hopes to transform the Burgstraße into a cultural mile that will span from the Burg Giebichenstein University art campus to its design campus, and which might even extend further south to connect with other important institutions. The Volkspark is a good starting point for this project, but the question remains: what role should it play? How can the Volkspark consolidate its advantages and become indispensable without imitating the existing cultural institutions—thereby attracting a constant stream of contributors and visitors? The building does not have to lose its name in the process. Instead, it can absorb and demonstrate what it means to be a place for people in an increasingly diverse society that (still) struggles to overcome social segregation. Doing this requires an intervention that overcomes boundaries and connects local inhabitants. Armed with an understanding of their needs and a collective pool of ideas, it becomes possible to create sustainable spaces that people identify with. The project aims to become a model for this kind of catalyst intervention.

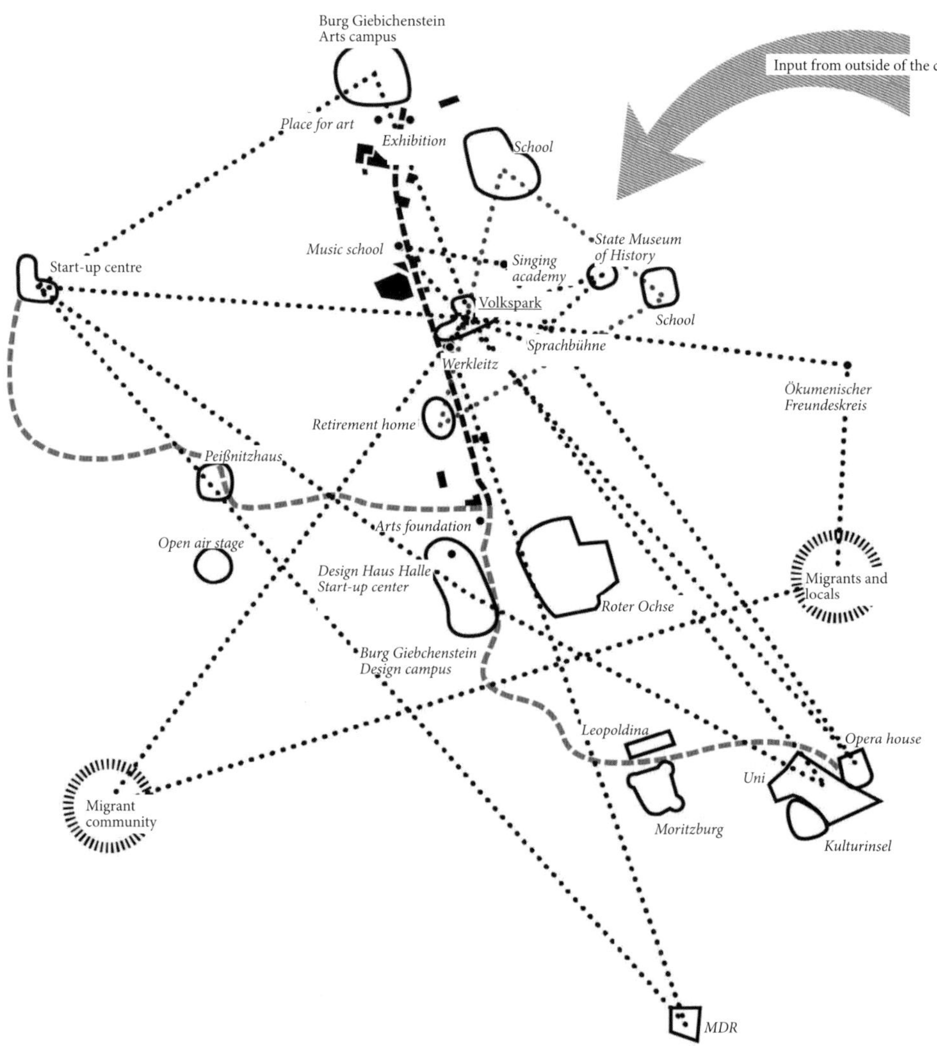

Figure 1
Connections through possible thematic collaborations
Graphic by the author

Figure 2
Section A-A
Concept design by the author

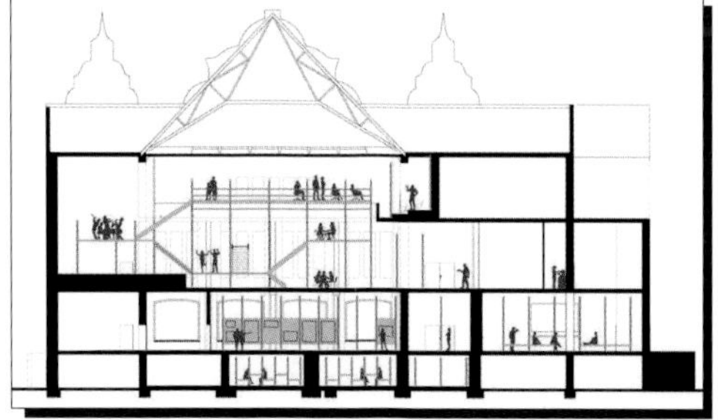

Figure 3
Section B-B
Concept design by the author

The main idea for the intervention consists of non-destructively dividing the spacious area of Volkspark using a temporary scaffolding structure that enables the creation of smaller, interactive, more easily adaptable spaces—and, therefore, more flexible use of individual rooms and sections of the park. The new configuration also makes it possible to guide visitors through the building in unusual ways, including through windows and back doors, giving them a new, "backstage-like" experience. The structure can be introduced to the public during a festival where performers and artists interpret the building in different ways and every visitor, whether independently or as a member of an association, institution, or similar group, has the opportunity to network with others and brainstorm ideas for collaborations and projects that can be hosted in the space. These new, collaborating groups could then apply for the use of different spaces within the site. After this event, depending on what connections have been made, the Volkspark can work in different modi operandi: as a whole, as individual rooms, or as a combination of spaces. In the latter configuration, parties with similar aims can share rooms to exchange ideas and try out new things. The allocation of the spaces should be time-limited—for example to a period of one year—and the parties encouraged to expand to other spaces on the Burgstraße in order to revive the unoccupied buildings and spaces. The introduction event can be repeated annually to provide an experimentation cycle.

FOOTNOTE
1_Source for the historical and actural aspects of Volkspark:
https://www.volkspark-halle.de/geschichte.html (01.08.2020)

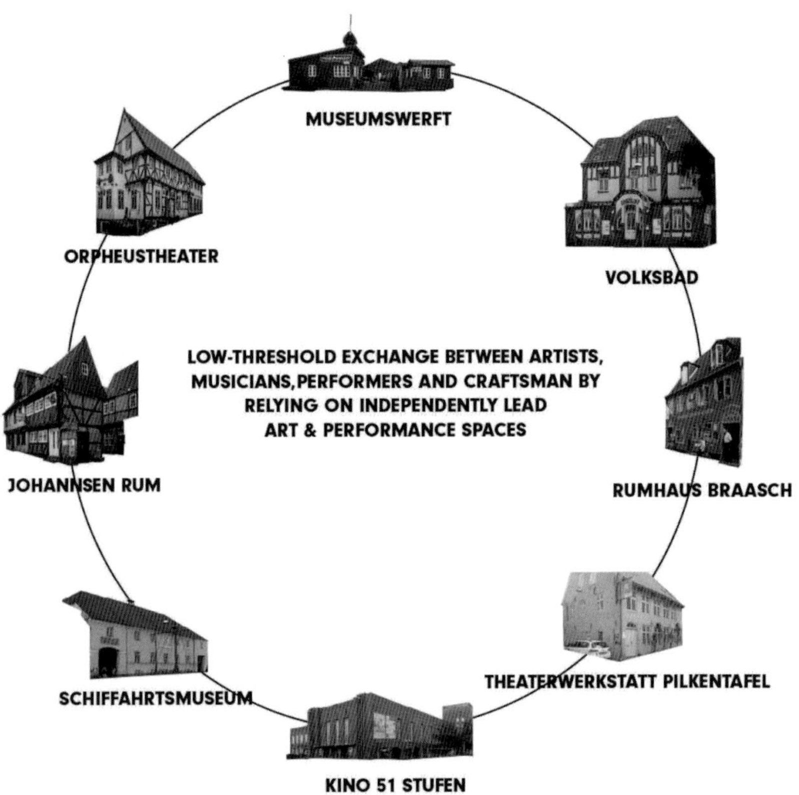
MUSEUMSWERFT
VOLKSBAD
RUMHAUS BRAASCH
THEATERWERKSTATT PILKENTAFEL
KINO 51 STUFEN
SCHIFFAHRTSMUSEUM
JOHANNSEN RUM
ORPHEUSTHEATER
LOW-THRESHOLD EXCHANGE BETWEEN ARTISTS,
MUSICIANS,PERFORMERS AND CRAFTSMAN BY
RELYING ON INDEPENDENTLY LEAD
ART & PERFORMANCE SPACES

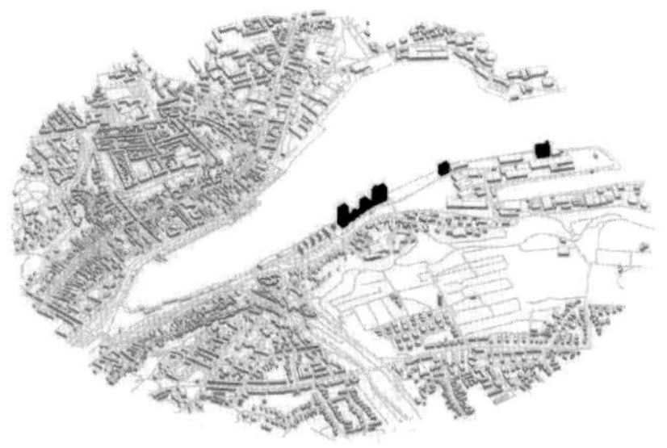

HARBOUR CULTURE TO CULTURE HARBOUR

JES HANSEN

This project is about transforming the (post)colonial harbour city of Flensburg. The aim is to establish a new link with the city of Charlotte Amalie and resolve the unsure future of the harbour region by both addressing the city's contemporary problems and finding new approaches to its past. That way, Flensburg can transition to a better future by rediscovering its history. The project consists of analyses of the (post)colonial spaces in both cities, a deeper spatial analysis of Flensburg's harbour region, and a proposal section in which programmatic and spatial changes to the harbour are suggested based on the earlier analyses. In the eighteenth and nineteenth centuries, Flensburg and Charlotte Amalie were linked through colonial trade activity. Flensburg, then a Danish city, imported rum, sugar, and molasses from the Danish colonies in the Danish West Indies. This made Flensburg the second-largest harbour in Denmark after Copenhagen. After Flensburg became German, it lost its trading rights—and with them its connections. While the colonial influence remains very visible in the (post)colonial spaces of Charlotte Amalie today, this shared history has largely been lost in Flensburg. It is retaining only traces of a colonial past that has largely been removed from the conscious history of the city. The project's aim is not only to create a new awareness of Flensburg's history, but also to generate new spatial realities using its (post)colonial past and present as catalysts.

The project consists of three major steps. In a first step, the "New Network" is established: a network for cultural exchange between the formerly linked cities of Charlotte Amalie and Flensburg that simultaneously raises awareness of the historical link and Flensburg's role in Danish colonialism. The second step is embedding the New Network in the city, first in the West Harbour region and later in

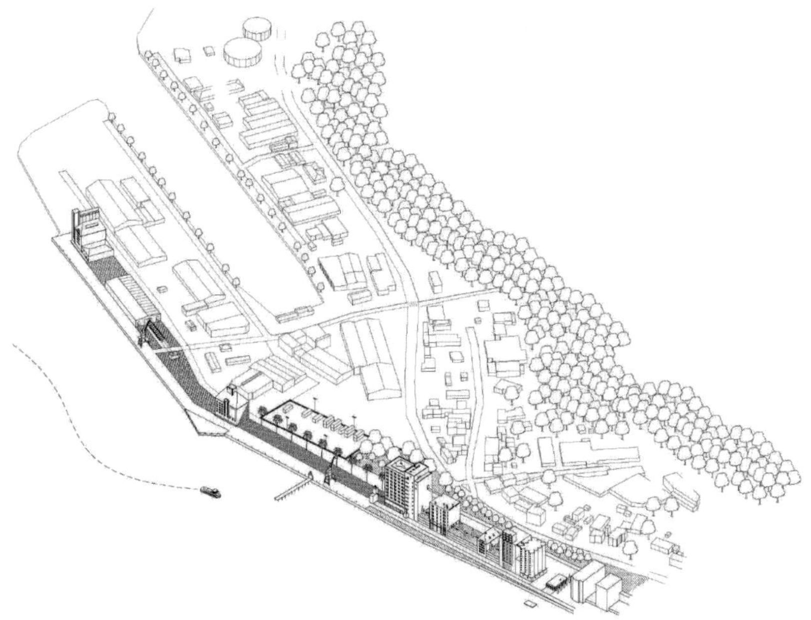

Figure 1
Proposal for the redevelopment of the East Harbour front
Concept design by the author

the East Harbour, in order to thoroughly anchor the network in the city's spatial and cultural fabric. The third step proposes a major programmatic and spatial redevelopment of the East Harbour front. To this end, the (post)colonial theories and methods developed and analysed in the first half of the project are used to generate new spaces in the front of the industrial East Harbour. By redeveloping former warehouses and finding new, expressive uses for the open and in-between spaces, the history of the harbour is preserved while at the same time becoming a key element of the city's future development. (Post)colonial theories applied to space are still a rarity in the field. It is even rarer for these theories to be applied to European spaces. This is likely to change in the future, as the history of a space always has the inherent potential to generate new spaces, better spaces, and future spaces. If we find new ways to engage with the city's history, we may find solutions to contemporary problems in very unexpected ways. As part of the first step, colonial markers have been identified in both cities. To do this, elements of the city that existed in the eighteenth century were singled out from the surrounding area. In Flensburg, the material markers consist mainly of former rum houses, warehouses, harbour infrastructure, and the *Kaufmannshöfe*. The immaterial markers are based on the area's self-identification as the *Rumstadt*, which betrays the Danish influences in the local language and placenames. By contrast, the city of Charlotte Amalie was founded for the sole purpose of the overseas exploitation of land and people by the Danish colonial power, prompting a different approach to colonial markers. Here, the focus was placed on material markers directly linked to colonial trade with Denmark. The influence of the Danish language is very recognisable in Charlotte Amalie's spaces. The focus area for the spatial concept developed in the proposal section is Flensburg's East Harbour. In contrast to the West Harbour, which features the historic city centre, the many cultural sites and scenic harbour front in this part of the city are dominated by twentieth-century industrial buildings. The first silos were built in the early 1930s, while the silo complexes now present are mainly a response to the need to store enough grain for the region during the Cold War. Many businesses linked to the harbour are located behind the silos. Further inland is the Volkspark, one of Flensburg's green spaces. This part of the city is facing major changes as the harbour industries are dwindling and new programmes and spatial offers have to be found for Flensburg's inhabitants.

The New Network will manage the cultural exchange between the two cities. In Flensburg, the New Network is made up of eight stakeholders that are already active, independent cultural players in the city. They are located primarily in the West Harbour area, where the main cultural institutions are to be found. Once established, the New Network will itself be headquartered in the city. It will initially be located in the Große Straße—the main pedestrian area on the West Harbour with many shops and restaurants—in order to anchor it in the city. Once the New Network becomes well-established, it will gain an experimental space in a derelict former administration building on the East Harbour, where it can support the participatory process for the East Harbour redevelopment. Both places will make the New Network visible in the city and the region. Three existing buildings on the East Harbour will be utilised by the New Network. These "Three Silos" will be re-purposed to provide spaces for living, culture, and work in the newly developed city quarter. The HaGe-Speicher will be transformed into three hundred flats, of which over a hundred will be publicly funded. The historic Stadtspeicher from 1932 will be transformed into a cultural exhibition space focusing on Flensburg's (post)colonial past and present. The Hübsch-Speicher in the north of the East Harbour will be remodelled into a co-working and maker space to provide a necessary location for industry 4.0 activities in cooperation with the university. All three buildings are part of the history of Flensburg's harbour and reusing them will retain their history for the city while giving them a new programmatic future. A central public space will link different uses and formulate a new spatial identity for the East Harbour. This will be an elongated space lined with southern European palm trees located between the residential HaGe-Speicher and the new cultural spaces in the historic Stadtspeicher. Named after St. Thomas, the central island of the former Danish West Indies, it will be the arrival point for visitors entering the city by ferry or boat. During the summer the space can be used for concerts and performances as well as for markets, and mobile street furniture will enable a multitude of possible spatial constellations. The space adjoins the Stadtspeicher and HaGe-Speicher, linking the two buildings and with them the city's twentieth-century history. Changing murals will be painted on the wall of the old warehouse.

As we see in the West Harbour, the harbour-related built structures do not need to be used as intended in order to create incredible spaces and atmospheres for both residents and visitors. In the West Harbour, the former warehouses and *Kaufmannshöfe* have found new uses in the today's city. Still emanating a sense of their history, they now contribute to the unique atmosphere of the historic city for inhabitants and tourists alike. We should learn from the West Harbour and transform the East Harbour into a contemporary, diverse, and active city quarter. Demolishing the built context of the East Harbour would cause Flensburg to lose a major part of its identity and its twentieth-century history. A city that owes most of its past to the harbour now owes the harbour its future existence. Giving these buildings new programmatic futures and rethinking the East Harbour with the concept of a shared (post)colonial history will allow Flensburg to maintain the harbour's history.

“CREATING COMMON GROUND FOR HIGHER EDUCATION.”

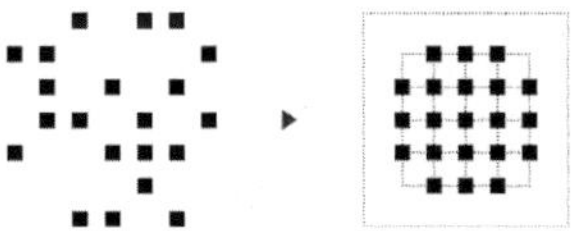

CONDENSE & CONNECT

ENNO ALTING, MATTHIAS TIPPE

Our world is undergoing remarkable changes. Due to the fast pace of digitisation, increasing numbers of students from all over the world, and developments such as the global pandemic, higher education institutions are facing major challenges. The study project "Condense & Connect" specifically focuses on the Leibniz University (LUH) in the city of Hanover as a case study. As such, our strategic design approach is not bound to one city alone, but can be interpreted as an adaptable catalogue that addresses these challenges in general and turns them into opportunities. One example of these approaches concerns the increasing shift in demand for space and a whole new way of teaching and learning. Future learning environments will have to stimulate students and teachers in various ways—from smaller, more private solutions for individuals to open, engaging group scenarios. Additionally, in order to meet the challenges of the ongoing fragmentation of higher education facilities—a development that is not only characteristic of Hanover—the key element of the proposal is condensing existing institutions of higher education and creating symbiotic proximity—both analogue and digital—that acts as the "resource" for the knowledge network and the overall public.

The project is divided into three action areas. The first focuses on future-proofing already-existing higher education buildings. For Hanover, we decided to show a transformation process based on the Conti high-rise and the adjacent lecture hall building. Higher education facilities with a high proportion of human sciences provision more likely to experience a structural shift. The Conti-Campus, therefore, represents not just one building but an entire branch of facilities with largely conventional teaching and learning methods. The open steel-frame structure provides a solid basis for future flex-

Figure 1
Vision of Georgengarten as "Common ground"
Concept design by the authors

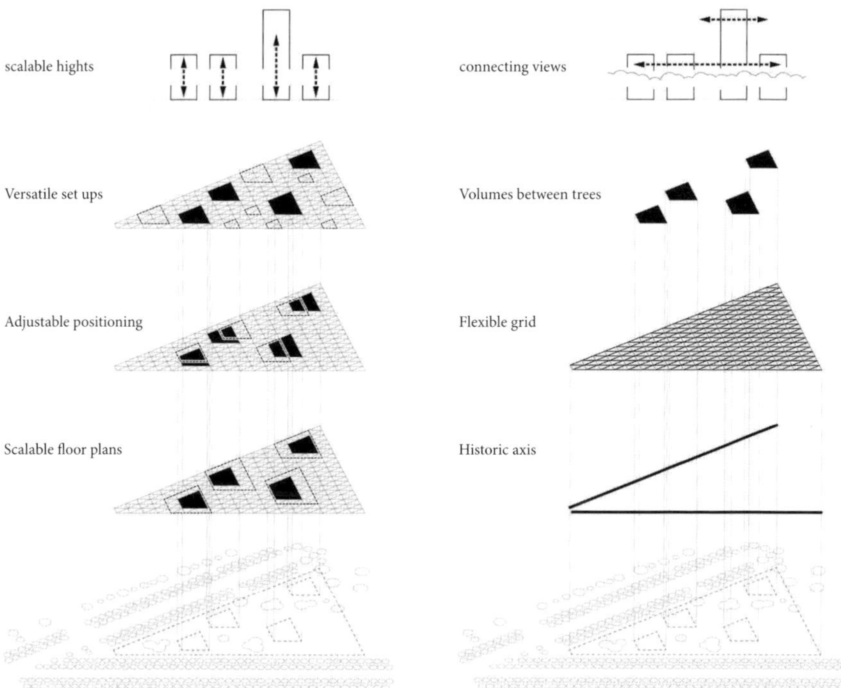

Figure 2
Embracing site constraints and structural adaptability
Concept design by the authors

ibility and adaptivity. With our approach, we aim to bring new life to the box-like architecture by filling it with units in sizes S, M, and L. These special modules are suitable for a wide range of uses from video-calling booths and small digital conference rooms to breakout spaces or even guesthouses and are designed to facilitate a future-proof campus experience.

With its vision of a more pedestrian-friendly city, traffic-calming measures, and transformed and activated streetscapes—specifically on the Nienburger Straße—the second action area focuses on an existing trend in city planning. Over two phases, the street could be converted into an active and recreational outdoor area with three different characters. The "Outdoor Gallery" creates a canvas for various exhibitions at the northern tip of the Nienburger Straße; the "Fun and Fitness" zone adjacent to the Welfenschloss provides much-needed activity spaces for students and the general public; and, finally, the "Green Zipper"—running the length of the Welfenschloss to the Schneiderberg—connects the previously divided Georgengarten and Welfengarten, forming one continuous recreational zone for students and visitors alike.

For the third action area, we suggest repurposing the existing parking lot at the Georgengarten. With a more pedestrian-centred design, huge car parks will become more and more obsolete, and the remaining spaces offer great opportunities for future development. Besides new ways of learning, the proposal includes a broadcast centre to support the production of digital media for online classes. The design consists of four towers connected by a public terrace that spans the size of the former parking lot. The height of the main tower corresponds with the other landmark buildings belonging to Leibniz University—the Conti-Hochhaus, the Welfenschloss, and the Hochhaus Appelstraße—creating a sense of community and belonging for both students and the public. The architecture of Leibniz University's newest location makes use of sustainable materials and contemporary construction methods based on the idea of "design for disassembly". The focus of the proposal addresses human experience: it aims to create different levels of stimulation with varying degrees of privacy, giving each student the option to choose between four types of learning environment. The open character of the area beneath the terrace—the Playground—provides an airy atmosphere for students and visitors alike. Spaces offering limited degrees of privacy are paired with a social component offering a range of interaction possibilities. The public terrace creates a common area for visitors of the new ensemble. Located within the new complex created by the four towers and framed by the surrounding trees, the spacious terrace includes various environments—ranging from more secluded areas to a very open main plaza. The fifth floor of all the towers is connected by a special element: the Bridge. Here, researchers, lecturers, and students can engage in open dialogue and move fluidly between different buildings. This open floor creates more private spaces than the terrace below and offers a more intimate learning and break-out environment. Finally, the towers make up the "brain" of the complex. Here, students and professors are provided with the most focused environment, providing space for concentration. The digital infrastructure paired with the modules of various sizes enables everybody to find the right amount of stimulation and interaction for them. All in all, our proposal for the LUH campus aims to provide a "common ground" with an inspiring spirit and welcoming atmosphere for students, professors, and visitors alike.

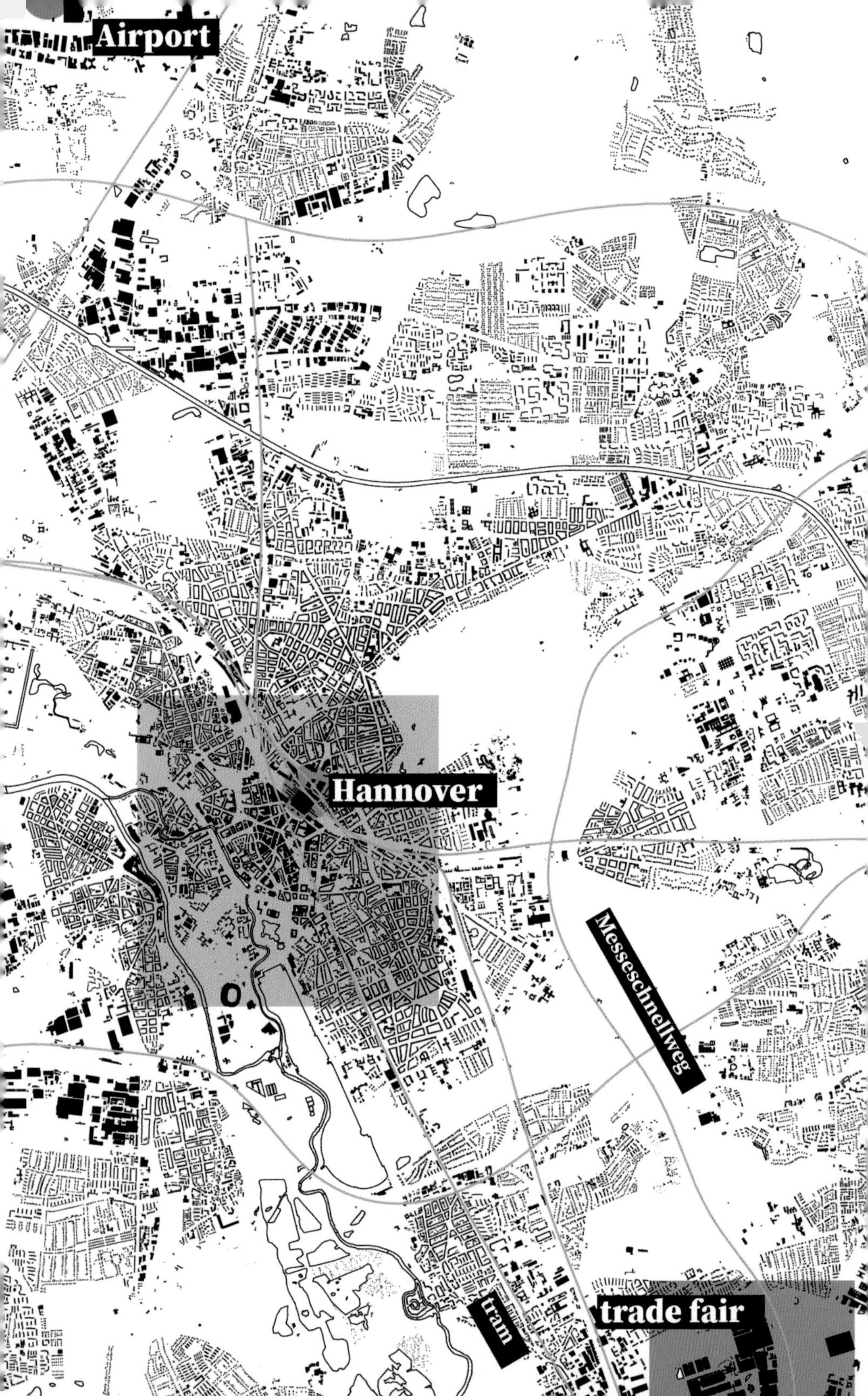

Airport
Hannover
Messeschnellweg
tram
trade fair

HANOVER TRADE FAIR REPORT

JULIA HERMANNS

The largest exhibition centre in the world: Hanover's globally unparalleled trade fair grounds are located on the city outskirts and have a capacity of over a million square metres. They are the largest in the world and have been attracting exhibitors and visitors from all around the globe for decades.

From the world to Hanover: In 1947, the government of the British Zone in Germany was looking for a symbolic way to present German industry and the country's economic upswing to a global public. Deutsche Messe AG was founded in Hanover, and the organisation's first export trade fair brought a huge amount of investment to the city, which had been heavily bombed in the war. To this day, the fair hosts one of the world's most important technology events. Every year, numerous leading trade fairs "made in Hanover" showcase their industry to the world and impress participants and observers with their individuality, internationality, and thematic variety. LIGNA, for example, is considered the leading trade fair for the wood industry, whereas infa has been the world's largest experience and shopping fair since 1981.

Optimised accessibility: Transfer to and from the exhibition grounds is based on a transport infrastructure characterised by Hanover's central location in Germany and an optimal network of different forms of mobility. The Messe Laatzen trade fair railway station provides a terminal for long-distance transit, and two modern city railway stations provide direct connections to the city centre and on to Hannover Langenhagen Airport. The Messeschnellweg, built in 1958, represents a further strategic project undertaken by the city.

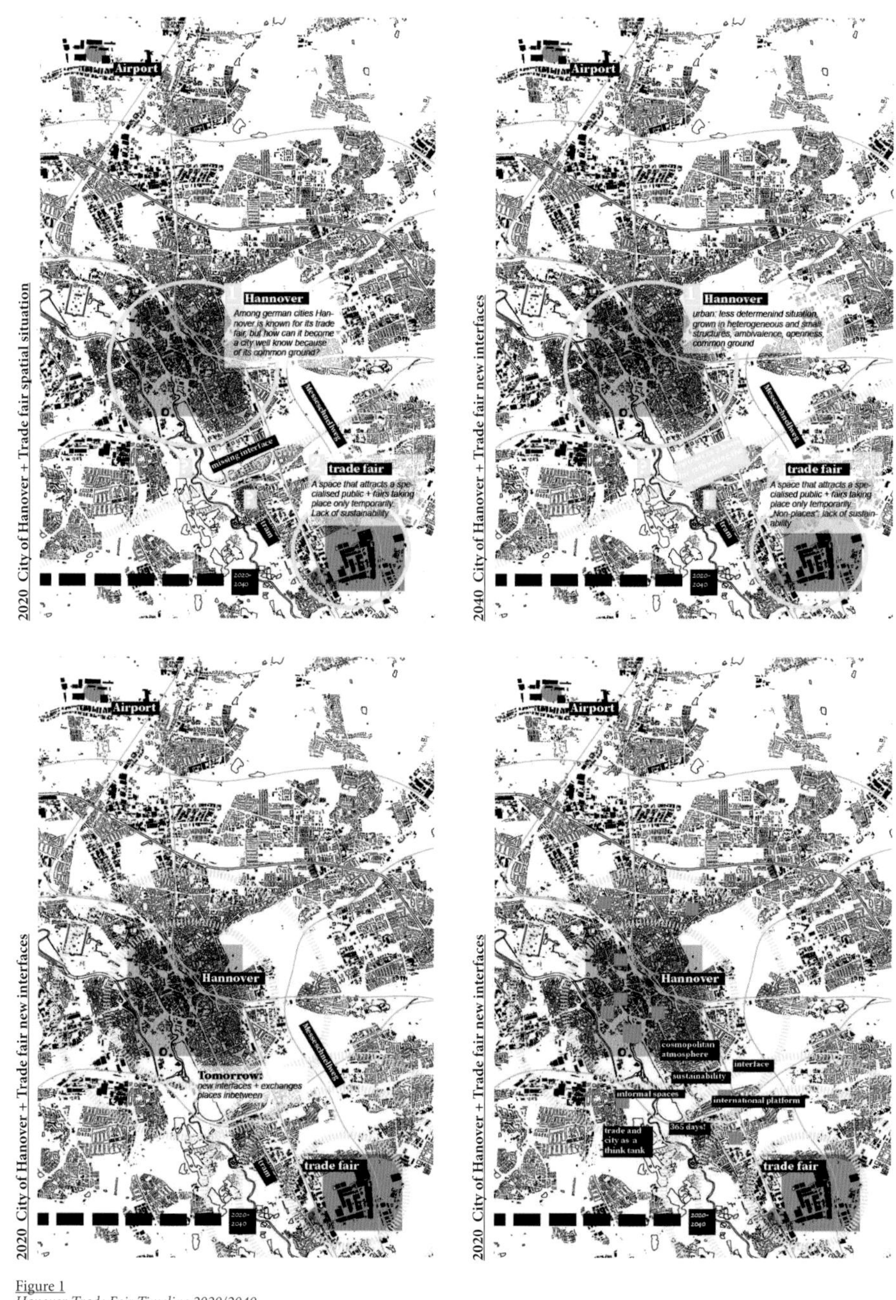

Figure 1
Hanover Trade Fair Timeline 2020/2040
Graphic by the author

Hospitality in a conservative time: In the 1960s, the fair set new records and counted more than a million visitors annually. While the hospitality industry established itself rapidly, it could still not meet the demand. Spontaneous establishments that could be considered to be an early form of AirBnB emerged: citizens known as "fair mums" welcomed guests into their private apartments and showed hospitality during an otherwise reserved and conservative period in the country's history.

International relations and expertise: In the 1970s, the fair aimed for greater diversity and intensified its trade relations beyond the borders of Europe. Joint events were held in Paris, New York, Melbourne, and in Brazil. An expansion to the Chinese market followed. During this time, the CeBIT computer expo became a world-leading fair in its field. The year 1996 brought a further new revolution: GLOBIS became the first virtual trade fair, with visitors able to call up product information online at any time. While we may feel today that an online expo ultimately cannot replace a trade fair, it provides an important platform—especially during the coronavirus pandemic. Since 2013, Industry 4.0 has been one of the most important keywords in the fair's activities.

The spatial situation of the city and fair today: The trade fair brings a range of diverse catalysts to the city, but how can we describe their current spatial relationship? The mapping indicates that the city and the exhibition ground can be described as two different spaces. On the one hand is the city: an urban and less-defined space that has grown in small, heterogeneous structures, patterns, and ambivalences. On the other hand is the trade fair: a very functional space that addresses a specialised audience. The fairs themselves are temporary and their events are not really transferred into the city; they are barely noticeable in the residents' everyday lives. International guests book hotels and bring their purchasing power with them, but most likely do not travel with the intention of taking a city break. As such, the Hannover Messe can be described as a collection of "non-places", begging the question: how can we justify this huge consumption of land if the area is not used throughout the whole year? And furthermore, how can we re-link the two poles spatially as well as programmatically? Both these questions demand new concepts and a stronger holistic vision.

A vision for promoting interfaces: In devising a vision for the future of Hanover and its Messe, the contrasts actually offer a promising basis for rethinking the interaction between the city and the fair: not contradictory, but complementary. We can already perceive a change in the practices and perspectives of the trade fair: modern events are smaller and aim to encourage more personal contact and networking in largely informal spaces. To take advantage of this trend, the fair should not be limited to a site that is distant from the city centre and its urban networks. Similarly, Hanover as city should be able to benefit from the resources, spaces, knowledge, and above all from the cosmopolitan atmosphere created by the fair over the past seventy years.

Ideas: Several approaches to making the fair more sustainable and changing its image should be considered. Such approaches aim to transform concepts in exhibition architecture in order to offer more possibilities for the use of the space. For example, they promote the implementation of permanent laboratories and workshops on site. In cooperation with the university, the trade fair could become a think tank and hotspot for visionary ideas. A network of many actors could create new synergies with and connections to the urban space. Another promising approach is the invention of new interfaces that offer space for innovation and entrepreneurship, as places to gather and connect.

03
EXPLORATIONS

ATMOSPHERE

ACCELERATORS

MAKERS

120–263

Murales in Palermo by Alessandro Bazan (detail)
Image © Alessandro Bazan. Photo by Barbara Lino

Matevž Čelik * Filipe Themudo Barata * Federica Scaffidi * Angela Alessandra Badami * Daniele Ronsivalle * Riccarda Cappeller * Marina Mazzamuto

Cosmopolitan Atmosphere

Triggering innovative spirit

COSMOPOLITAN INSTITUTIONS AS AGENTS OF CHANGE

MATEVŽ ČELIK

Today's cultural institutions have great and untapped potential. There is a huge need for them to play an active role in addressing the most pressing challenges facing humanity today. As the President of the European Commission states in her op-ed on the New European Bauhaus, "The European Green Deal must also—and especially—be a new cultural project for Europe" (von der Leyen 2020). In modern history, we have seen cultural institutions playing diverse roles that testify to their importance in urban and community development, whether in regenerating deprived urban areas, changing the urban economy in deindustrialised areas, or supporting community recovery from natural disasters. All of this highlights the need for new missions and functions for cultural institutions in the communities of the future.

Public space is of great importance to the role of institutions today, as shown by a number of impressive examples from which cultural institutions can draw important lessons. The Europe City project,[1] run between 2013 and 2015 by three European cultural institutions, explored the idea of public space as an invention of European civilization that both played a role in the region's democratic development and in many places still represents a physical proof of democracy. In a book published at the end of the project, Zygmunt Bauman claims that "public spaces in the city which allow free access to everybody, while attracting and encouraging the city residents to make use of the facilities put at their disposal, are urban variations of the 'commons'" (Bauman 2015, p. 183).

According to Bauman "we currently inhabit what in all likelihood is an irrevocably and irreversibly multicultural world, a product of the massive migration of ideas, values or beliefs, as well as their human carriers" (ibid. p. 187). The winner of the last competition for the European Prize for Urban Public Space, Tirana's Skenderbeg Square, is a physical space that eloquently reflects contemporary multiculturalism. Around the square we see a minaret and a bell tower, capitalist skyscrapers, and Stalinist public buildings built under the regime of Enver Hoxha. The basic urban features of the square were created during Mussolini's occupation of Albania, and the square was recently redesigned by the Belgian Architectural Office 51N4E. The architects formed a deep understanding of this complex space and transformed it into an urban commons for the future. They have created a

Figure 1
Open-Air Library, Magdeburg, Germany
An open air library collectively prototyped by the citizens of Magdeburg on the former premises of a shop.
Photo by Thomas Voelkel

innovative institutions cultural system public space

space that reflects the identity of Albania through materiality. Above all, they have created an *agora* that allows citizens to meet, celebrate, or protest together, and to understand and be reconciled with their history. The modern *agora* is also made up of public cultural institutions. Sociologically speaking, institutions are collectively constructed normative action systems made up of norms and social practices (Tuomela 1997). The Magdeburg Open-Air Library, built by the citizens of Magdeburg themselves, demonstrates how it is possible to collectively build a public space through a "normative action system" that already hints at an institution. The abandoned store premises adjacent to a former library space were used to organise a book collection drive and gather residents in an open participatory process. A 1:1 model of the design most liked by the residents was produced at the final location using more than a thousand beer crates. Based on this campaign, residents received funds to build the facility. It was a way of dealing with social depression in the neighbourhood (Cachola Schmal 2010).

When looking for a new model for responsive and open cosmopolitan cultural institutions, we cannot overlook the initiative and responsiveness of communities and cities themselves. It is in the most critical situations that it becomes especially apparent how a "normative action system" can work in society. The ability of society to solve the pressing challenges of an interdependent world incredibly quickly and efficiently is proven by people's desire to solve the problems they are confronted with on a daily basis. During times of migration crisis, some places on Italy's southern coast have undergone transformations that they themselves have encouraged by agreeing on a system that offers refugees training and empty housing in the villages. By doing so, they have restored the population and the economy in the almost-abandoned settlements. From places such as Riace, institutions can learn that, in order to solve problems, survive, and thrive, you need to stay hospitable and pragmatic, collaborate and network, and create and innovate.

Many transformative actions require only a comprehensive understanding of the context and the use of existing institution resources in a different way. In April 2019, people lay down on the ground under the skeleton of a blue whale in the Hintze Hall of the Natural History Museum in London. But these were not ordinary museum visitors. They were activists staging a protest to warn of the mass extinction of living beings caused by global warming. This event points to potential new relationships between the museum and citizens and reveals the new expectations citizens have of museums. The blue whale's skeleton testifies to the museum's traditional activities in acquiring, conserving, researching, communicating, and exhibiting heritage of humanity.[2] But the skeleton, its preservation, and its study have a whole new meaning in the context of the threat of species extinction and in the context of the protest.

The challenges institutions face today are systemic (Boyer, Cook, Steinberg 2011). Perhaps not so long ago, museums could increase their impact, reach, and visitor numbers with a new building, an update of their exhibits, new technologies, or new highlights added to their galleries. That is no longer enough: museums now need to rethink themselves as institutions and build an objective and comprehensive understanding of themselves and their activities in physical and digital venues. Cultural institutions today should have the responsibility and power to become agents of change. In order to become such, cultural institutions must first and foremost be bold and brave—and take risks that can lead to really interesting projects. One of the key challenges for cultural institutions

Figure 2
Open-Air Library, Magdeburg, Germany
Designed by KARO with Architektur+Netzwerk.
Built in 2009. An open library as a collectively constructed normative action system that already hints at an institution.
Photo by Thomas Voelkel

today is that it is becoming increasingly difficult to understand the context in which we live and which we have experience with, as well as the risks that it contains. The context within which museums operated and developed a few decades ago was evolving very slowly compared to the speed of transformation today. The operation of museums was once so static that most of their activities remained unchanged for decades. Today, the dynamics of change are so rapid that museum managers, cultural producers, and curators can no longer learn from the case studies that benefited their predecessors. The context in which they now operate is too different, so past practices can no longer be easily transferred to the present day. However, this uncertainty should not paralyse the functioning of these institutions. In order to be able to fully carry out their mission in today's context, they must make important decisions about their new functions, the new types of events they can host, and the new tools they can use to address their audiences. The new cultural policies and programmes of cosmopolitan institutions should focus on great human challenges, such as saving the

Figure 3
Museum of Architecture and Design, Ljubljana
Courtyard renovation by Julio Gotor Valcárcel.
Renovation of the courtyard as part of an exhibition on architectural renovation. The installation acted as a live display and experience of modern renovations interpreted in the exhibition.
Photo by Miran Kambič

planet, multiculturalism, helping vulnerable groups, supporting young professionals, and actively involving the elderly in the face of demographic change. As the President of the European Commission pointed out in the announcement of the new European Bauhaus, culture will play an important role in a vital economy and in the healthy development of society. So far, however, there are far too few proposals and examples of change and innovation in the public sector, and cultural institutions are no different. We need to be aware that social innovations are more than necessary in order to tackle seemingly impossible challenges. Innovation in a museum today does not mean improving heritage protection standards or introducing new technology into the exhibition space. It is more complex.

The introduction of innovation into institutions primarily "requires observation and a fundamental understanding of people, things and decisions as situated in time and space and therefore connected to and influenced by their context, environment and mental state of being" (Boyer et al 2011, p. 47). It is necessary to build coalitions of organisations and individuals who will work together to create and implement new proposals and ideas. The aim is to draw up a roadmap for the collective transformation of norms so that the action system of cultural institutions can be integrated into today's context in the short and long term. Such an insight into the responsiveness of cultural institutions will help unleash their full potential.

One of the great advantages of cultural institutions is that their concept—the concept of a museum, the concept of a library, or the concept of a theatre—regardless of any definition, is a relatively open institutional concept. This concept allows cultural institutions to be spaces that facilitate and support experimentation, the testing of new concepts, and open discussion of those concepts. Therefore, cultural institutions should be the first to resolutely innovate and modernise their function in the culture system.

FOOTNOTE

1_Public Space (2013) "The new programme "Europe City" has been launched to uphold a European idea of the city". Available online at:_https://www.publicspace.org/web/guest/multimedia/-/post/the-new-programme-europe-city-has-been-launched-to-uphold-a-european-idea-of-the-city (28.12.2020).

2_ICOM, *Museum Definition*. Available online at: https://icom.museum/en/resources/standards-guidelines/museum-definition/ (28.12.2020).

BIBLIOGRAPHY

Bauman Z. (2015) "Cities in the Globalized World of Diasporization". In: Gray D. ed. (2015) *Europe City, Lessons from the European Prize for Urban Public Space*. Zurich, Lars Müller Publishers, p. 183.

Boyer B., , Cook J. W., Steinberg M. (2011) "In Studio: Recipes for Systemic Change. Helsinki, Sitra". Available online at: http://www.helsinkidesignlab.org/peoplepods/themes/hdl/downloads/In_Studio-Recipes_for_Systemic_Change.pdf (28.12.2020).

Cachola Schmal P. (2010) "Books against Depression". In: Anglès M. ed. (2010) *In Favour of Public Space, Ten Years of the European Prize for Urban Public Space*. Barcelona, Actar, pp. 55–59.

Tuomela R. (1997) "Searle on Social Institutions". In: *Philosophy and Phenomenological Research* 57(2). pp. 437. Available online at: http://www.jstor.org/stable/2953733 (28.12.2020).

von der Leyen U. (2020) "A New European Bauhaus". Op-ed article by Ursula von der Leyen, President of the European Commission. Available online at: http://ec.europa.eu/commission/presscorner/detail/en/AC_20_1916 (15.10.2020).

MANAGING OLD AND NEW URBAN ENVIRONMENTS IN THE CITY OF ÉVORA: DIFFICULTIES IN FIXING LONG-TERM COSMOPOLITAN PUBLIC POLICIES

FILIPE THEMUDO BARATA

My participation in the initiative *Cosmopolitan Habitat* is based on a story that is both personal and at the same time aims to be a testimony from which I will try to organise a reflection on public policies and the capacity for urban innovation.

My testimony refers to four points:

- **How to promote efficient public policies;**
- **The difficulties of changing public uses and practices;**
- **The importance of finding methods and tools to organise and promote negotiation in the civil society;**
- **How to enhance the importance of heritage and cultural industries.**

The story unfolds in the city of Évora. The details of the foundation of the city are lost in time, but by the end of the Second World War, its buildings were practically confined by walls built in part by the Romans, in part by the Arabs, in still other parts by the Portuguese medieval kings, and by the intervention of yet more architects in the eighteenth century. This is shown on the left side of the aerial photograph taken by a public service that has already disappeared (Fig. 1). However, during the decades that followed, around fourteen largely informal neighbourhoods had begun to grow around the city. It is this situation that the second image illustrates (Fig. 2).

My story begins in the late 1970s, when the Évora City Council—at the time led by the Communist Party—took the initiative to draw up a Strategic Plan for the city. The plan's main function was to integrate the peripheral neighbourhoods into the city. When the work started, the existing situation was of great concern: while the population of the municipality was growing somewhat overall, that of the historic centre was clearly decreasing (Fig. 3). The situation in the historic centre was serious, with an aging population—with limited education and skills, few resources, and no ability to renovate their homes—very degraded structural heritage, and low demand for accomodation in the neighbourhood. The maintenance difficulties were clear; narrow streets of less than five metres in width were added to the lack of national guidelines for this kind of undertaking. At the time, there was not

Figure 1
Évora view from the air , 1946
Source: DGEMN, Miranda 2014, p. 24

public policies public practices civil society cultural industries

Figure 2
Evolution of urban expansion outside the walls, 1950
Source: Simplício 2009, p. 22. CME/PDM, Rel. nº 6, 1978/79

Municipality territory	
Years	Population
1960	50 095
1970	46 900
1981	51 575

Historic Centre	
Years	Population
1960	15 096
1970	12 696
1981	10 687

Figure 3
Population of Évora
Source: CME/PDM

even national legislation in place to guide the framing of strategic plans. On the other hand, however, it was evident that there was an awareness of the patrimonial importance of the area. What makes this situation so special was the approach taken to this situation: the courageous, unprecedented, and innovative decision to develop a Strategic Plan, later called the Municipal Master Plan, that would position the historic centre and its heritage as its main development pillar. But one question remained: what could the council do to promote this option and organise innovative and cosmopolitan public policies?

Interesting measures were taken immediately. The aims of 1978 were to:

- launch an international competition to develop the plan. The decision was to recognise the need to learn about other experiences at international level;
- recruit competent technical staff, as there was a clear need for technical skills in municipality offices;
- recover the social urban and built tissue. It was clear that the new policies should be promoted with the population, and above all, it was imperative to avoid evicting the population from the historic centre;
- preserve and survey urban heritage; before this point, there had been no rigorous scientific survey of the area;
- simultaneously create conditions for economic, social, and cultural revitalisation, because heritage cannot exist on its own; and
- maintain Évora as a regional pole and functional centre.

Briefly, here are the main outcomes:

- The City Master Plan—the first in Portugal—was approved (February 1985)
- Évora applied to be included in UNESCO World Heritage List (February 1985)
- The Historic Centre of Évora Centre was included in the UNESCO World Heritage List (November 1986)
- The interesting decision was made to build a housing estate to be the symbol of these “new times”, remembering the links between past, present, and future. The resulting Quinta da Malagueira estate was a masterpiece by the architect Siza Viera; the project was one of the 1992 Pritzker Prize laureate’s first works.

In 1984 I began collaborating with the City Council in several ways: organising meetings, receiving the city’s support to carry out special training sessions, helping to establish a UNESCO office, participating in heritage survey projects, and valorising heritage sites. That cooperation has continued to this day, even when working with the leaders of different parties. During this time, of course, the city continued changing, growing, introducing new industries, greatly increasing its tourism numbers, creating new hotels and restaurants, and building shopping centres, apparently continuing to modernise and innovate.

This went on until two years ago, when the city of Évora decided to organise an application for the title of European Capital of Culture in 2027. The dossier was to be submitted by November 2019.

Figure 4
Évora view from the air, 2006
Source: Municipal Archive, Miranda 2014, p. 42

Municipality territory		Historic Centre	
Year	Population	Year	Population
1960	50 095	1960	15 096
1970	46 900	1970	12 696
1981	51 575	1981	10 687
1991	53 754	1991	7 841
2001	56 519	2001	5 671
2011	56 596	2011	4 738

Figure 5
Population of Évora, 1960/2011
Source: CME/PDM

I joined the Executive Committee for this initiative and the first thing we did was diagnose the existing situation. For me, at least, the results were shocking: when looking at the population data, the old trends—similar to those of 1980—have only become more pronounced (Fig. 5). Of course, I immediately started wondering what had happened. In seeking answers, a number of issues became clear. The city has lost its cultural references, including the awareness of the symbolic value of the historic centre. Before, Évora had been the only city in Portugal to set up a development strategy based on cultural heritage. Secondly, the city has decreased its connections to UNESCO; for a large number of reasons, even the university and city hall have diminished their cooperation level. As time passes and the experts at the city hall age, the city is losing its innovation skills. There are still difficulties for new poltical and ecomomic actors—since élites compared to 1986 have changed—to adapt to changing social and political environments. At the same time, however, economic diversification has increased overall wealth; many people were in favour of new construction of buildings and quickly moved away from options linked to heritage values.

The impact of this situation is, in my opinion, terrible. The old approach of promoting a constant dialogue with the population has waned, particularly after the disappearance of the previous flexible structure that enabled intervention by associations, centres, and public or private institutions. Furthermore, there is now no practice to gather all stakeholders in order to promote and implement policies concerning heritage, or even to discuss conservation, recovery, and valorisation issues. It is also clear that negotiation practices and dialogue mechanisms linking different approaches, opinions, and interests no longer exist. This situation has the consequence that the municipal administration is not accessing diversified legal tools, human resources, or financial means, leading to a kind of isolation from heritage and creative and cultural industries.

For someone like me, who had worked with the city for so many years, it is clear that opportunities, skills, and instruments for intervention have been lost. Capacities for innovation, technical means, the way people look and feel the city, and governance systems have vanished.

Now, the work will be much more difficult. What needs to be done?

- Local and regional cultural legislation needs to be reinvented.
- Ways of increasing links with communities must be found; this is a long-term project requiring the creation of groups, institutions, and associations.
- “Smart culture” needs to be improved (paying attention to digital skills and professions) and more attention needs to be directed to intangible heritage.
- The implementation of technology and digitalisation must be improved, enabling a reduction of the movement of people to larger cities and attracting young people to take part in the urban project.
- Policies that prevent the gap between generations from growing need to be discussed and promoted.
- New decision and negotiation mechanisms, such as living lab strategies, should be discovered.
- Civic involvement and partnerships need to be promoted.

Hard work that will keep us busy for years!

BIBLIOGRAPHY

Barata F. T., Marsh J., Molinari F., Cabeça S. (2017) *Creative Innovation and Related Living Lab Experiences: A Mediterranean Model.* Évora, UNESCO Chair.

Lucas R. S. (2009) *Regeneração urbana e ambiental de áreas de pequena indústria. Évora, caracterização e oportunidades.* Master’s thesis. University of Lisbon, Architecture Faculty.

Miranda E. R. V. (2014) *O Centro Histórico e as Centralidades em Évora Dinâmicas Urbanas e Organização Espacial.* Master’s thesis. Lisbon. University of Lisbon, IST.

Simplício M. D. (2009) *Evolução da Estrutura Urbana de Évora: o século XX e a transição para o século XXI.* Évora, University of Évora. Available online at: https://dspace.uevora.pt/rdpc/bitstream/10174/2668/1/Evolucao_Estrutura_Urbana_Evora_secXX_XXI.pdf (02.01.2021).

PALERMO-HANOVER: URBAN STORIES FROM COSMOPOLITAN PEOPLE

FEDERICA SCAFFIDI

Recently, there has been renewed interest in cosmopolitan issues and migration. Cosmopolitanism is often heralded as the sociocultural ability to transform a space and make it open and welcoming. This article attempts to show how cosmopolitanism can be expressed in intangible aspects, such as feelings, perceptions, interactions, and behaviours, and in tangible ones, where urban spaces and architecture are physically transformed by the human and cultural flows that cities experience over the centuries. With this purpose in mind, this research investigates the cosmopolitan features of two medium-sized European cities characterised by their sociocultural diversity, migratory flows and international vibes. The case studies selected for this DAAD funded research project are Palermo and Hanover. The research adopted qualitative methods based on semi-structured interviews of cosmopolitan people. This article is not designed as a final report, but as an initial contribution to the body of knowledge and as a basis for future research on *Cosmopolitan Habitat*.

Many cultures and communities have succeeded one another, shaping human behaviours, architecture, streets, and squares and making urban spaces dynamic, resilient, open, and cosmopolitan (Schröder 2018). The dynamic culture of cities is subjected to ongoing changes that progressively influence their identities and urban contexts. According to François Jullien (2016), there is no culture that is not transformed by others; there is no society with a primordial, unchanged culture that resists change. Jullien recommends using the term "cultural resources" to understand the homogenisation of territorial spaces, instead of "cultural identity", because the identity of a place can be influenced by globalisation (Craig, Siok Kuan 1999). In order to better understand cosmopolitanism, it is necessary to observe the territorial resources and spaces that keep the legacy of the place in question alive (Barata 2017). Cosmopolitanism is often said to be the sociocultural ability to transform a space and make it open and welcoming. This characteristic makes people feel a deep sense of belonging to the place. The idea of cosmopolitan citizenship first appeared in Ancient Greece in the fourth century BC, when the philosopher Diogenes called himself a citizen of the world (Linklater 2002). This article aims to observe the cosmopolitan characteristics of the cities of Palermo and Hanover and to describe how their human flows have given rise to the cities' heterogeneous urban structures. There

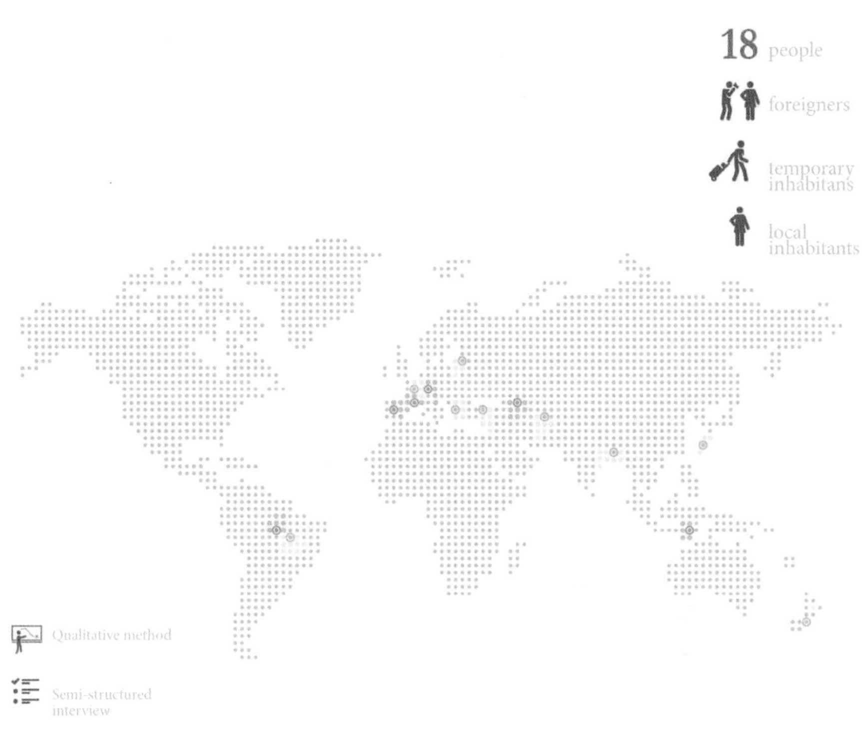

Figure 1
Nationality map of interviewees
Graphic by the author, 2020

international people integration

is a growing body of literature that recognises the importance of this topic in relation to human, cultural, and migratory flows and atmospheres (Böhme 2005; Norberg-Schulz 1979). This study aims to contribute to this growing area of research by exploring the topic of cosmopolitanism in relation to Palermo and Hanover. The study provides new insights into *Cosmopolitan Habitat*, investigating the main characteristics of these urban contexts through the eyes of cosmopolitan inhabitants. This study uses a qualitative approach to investigate the atmosphere of cosmopolitan cities through semi-structured interviews1 with eighteen people from all over the world (Fig. 1). The selection criteria for the interviewees was their place of origin and their living or having lived in Palermo or Hanover. The study is a starting point and basis for future research, which will include more interviewees in order to further understanding of the topic.

Palermo and Hanover: cosmopolitan cities

Palermo and Hanover are two mid-sized European cities characterised by a history of steady migratory flows (Fig. 2). Hanover has 536,000 inhabitants, of whom 13% are foreigners.2 A significant proportion of these are Turkish, but there are also many Asians, Poles, Greeks, Russians, Italians, and other nationalities. The new mayor of Hanover, Belit Onay, is the first ethnically Turkish German to lead a state capital. One interviewee said that Hanover contains many communities from different countries and religions. This is an important element of the cosmopolitan characteristics of a city, as the co-existence of different cultures and people helps to create the *Cosmopolitan Habitat*. Another important aspect is the feeling of integration and openness experienced by the new generations of migrants. As one interviewee put it: “There are a lot of students from all over the world. It’s somehow an international city. … It’s not that hard to find new friends here.” The opportunity to interact with many people and easily get in touch with other foreigners makes the city open and cosmopolitan. The international context makes people feel comfortable, as well as well-connected socially. Despite this, some people expressed concerns about the difficulty of creating deep relationships with Germans. Language is a huge barrier, but cultural differences between communities can exacerbate this further.

This issue does not always emerge in the interviews, however, as most people focused on the opportunities the city offers. When talking about the topic, one interviewee said: “I joined the community of my sons’ kindergarten. … they have many kinds of interesting activities, drawing or Zumba once a week. … They are from many countries, but most of them are from Germany”. Schools, as well as universities, play a major role in the integration of foreigners. The possibility of having a strong community of students, professors, and parents creates the basis for further interactions. Moreover, cultural activities organised by these institutions create an open and comfortable space where people can talk, share hobbies, and feel integrated. The city of Hanover works hard to achieve this. It is a UNESCO City of Music where many events, urban festivals (e.g., the Fête de la Musique) and night-time tours in cultural places are organised. The university also creates innovative opportunities for interaction through language courses, sports activities, and many other cultural events. As the interviewees note, people can even feel these cosmopolitan vibes in the city streets of areas such as Nordstadt and Linden. Cosmopolitanism was mainly associated with the openness of a place, the possibility of finding people and shops from different countries, and being able to feel the integration among communities. This came up in the following interview excerpt: “The neighbourhood in which I live is Linden. It’s multicultural, and a nice place with a good cohabitation of Germans and

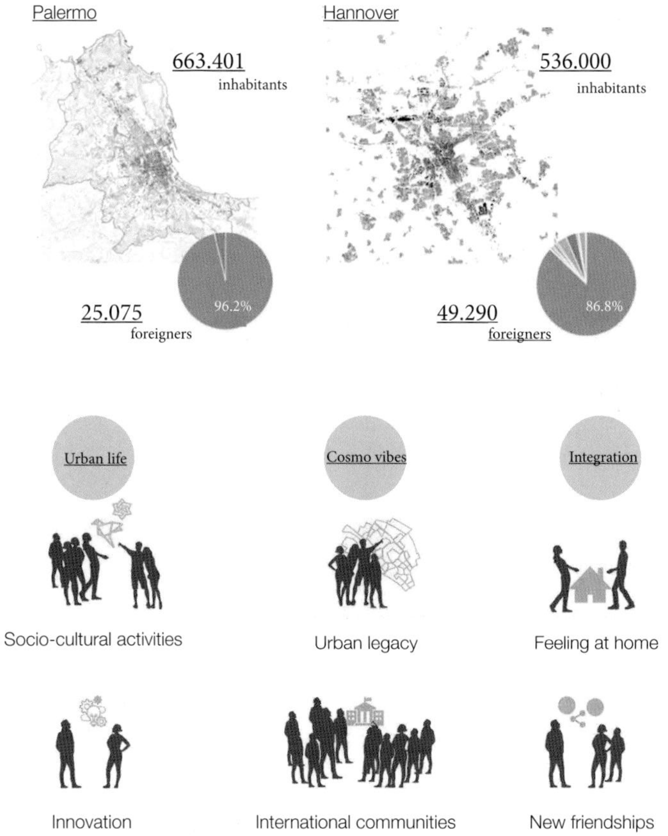

Palermo
663.401
inhabitants
96.2%
25.075
foreigners
Hannover
536.000
inhabitants
86.8%
49.290
foreigners
Urban life
Cosmo vibes
Integration
Socio-cultural activities
Urban legacy
Feeling at home
Innovation
International communities
New friendships

Figure 2
Cosmopolitan atmosphere
Graphic by the author, 2020

POSITIVE ASPECTS
Socio-cultural activities
Innovation
International communities
Urban legacy
New friendships
Feeling at home
interviews
Cultural barriers
Multi-ethnicity in specific districts
No connections among communitie
Language barriers
NEGATIVE ASPECTS

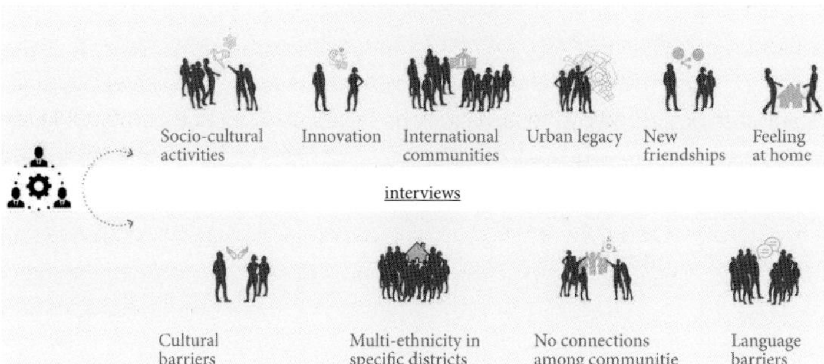

Figure 3
Positive and negative aspects
Graphic by the author, 2020

foreigners. It's a cosmopolitan place with a fairly open mind. There is a lot of life. It's a nice place, with many bars, supermarkets and shops." Another interviewee, when asked to identify cosmopolitan spaces in Hanover, said: "The Limmerstraße is somewhere very important for Hannover. They have a verb—'Limmern', used among young people—that means to walk in the Limmerstraße, drinking and talking." It is interesting how urban spaces can influence language and create new words, identifying cosmopolitan behaviours and places. The presence of different communities and heterogeneous sociocultural activities creates social mixing. These cosmopolitan vibes and spaces influence each other, defining innovative and welcoming urban habitats.

Palermo, for example, is recognised as a welcoming city. The mayor, Leoluca Orlando, has tried to make the city a comfortable place to live since his first term. He has created a city that is open to international students, academics, entrepreneurs, artists, and rescued migrants. "Every time a ship with rescued migrants enters the harbour of Palermo, the mayor welcomes them saying 'The worst is over. You are citizens of Palermo now'" (Van der Zee 2017). In 2015, the city of Palermo wrote the Charter of Palermo, which states the right to international human mobility and aimed to abolish the requirement of a residence permit. As one interviewee said: "Palermo gives you this opportunity; it does not make you feel foreign. It makes you feel at home. This is fundamental for me, that's why I don't suffer while living in Palermo. I am at home". This interview shows that Palermo makes people feel at home. Home is a very intimate place; it is a space where people feel comfortable and welcome. As such, the feeling of belonging is an important part of a cosmopolitan city. Integration is another significant characteristic of cosmopolitanism.

The mixture of cultural activities, spaces, and behaviours creates close relationships with the urban context. This was felt by the following interviewee: "For the first time, I stayed about one year. After the summer vacation, I came back to Palermo and they still remembered me. This kind of close relationship makes me consider myself a local resident, while in other cities I felt like an outsider." These cosmopolitan vibes can be experienced in many spaces in the city of Palermo. According to Ola Söderström (2009), Palermo has been the centre of many flows: flows of people, of ideas, and of capital. Every single element of these flows has changed and influenced its spaces, its people's minds, its urban structure and architectural forms (De Carlo 1999). This multi-level stratification is visible in many aspects of the Sicilian capital (Carta 2019). It can be observed in both the intangible and tangible heritage: when crossing the street, when enjoying a *pièce de théâtre* with Sicilian puppets, when tasting traditional food, and when getting carried away by the smells of the city—such as those of Tamil cuisine—or when hearing the sounds of the local markets that make people feel like they are in an Arabic souk (Scaffidi 2020). Commenting on this aspect of the city, one of the interviewees said: "I really love the food and the vibe of the people; even though it was hard to communicate, in the end you can communicate with everyone." This multi-ethnic heterogeneity builds the character of Palermo, reveals the real soul of the city, and explains how the ways people live in these cities turns them into *Cosmopolitan Habitats*. Urban legacies such as the local architecture and urban stratifications make the city authentic. As one interviewee put it: "I think that one of the main things that attracted me was the atmosphere. The ambiance of walking through the city at night or during the day felt vibrant and alive. I really liked the architecture and I liked the fact that it feels very rich and deep and authentic." Nevertheless, the interviews also reveal some cultural and linguistic barriers, and the difficulties in establishing close relationships.

Overall, the findings show that Palermo and Hanover are cosmopolitan cities because they possess the following characteristics (Fig. 3):

- sociocultural activities (events, informal street events);
- international communities (students, academics, cultural and religious communities);
- urban legacy (architecture, urban stratification);
- friendly behaviour and spaces (friendly people, open communities and spaces);
- a sense of belonging to the place (feeling at home).

The findings also show some negative aspects related to language and cultural barriers, the presence of multi-ethnicity only in specific districts, and the lack of deep and close connections between foreigners and locals.

Conclusions

This research was undertaken to examine the cosmopolitan characteristics of two mid-size European cities characterised by sociocultural diversity, migratory flows, and international vibes. This study has shown that Palermo and Hanover possess many positive and negative aspects that characterise their vibrant and multi-ethnic habitats. These findings have significant implications for the understanding of how cosmopolitan atmospheres are perceived by cosmopolitan people. The methods used for this study may be applied to other places in the world, or extended for the chosen locations by increasing the number of interviewees. Despite its limited sample size, this research offers valuable insights into the topic of *Cosmopolitan Habitat*. As such, the research presented here is not considered a final report, but is designed as a contribution to the body of knowledge and as basis for future research.

FOOTNOTES

1_The selected interviewees have different nationalities. They come from New Zealand, Brazil, Bangladesh, Indonesia, Italy, Taiwan, Greece, Pakistan, Lithuania, Turkey, France, and other countries.

2_The city of Hannover has 49.290 foreigners, representing 13% of the entire population. Source: citypopulation.de.

BIBLIOGRAPHY

Barata F. T. Carvalho A. (2017), "Ethics in Intangible Cultural Heritage Public Policies: Interview with Marc Jacobs". In: *Revista Memória em Rede* 16, pp. 165–180.

Böhme, G. (2005) "Atmosphere As The Subject Matter of Architecture". In: Ursprung P. ed. (2005) *Herzog & DeMeuron: Natural History.* Zurich, Lars Müller Publishers, pp. 398–406.

Carta M. (2019) "Palermo, Aziz. The archipelago city of diversity and creativity". In: Carta M. ed. (2019) *Futuro. Politiche per un diverso presente.* Soveria Mannelli, Rubbettino.

Craig J. T., Siok Kuan T. (1999) "Trying to Be Cosmopolitan". In: *Journal of Consumer Research* 26, pp. 214–241

De Carlo G. (1999) *Io e la Sicilia.* Catania, Maimone Editore.

Jullien F. (2016) *Il n'y a pas d'identité culturelle.* Paris, Éd. de l'Herne.

Linklater A. (2002) "Cosmopolitan Citizenship". In: Isin E. F., Turner B. S. (2002) *Handbook of Citizenship Studies.* London, SAGE.

Norberg-Schulz C. (1979) *Genius Loci: Towards a Phenomenology of Architecture.* New York, Rizzoli.

Van der Zee R. (2017) "He fought the mafia and won. Now this mayor is taking on Europe over migrants". In: *The Guardian*, 18 April 2017. Available online at: https://www.theguardian.com/global-development-professionals-network/2017/apr/18/he-fought-the-mafia-and-won-now-this-mayor-is-taking-on-europe-over-migrants (30.12.2020).

Scaffidi F. (2020) "Palermo: Flow of Cultures, Energies, Ideas and Cosmopolitan Spaces". In: Schröder J., Scaffidi F. eds. (2020) *Palermo Open City.* Hannover, Regionales Bauen und Siedlungsplanung Leibniz Universität Hannover, pp. 13–17.

Schröder J. (2018) "Open Habitat". In: Schröder J., Carta C., Ferretti M., Lino B., eds. (2018) *Dynamics of Periphery. Atlas of Emerging Creative and Resilient Habitats.* Berlin, Jovis, pp. 10–29.

GIBELLINA: VANGUARD OF A COSMOPOLITAN CITY

ANGELA ALESSANDRA BADAMI

Gibellina is a city formed by orogenesis. It was reborn after a dramatic earthquake and shook the sediment off urban theory, becoming a city open to the world and to the worlds of contemporary culture; of architecture, art, theatre. To understand its revolutionary force, we must immerse ourselves in the context of 1968, when an earthquake hit the Belice Valley[1] with a violence capable of damaging fourteen cities and razing four of them—including Gibellina—to the ground.[2] The earthquake marked a sharp break in the historical continuity of the small, rural centre of Sicily. The original site of the town was abandoned and another city was built from scratch for the surviving inhabitants. The city was "other", alien to the sociocultural and environmental context; a dystopian transplant of an urban utopia. The reconstruction process[3] was managed entirely by the Italian state, without any dialogue with the inhabitants. While the futuristic plan for Gibellina won much acclaim for its technical perfection, it nevertheless produced an urban landscape that was alienating, fragmented into terraced houses, and dispersed across vast empty spaces, oversized streets, and useless public services.

The futuristic vision of Ludovico Corrao, who was mayor of Gibellina almost continuously from 1970 to 1994, interrupted this scenario. The intention was to build a new identity for the city—at the cost of unhinging social conventions, but ultimately opening Gibellina to the world. The mayor believed it necessary to promote a new local development, capable of supporting the community economically and culturally and providing the reasons for people to put down roots in the new settlement.

Despite numerous controversies regarding the priorities of the reconstruction (many citizens believed that it was necessary to first build the houses and essential services and postpone anything that could be considered superfluous), Corrao made a choice that initially seemed superficial but eventually proved far-sighted: he invested in contemporary art for the city. This approach could only have been prompted by a unique mindset. Corrao's choice to renew local traditions, inserting them into international contemporary art circles, was acclaimed by the cultural world, which viewed the case of Gibellina with renewed interest. Corrao's goal was achieved through the promotion of contemporary art in all its forms (architecture, sculpture, painting, applied arts, theatre, scenography, dance, music,

Figure 1
Great Cretto. Land Art work by Alberto Burri, 1985/2015)
Image by Sandro Scalia, 2018

contemporary art local traditions intercultural exchange

Figure 2
Gibellina, Belice/EpiCentro della Memoria Viva Museum
Photo by the author, 2018

Figure 3
Gibellina, Museum of Mediterranean Textures
Photo by the author, 2018

and poetry), calling together the most renowned architects and artists of the Italian and international art scenes. In search of a *genius loci*, the so-called "Charge of the Five Hundred" experimented with new pathways for art in Gibellina, projecting an international and cosmopolitan dimension onto the city. As Corrao used to say, he wanted Gibellina to be reborn "from the creative breath of art" (Corrao, Carollo 2017), creating a unique place: a settlement where architecture and hundreds of contemporary works of art are distributed *en plein air* and in museums. As a precursor of artistic trends, behaviour, values, and forms of expression the introduced Gibellina in modernity.

Today, many questions arise on how to implement and metabolise innovations suddenly introduced to Gibellina in the field of urban planning, architecture, and art. It is necessary to reflect on how these new values can be grafted onto the cultural traditions of the local population, and how they can be applied to a patrimonial concept in which they can be identified and valued as resources and used to create new heritage.

Gibellina's cultural institutes are the cultural mediators and ambassadors of its cosmopolitan identity in the world. The first of these to be established were the Civic Museum of Contemporary Art and the Ethno-Anthropological Museum, both in 1980. In the 1990s, the Orestiadi Foundation (1992) and the Museum of Mediterranean Textures (1996) were opened on the initiative of Ludovico Corrao. The Belice/EpiCentro della Memoria Viva Museum was established in 2011, promoted by CRESM,[4] and finally, in 2019, the *Great Cretto* Museum, sponsored by the municipality, was inaugurated at the site of the original old town. Gibellina's museums act as amplifiers that demonstrate the international openness and cosmopolitan dimensions of the city and testify how, through contemporary culture, it has opened the local dimension up to the world. Museums constantly feed the artistic heritage and involve new users by promoting cultural events and activities, making spaces available for formal and informal education, and providing places for cultural mediation. In Gibellina, the concept of a museum does not correspond to its usual meaning; Gibellina is itself a museum. The Civic Museum of Contemporary Art is only one of its components; it contains works that cannot be exhibited outdoors. Furthermore, the museum's collection is unique: all the works it holds (more than 1,800 pieces of art, including paintings, graphics, sculptures, installations, sketches, and models) were made in or for Gibellina. The Ethno-Anthropological Museum reproduces the typical environments of peasant life by displaying common objects used in the area and testifies to the peculiarities of traditional arts and crafts. The fact that this museum has been present from the first years of the new settlement represents the desire to preserve the local culture and popular traditions that have evolved over the centuries and were threatened by the fractures caused by the earthquake.

The Orestiadi Foundation is based at the Baglio Di Stefano. The Baglio is a testimony to rural architecture, the agricultural economy, and the traditions of working in the fields of the Sicilian hinterland. In order to give Gibellina a link to the past, Corrao has restored the building and made it the town's headquarters for cultural activities. The mission of the Orestiadi Foundation is to promote intercultural exchange between the peoples who inhabit the complex geography of the Mediterranean first and foremost by involving the younger generations and sensitising them to the themes of art as a vehicle for knowledge, sharing and brotherhood. The Museum of Mediterranean Textures proposes an unprecedented reading of the history of the Mediterranean Sea through the exhibition of finds from the various countries that overlook it. The museum features decorative art objects, costumes, jewellery, fabrics, ceramics, and artifacts from Sicily, Tunisia, Palestine, Albania, Algeria, Spain, and Morocco. Comparing the items in the collection reveals the coexistence and continuity of decorative design languages that, despite having evolved into individual compositions in different cultures, demonstrate the permanence of common matrices. The museum thus celebrates these different forms of human culture and presents itself as an ideal cosmopolitan space that fosters coexistence between different peoples, breaking down the distrust of difference by asserting the permanence of common roots and becoming a metaphor for an ethical attitude free from prejudice, fundamentalism, and discrimination.

In this way, the stories and destinies of different Mediterranean cultures are intertwined in the city. But the city also tells its own story. The operators of CRESM wanted to display and make available to the public the documentation relating to the intense season of participatory democracy and bottom-up planning of the 1950s and 1960s, the tragedy of the earthquake, and the reconstruction events that followed. Gibellina's past and present are compared in a permanent interactive exhibition with the evocative title "Belice/EpiCenter of Living Memory".

The establishment of the most recent museum, dedicated to the *Great Cretto* land art installation by Alberto Burri, was commissioned by the municipal administration in order to promote knowledge of the artwork. The exhibition narrates the genesis of the *Great Cretto* from its conception to its realisation, and presents to the public the symbolic value of the work of art that has resemanticised the remains of the old city into a memorial, immortalising the memory of a city erased from the ground. Thanks to its new and highly unique identity, Gibellina has become a centre of gravity for the production and enhancement of contemporary culture and, as such, is capable of exerting a powerful magnetic force. The city, created by the visionary dream of Ludovico Corrao, will be able to proceed towards its destiny if it will be able to expose its potential to the international scene. The comparison with the main cultural production centres will allow Gibellina to promote its identity. Today, in order to ensure that the image of Gibellina "born from art" will not disappear, it is necessary that the dream of Corrao becomes a collective dream: only in this way Gibellina can remain the protagonist of a new cosmopolitism based on culture.

FOOTNOTES

1_The Belice River Valley occupies a large area of western Sicily between the provinces of Palermo, Trapani, and Agrigento.

2_The urban centres damaged by the earthquake were Calatafimi, Camporeale, Contessa Entellina, Menfi, Partanna, Salemi, Sambuca, Santa Margherita, Santa Ninfa, and Vita. The urban centres with over 90% of the houses destroyed were Gibellina, Montevago, Poggioreale, and Salaparuta.

3_For the analysis of the events of the earthquake and the post-seismic reconstruction of Gibellina, see the volume: Badami A. (2019) *Gibellina: la città che visse due volte*. Milano, FrancoAngeli.

4_CRESM: The Centre for Economic and Social Research for the South, founded in 1973. The Centre is based in Gibellina.

BIBLIOGRAPHY

Badami A., Picone M., Schilleci F. eds. (2008) *Città nell'emergenza. Progettare e costruire tra Gibellina e lo ZEN*. Palermo, Palumbo.

Badami A. (2012) "L'investimento in arte e cultura per fondare una città e generare una comunità a Gibellina. Intervista a Ludovico Corrao". In: *Archivio di studi urbani e regionali* 105. pp. 66–86.

Badami A. (2019) *Gibellina: la città che visse due volte*. Milano, FrancoAngeli.

Corrao L. (2008) "La ricostruzione è un'eterna metafora. La memoria di Gibellina". In: *Riso/Annex, I quaderni di Riso, Museo d'Arte Contemporanea della Sicilia*, n. 1/2008, pp. 38–42.

Corrao L., Carollo B. (2017) *Il sogno mediterraneo*. Alcamo, Ernesto Di Lorenzo.

Pes A., Bonifacio T. eds. (2003) *Gibellina dalla A alla Z: catalogo della collezione del Museo d'arte contemporanea di Gibellina*. Gibellina, Museo d'arte contemporanea.

Sorgi O., Militello F. eds. (2015) *Gibellina e il Museo delle Trame mediterranee*. Palermo, CRICD.

Figure 4
Gibellina, Museum of Mediterranean Textures
Image © Fondazione Orestiadi

HISTORIC URBAN LANDSCAPES: HOW TO IMPROVE NEOCOSMOPOLITANISM IN HISTORIC CENTRES

DANIELE RONSIVALLE

The novel coronavirus is not only a biological entity, but a social event that arose when it spread across the Northern Italy and Europe in January 2020. At the time, the media identified it as the expected "black swan" of the millennium. However, Covid-19 is not a black swan—an unexpected event caused by malevolent fate—but rather the predictable effect of the apical phase of the pandemic "polycrisis" in which we live. As Maurizio Carta underlines in this book, we have in the past months come to understand that Covid-19 is only the most recent and disruptive evidence of a "syndemic", and is making it clearer and clearer how many troubles exist in our contemporary cities.

The context: Covid-19 as a social event

As we know, the increased population density caused by the combination of predatory capitalism and the hyper-rational design of contemporary cities—starting with the rigid zoning of spaces and functions—began in the eighteenth century. Since the 1960s, the idea has spread that the Industrial Revolution was not, per se, a negative event, because the concentration of its effects caused the rise of the Anthropocene (Crutzen, Stoermer 2000). To understand this perspective, we may refer to a particularly significant topic in the history of technology. In the Hellenistic age, Heron of Alexandria invented the aeolipile, a steam-powered device. While it is a perfect example of the use of steam power, it was irrelevant in the Hellenistic innovation process, as no needs were fulfilled by the device.

By contrast, many centuries later in the early eighteenth century, fossil fuels (really!) represented an innovative solution for deforestation: coal was seen as a good, sustainable means of preserving English woods, just as the steam machine and internal combustion engine were seen as positive solutions that improved the quality of work and reduced pollution by animal manure in the overcrowded metropolis. In other terms, just as Marco Polo wrote about the unusual use of crude oil found in the Persian desert as beauty cream, each resource on Earth could be a considered fortune or a misfortune for mankind depending on the age. In the end, a sociodemographic and economic critical mass was reached in the Sixties, and the application of a global econometric development model produced social inequalities and resulted in a consumption of physical, social, and cultural

Figure 1
View of the urban context from High Line New York
UNESCO considers the regeneration of the High Line Park and its environs is an example of the use of civic engagement and financial tools in relation to a Historic Urban Landscape.
Photo by David Berkowitz via Wikimedia Commons[1]

human environments historic centres good practices

Figure 2
The location of the three studied historic urban landscapes (HULs) in Alexandria
Elaboration by the author based on Hussein et al. 2020

resources that went beyond the limits of the planet. The effects are now universally apparent, and global organisations are now warning nations of the collapse effects generated by the acceleration of the Anthropocene with increasing urgency.

The cultural aspects of combating the rise of the Anthropocene

For the past fifty years, UNESCO and the Council of Europe have declared the social and cultural aspects of landscape and cultural identity preservation to be fundamental rights (Council of Europe 2000), and governments have approved laws and adopted operative rules to protect cultural identities and support local-culture-based policies. In Italy, for example, the heritage, landscape, and cultural identity are protected by Article 9 of the Constitution: as a consequence, that the national government must promote regional and local-culture-based policies. However, cultural identity has not yet become a catalyst for local developments aiming for cultural transition. In 2012, UNESCO announced through Director-General Irina Bokova that tangible and intangible heritage are sources of social cohesion, factors of diversity, and drivers of creativity, innovation, and urban regeneration (UNESCO 2013). As a number of references show, historic centres are studied and planned as a concentration of tangible and intangible heritage: By identifying and defining paths, edges, districts, nodes, and landmarks as modules of the urban project Lynch (1960) revealed how people live in cities and what topics are most important in urban design. Furthermore, when Lynch analysed the quality level of urban spaces using his qualitative assessment model, a higher quality of the urban space corresponded to better evaluations from inhabitants. This is especially true in historic centres. The following year, Mumford argued in *The City in History* (1961) that the evolution of cities never produced "perfect" cities, but that each transformation was based on multifaceted—not merely functionalist—conditions. Historic urban spaces therefore exhibit a complex and stratified environment resulting from these conditions. Houses, squares, and streets in historic centres represent a well-combined fabric and are enriched by mixed uses. After fifty years of study and research on historic centres and in accordance with UNESCO historic urban landscape (HUL) policy, we are conscious of the quality and relevance of our historic centres that results from their stratified and well-settled environment. The development of a new, integrated approach in regeneration would be helpful, as it would offer a conceptual framework for contemporary urban heritage conservation, provide guidelines for urban heritage management, and serve as a regulatory instrument implemented at different levels by political authorities (Sonkoly 2017).

Could HUL policy be a good approach to Neocosmopolitanism?

Quality of life, openness to multiculturalism, a multi-layered historic identity; "...multi-species communities that are open to the possibility of meeting each other and of mutual cooperation, as well as willing to face the plurality and hybridisation of public space and new places of living..." (Carta, p. 27 in this book). With these characteristics of the cosmopolitan city in mind, an HUL policy could suit the needs of Neocosmopolitanism; and, more specifically, the UNESCO Recommendation on the Historic Urban Landscape (36 C/ Resolution 41) calls on Member States to integrate the conservation and management of cultural heritage into cities and settlements through policies and practices for sustainable urban development. In fact, the Neocosmopolitanism approach can support the HUL, with "the streets, the squares and the courtyards, the city gates and places that generate flows (ports, airports, stations, etc.), the places of culture strengthened by a new distributed localisation of services (theatres that extend into the streets, museums that meets the suburbs, schools that extend their activities to the outdoors, etc.), as well as gardens and parks that are connected through an urban ecological network and enter buildings or climb onto roofs, becoming places for free time, culture, and education" (Carta, p. 27 in this book). In the middle, there is Palermo's historic centre, a place where history and communities have repeatedly overwritten a complex palimpsest which Nature and Culture, in a cosmopolitan way, walk through without barriers and frontiers (Guarrasi 2011).

Because the historic urban landscape approach goes beyond the preservation of the physical environment and focuses on the entire human environment—with all of its tangible and intangible qualities—the Neocosmopolitan approach helps increase the sustainability of planning and design interventions by taking into account the existing built environment, intangible heritage, cultural diversity, and socio-economic and environmental factors, along with local community values. As such, an HUL policy framework would address the challenge of Neocosmopolitanism in Palermo. The historic centre of Palermo exhibits a "plural coexistence" and the concept of plural cultures has been widespread for last ten years. Palermo's historic centre is enriched by places of hospitality, sharing, and exchange, and the local community is almost completely integrated with new, incoming communities. The challenge of Neocosmopolitanism (Carta, p. 27 in this book) is taken up by many communities from Asia, Africa, and Europe who share traditions, culture, and ways of life and are proud to show their identity. Furthermore, the historic centre hosts cultural world-places, universities and musical and artistic colleges, UNESCO sites, festivals, movie sets, and other expressions of culture.

Some suggestions for how an HUL policy could be implemented in the historic centre of Neocosmopolitan Palermo

As an approach, HUL considers cultural diversity and creativity key assets for human, social, and economic development. This can help prevent "zoning" places into separate conservation areas, which thereby become ghettos of historic preservation. A Neocosmopolitan approach to Palermo's historic centre would support the integration of environmental, social, and cultural concerns into the planning, design, and implementation of urban development. This approach has had very positive and encouraging results in many cities; in each local situation, a balance was reached between the preservation and protection of urban heritage, economic development, functionality, the liveability of the city, and respect for social and cultural identities. Thus, the approach tends to the needs of existing communities while sustainably enhancing the city's natural and cultural resources for future generations. The different aspects of the approach—heritage, economic, environmental, and sociocultural—do not conflict; they are complementary, and their long-term success is dependent on them being linked together.

There are many global examples of good practice. The High Line in New York City is a historic site that was put in danger by a potential development programme. Participating in a bottom-up approach, the Friends of the Highline association fought for the historic structure's preservation and transformation at a time when it was under threat of demolition. In addition to overseeing maintenance, operations, and public programming for the park, Friends of the High Line works to raise the essential private funds needed to support more than 90% of the park's annual operating budget. The more than three million annual visitors to the High Line annually have rejuvenated this former brownfield site. In Istanbul, the Play the City foundation introduces serious gaming into city-making to test the rules and constraints of a given complex urban question and co-design a solution with stakeholders. One of these games focuses on the question of how Istanbul's vast number of newcomers can be accommodated in a city that is already highly dense and at risk of earthquakes, especially in the historic centre (UNESCO 2013). In Alexandria, many applied research projects are focusing on HULs in order to understand what approaches are necessary to preserve feelings of responsibility and rootedness. The risk of transformation and erasure is countered by citizens' self-awareness (Hussein et al. 2020).

Evidence increasingly points to a link between regeneration and social aspects—so, in accordance with HUL policy, a new policy programme for the Neocosmopolitan historic centre of Palermo will undertake a full assessment of the city's natural, cultural, and human resources, using stronger participatory planning and stakeholder consultations to decide on conservation (and transformation) aims and actions. The plan would take into account the vulnerability of urban heritage to socio-economic pressures and the impacts of climate change: water and geological sensitivity are key concerns in a historic centre crossed by two underground rivers that pose a silent risk. Ultimately, a Neocosmopolitan plan would integrate urban heritage values and their vulnerability status into a wider framework of city development, as well as prioritise conservation and development policies and

Figure 3
Interior view of Hagia Sophia, Istanbul
The "over-written" palimpsest of the building is a relevant metaphor for contemporary HUL policy in Istanbul, where the social fabric is changing in an already high-density metropolis, particularly in the historic centre.
Photo © Türkiye Kültür Portalı[2]

actions, including good stewardship, and establish appropriate public-private partnerships and local management frameworks. The developed mechanisms for coordinating various activities between different actors should be restarted based on a "community" concept: the historic city could be divided into different thematic design areas based on similarities in design issues and social context, and its public spaces could be used for multiple and changing uses throughout the day. Squares and streets designed to be enjoyed and open spaces that allow different formal and informal uses would modify the historic centre and express Palermo's ability to be extremely flexible. Palermo has been starting to experiment, with some success, with a new way of developing the historic centre, but we need to increase its collaborative component in order to launch a Neocosmopolitan historic urban landscape strategy.

FOOTNOE

1_https://commons.wikimedia.org/wiki/File:High_Line_Park_-_New_York_City_-_July_09.jpg

2_https://www.kulturportali.gov.tr/turkiye/istanbul/gezilecekyer/ayasofya-muzesi

BIBLIOGRAPHY

Council of Europe (2000) *European Landscape Convention*. Available online at: https://www.coe.int/en/web/conventions/full-list/-/conventions/treaty/176 (10.05.2020).

Crutzen P. J., Stoermer E.F. (2000) "The Anthropocene" In: *IGBP Newsletter* 41. pp. 17–18. Available online at: http://www.igbp.net/download/18.316f18321323470177580001401/1376383088452/NL41.pdf (18.08.2020).

Coruhlu Y. E., Uzun B., Yildiz O. (2020) "Conflict over the Use of Hagia Sophia: The Legal Case". In: *Land* 9(10). p. 350.

Guarrasi V. ed (2011) *La città cosmopolita. Geografie dell'ascolto*. Palermo, Palumbo.

Hussein F., Stephens J., Tiwari R. (2020) "Grounded Theory as an Approach for Exploring the Effect of Cultural Memory on Psychosocial Well-Being in Historic Urban Landscapes". In: *Social Sciences* 9(219). Available online at: https://doi.org/10.3390/socsci9120219 (09.12.2020).

Lynch K. A.(1960) *The Image of the City*. Cambridge, MIT Press.

Morin E. (2020) *Sur la Crise: Pour une Crisologie Suivi de Où Va le Monde?* Paris, Flammarion.

Mumford L. (1961) *The City in History*. San Diego, Harcourt.

Sonkoly G. (2017) *Historical Urban Landscape*. London, Palgrave Macmillan.

UNESCO (2011) *Recommendation on the Historic Urban Landscape (36 C/Resolution 41)*. Available online at: http://portal.unesco.org/en/ev.php-URL_ID=48857&URL_DO=DO_TOPIC&URL_SECTION=201.html (06.12.2020).

UNESCO (2013) *New Life for Historic Centres*. Paris, UNESCO.

URBAN BRICOLEURS

RICCARDA CAPPELLER

In order to grasp the character of urban spaces, it is not enough to look at images and plans, read descriptions, or even to browse the area on Google Earth and in 3D, as has been necessitated by the recent global restriction of people's mobility. Just as we form a first impression when meeting a new person, there is something in every spatial situation that we can only experience in the place itself as we are moving through it, perceiving it both subconsciously and with all our senses: its atmosphere. Constituted not only by built elements, but also by social relations, networks, and activities, atmosphere is what we deal with as architects and urban designers (Wolfrum 2016, pp. 48–51), and something that must be defined in a social and spatial sense when approaching *Cosmopolitan Habitat* and its cross-cultural and mobile dimension. In order to do this, a new kind of knowledge creation and application is necessary and will be looked at through a process-oriented, multiperspectival, and interdisciplinary understanding and designing or way of interacting with space , connected to the concept of "urban bricoleurs" as practitioners dealing with cosmopolitan atmospheres.

Characterising the cosmopolitan atmosphere

Starting from cosmopolitanism as an ideal—a political and cultural aim towards a universal human community, global citizenship, and societal pluralisation (Delanty 2006)—we as architects and urban designers must reconsider and recreate our habitats: the political organisation and spatial structure of the environments we live in, the way we inhabit, access, process and change them, and how we communicate these elements to indicate a future lying ahead. Building upon these requirements, the cosmopolitan atmosphere I envision is characterised by:

1. creating a contextual relation between existing social and spatial resources, to generate new ones;
2. urban complexity and diversity in which circulatory dimensions come together; and
3. the presence of creative agency and constantly changing networks that foster engagement and a collective exchange, creating bridges between distinct realities, building on ideas of democracy and "political equality" (Allen 2020).

Figure 1
Narrative elements
Photo by Riccarda Cappeller

"The bricoleur as cultural agent."

Using existing social and spatial resources to generate anew

The creation of new living spaces today is based on reworking, reinterpreting, altering, and adding onto what already exists, understanding its past and present in order to project its future use. The perception of these spaces, their patina, and their further development introduces both a new sensibility and variable forms, opening up possibilities for different uses and events. Referring to the As Found concept introduced in the 1950s by Alison and Peter Smithson, this reworking is about discovering qualities and values within ordinary everyday situations and reflecting upon the world as experienced in order to transform it. What becomes important here is the comprehension of the local context as the preliminary setting of each space, a subjective approach, and a strong conceptual idea used for its communication. There is not just one identity to be transmitted, but a composition of (cultural) resources in dialogue that form society—and, with it, the urban space. What needs to be developed is an intercultural discourse and mode of exploration, integrating people of all kinds of affiliations (Jullien 2016), as well as an effort to seek appropriate spatial translations.

Urban complexity and diversity connected through circulatory dimensions

Urban life is seen as irreducible product of mixture, containing unpredictable elements that are constantly transforming. (Amin, Thrift 2008, p. 3) The people, practices, and ideas that come together in one specific spatial setting are interconnected not only on a local level, but also globally. Through various flows and the circulatory dimensions of the city—encompassing market liberalisation (the flow of capital), international migration (the flow of people), cultural globalisation (the flow of ideas), and urban entrepreneurism (the flow of images)—a multifaceted process becomes visible (Guggenheim, Söderström 2009). This process is no longer concerned with national constraints, the privileges of states or people, fixed preconditions, norms and regulations, and profit- or business-oriented interests, but with the coexistence of contradictions, and a continuous re-examination of the social and spatial relations experienced in the everyday of built environments.

The presence of creative agency in changing networks

Based on openness towards otherness as well as on a shared ethos, we move towards a collectively shared, creative activity (Derrida 2001, p. 12) realised in the built environment. Especially in times when digital connections might be stronger than physical ones, real engagement, human interaction, and spatial interventions become indispensable in addressing segregation and inequality, as well as the fragmented character of urban space. They are the starting point for a different attitude in the production of space: an attitude based on collaboration, continuously changing networks and flexibility. Even in times of social distancing (due to the pandemic), ways to create public encounters on a small scale have to be thought of. Smaller cultural agencies that are focused on neighbourhood activities already do this by encouraging single actors to take action and create bridges between people or groups who normally would not interact. Taking these challenges as potentials, we as architects and urban designers need to develop new design modes, and must base the tools and approaches we use on spatial, social, cultural, and political hybridity and exchange, as well as on curiosity about the unplanned and on readiness to allow unexpected improvisation and experimentation to occur (Wolfrum 2016, p. 43). This inventive way of thinking and doing, and of being released from obligations and predefined (spatial) uses or thematic labelling, can be learned from the arts. This is not a new insight: for example, the Situationists in the 1970s worked with artistic approaches in order to create new spatial perspectives and dimensions.

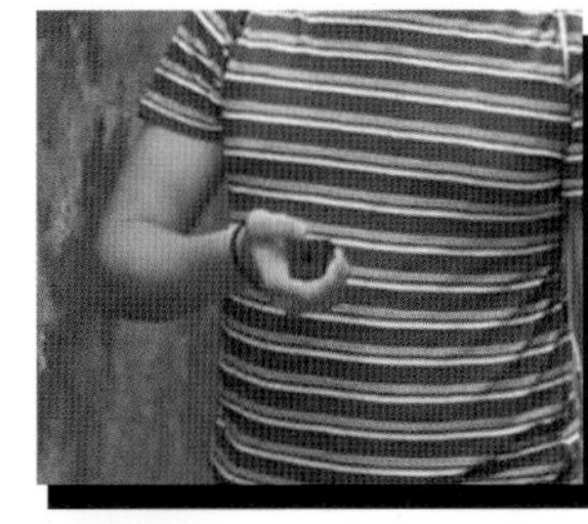

Figure 2
Collecting Activities
Photos by Riccarda Cappeller

"It is an agency that survives on its operational, transforming, and incidental character, able to establish sets of relations, networks, and programmes for a future liveable space with a cosmopolitan atmosphere."

Their work back then did not reach broader education and practice in the discipline, but now has become an real task as well as a movement; there is almost a fashion for working with the everyday. In this text, the focus is on an interdisciplinary and socially connected imagination of space, alternative ways of putting together its multiplicity, and the agents involved in this process. As architects and urban designers, we have to detach ourselves from our products and the "what" we produce, instead looking at "how" and "why" we do it, as well as at the abilities we need to learn to do so.

The bricoleur as cultural agent

The concept of the bricoleur, coined by Lévi-Strauss (1966), is of high relevance to this discussion. The activity of the bricoleur involves making do with materials already at hand, constantly re-using them to create something new. The bricoleur is "not only speaking with things, but through them" (Lévi-Strauss, in Dezeuze 2008, p. 31), opening up a different and more affective approach towards the atmosphere of physical space. An example from the arts is the Argentinean artist Antonio Berni, who in the 1960s developed a new language through his "Xilocolage": a combined technique of printing and paint. He created a series made from prints of trash materials found at the site the images reference, also drawing on these prints. One important figure in these images is Juanito, a poor boy from the slums of Buenos Aires, with whom Berni tells the story of the working class, directing a critical eye to the division of society in one specific place while referring to a global problem. Through his work, he critically brings together the material, social reality, and fiction, creating a narrative that is easy to understand and to build discussions on. Following Kincheloe's definition of the bricoleur, he is an "expert on relationships, connecting the cultural context, meaning making, power and expression within disciplinary boundaries" (2011, p. 684) while cultivating difference and developing tools for the work to be done at the boundaries. Returning to the architects and urban designers designing future *Cosmopolitan Habitat*, we could say that their responsibility is nearly equal to that of the bricoleur in assembling apparently incompatible aspects into something new: They discover potentials in existing spatial settings and the related political processes and organisational structures, setting up innovative concepts and new programmatic ideas. Moreover, they search for a refined way of developing and realising space with a process-oriented approach that keeps open possibilities for improvisation and allows to integrate the communication of spatial qualities, values, and the cultural capacity, including intangible aspects. In managing these topics, the urban bricoleurs become cultural agents handling the collected built materialities, conceptual ideas, and projected narratives that may be reanimated through public interest, as well as convincing authorities or financiers of the motivations, metaphors, and dreams that are later transformed into spatial designs and eventually become realised.

The urban bricoleur's agency, which strongly depends on communication and collaboration—as demonstrated by recent nominations of curating collectives for art events such as the *Documenta* exhibition—addresses a shift within the practice. One that is directed towards enabling a spatial knowledge production that reaches beyond its materiality and understands the principles of society as based on human values. The intention here is not to clearly identify and define this new direction, as it is an agency that survives on its operational, transforming, and incidental character, able to establish sets of relations, networks, and programmes for a future liveable space with a cosmopolitan atmosphere. What needs to be stressed instead, as has been done through the image of the bricoleur as an example here, is the search for new design modes.

BIBLIOGRAPHY

Allen D. S. (2020) *Politische Gleichheit*. Berlin, Suhrkamp.

Amin A., Nigel T. (2002) *Cities: Reimagining the Urban*. Oxford, Blackwell Publishing Ltd.

Derrida J. (2001) *On cosmopolitanism and forgiveness*. London, Routledge.

Delanty G. (2006) "The Cosmopolitan Imagination: Critical Cosmopolitanism and Social Theory". In: *British Journal of Sociology* 57(1), pp. 26–47.

Dezeuze A. (2008) "Assemblage, Bricolage, and the Practice of Everyday Life Source". In: *Art Journal* 67(1). New York, College Art Association, pp. 31–37.

Guggenheim M., Söderström O. (2009) *Re-Shaping Cities. How Mobility Shapes Architecture and Urban Form*. London, Routledge.

Jullien F. (2016) *Es gibt keine kulturelle Identität*. Berlin, Suhrkamp.

Kincheloe J. L. (2001) "Describing the Bricolage: Conceptualizing a New Rigor in Qualitative Research". In: *Qualitative Inquiry, 7*. Available online at: https://journals.sagepub.com/doi/10.1177/107780040100700601 (30.11.2020).

Watt K. (2010) "Cosmopolitanism and the architecture curriculum". *Spandrel: Journal of the School of Planning and Architecture* 1(1), pp. 35–44.

Wolfrum S. (2016) *Die Architektur der Stadt*. Stuttgart, Karl Krämer Verlag.

OVERTOURISM IN CONTEMPORARY CITIES: PARADOXES OF AN ANTI-COSMOPOLITAN PHENOMENON. CAUSES, CONSEQUENCES, AND TREATMENT

MARINA MAZZAMUTO

In recent months, pandemic paralysis has forced us to question, among other issues, the limitlessness of international mobility—and, consequently, the established idea of cosmopolitan practices. Tourism, in particular, has been the practice most affected, and its crisis has unveiled several contradictions in the current paradigm. Most of the completely "tourist-oriented" historic centres all around the world have found themselves suffering from the recession and subsequent desolation of a fragile, monocultural economic system. Some interesting questions may arise from this scenario: were contemporary cities' atmospheres moving towards a truly cosmopolitan model, as certain narratives may suggest, or just a globalised one? In an organic, breathing structure, where cities need to be able to absorb contractions and expansions of inhabitants and economic activities, can tourists be considered and involved as a different kind of temporary citizens of the universal *polis*—as discussed in regard to cosmopolitanism by several philosophers? What are the practices that can catalyse a truly sustainable touristic model?

The present work is linked to a thesis project that studies overtouristified cities in Southern Europe in order to elaborate new models for sustainable urban tourism. This article, which constitutes a portion of the theoretical framework of the research, tracks the cultural roots of overtourism down to the progressive distortion of what the article puts forward as cosmopolitanism's philosophical concept. It then traces the evolution of the conceptualisation of this urban phenomenon through a sequence of previous studies that have described and analysed it. The paper ultimately attempts a provisional inventory of practices that have been implemented by different cities in the past years and concludes that, in order to develop appropriate responses, a wider contextualisation of the issue within the current change in paradigm pertaining to contemporary cities is necessary.

Tourism and cosmopolitanism

Cosmopolitanism has always been linked, from its first conceptualisation, to the practice of travel. The concrete increase in the volume of movement and exchange during the Hellenistic Era was, in fact, no less important in the gestation of cosmopolitan philosophy than the geopolitical changes

LE

COSMOPOLITE

OU LE

CITOÏEN

DU

MONDE.

Patria eſt ubicunque eſt bene.

Cic. 5. Tuſcul. 37.

Aux depens de l'Auteur.
MDCCL.

Figure 1
Frontispiece of "Le Cosmopolite" by Louis Charles Fougeret de Monbron, 1776

touristification
overtourism
sustainability
neo-nomadism

catalysed by the imperialism of Alexander the Great generally associated with the elaboration of this philosophical idea (Brown 2012). This broad spatial, productive, and cultural expansion of mobility did not correspond, as is often claimed, to the institutional decline of the *polis*. During the reign of Alexander, and even during the Roman Empire, the Greek *poleis* maintained, alongside their new cosmopolitan vocation, considerable citizen involvement and great local political vitality. Stoic cosmopolitanism, rooted in Socratic philosophy and the first true crystallisation of cosmopolitan thought (although the very term *kosmopolites*, "citizen of the world", is historically attributed to the cynic Diogenes), preached a double level of political involvement both in the local and in the global *polis*. The original meaning of cosmopolitanism was then completely distorted during the eighteenth century: one of the ramifications of Enlightenment thought was the identification of cosmopolitanism with a predatory and totally apolitical idea of the travelling experience as an appropriative and cultural levelling process in service of the *loisir* of an aristocratic elite. In his autobiographical report Le Cosmopolite (Fougeret 1753), Fougeret de Montbron, who seems to prophesy an *ante litteram* version of the contemporary transnational lifestyle gentrifier (Lees et al. 2016; Sigler, Wachsmuth 2020), calls himself a cosmopolitan and describes how he travels everywhere without being committed to anywhere, declaring, "All the countries are the same to me" and "[I am] changing my places of residence according to my whim" (Fig. 1).

This negative version of cosmopolitan philosophy has grafted onto a historic context that saw the growth of colonialist policies, the theoretical formulation of capitalism (Smith 1776), and, not surprisingly, the advent of the practices of the Grand Tour. A seed that, germinating over the next two centuries, evolved into the practices of the current mass tourism industry. This gradual process, following what may be called the neoliberal atomisation of social life, established both an individualistic conception of leisure in the global *polis* and a detachment from the collective seasonal rituals in the local *polis*. The distortions of cosmopolitanism reaching contemporary urban dynamics, such as the standardisation (Nofre, Sequera 2018) and "Disneyfication" (Semi 2015) of tourist sites, have revealed modern cosmopolitanism's internal contradiction and its distance from classic cosmopolitan philosophy. In the last decade, uncontrolled tourism, smoothing over differences in the urban fabric (especially in historic centres) and generating friction between tourists and locals, has become completely detached from the stoic ideal of a universal, "glocal" harmony and now threatens the component of cultural richness that ultimately makes travelling a cosmopolitan practice. We can therefore affirm that urban tourism and its current invasive phenomenology, contrarily to what it may seem, has degenerated into an anti-cosmopolitan phenomenon.

Urban tourism becomes overtourism

Though traditionally linked to a narrative of extra-urban escape, recreation, or mass tourism, in recent decades mass tourism has strongly veered in the direction of the urban habitat. If tourism became an urban phenomenon of great importance from the 1980s onwards (in parallel to the first major urban redevelopment interventions and as a consequence of the new role assumed by leisure services in post-industrial cities), it is only in the last two decades that it has experienced a sensational surge: the so-called "world tourism cities" absorbed 17% of total international arrivals in 2017. In the context of a general increase in the volume of touristic travel (1.4 billion global arrivals per year in 2018; Butler, Doods 2019), Europe (which accommodates 50% of tourist arrivals) has been one of the most representative examples of this transformation (ibid. 2019). This scenario did not come about by accident: the Lisbon Treaty of 2009, first of all, sanctioned a change of course from previously feeble community policies on tourism promotion. Following the economic crisis in 2010, these changes were consolidated with the COM(2010) 352 framework, which enshrined as a key objective the affirmation of the touristic competitiveness of European countries. As a consequence of these development policies, various European cities (Barcelona, Venice, Berlin; see Fig. 2) have since the summer of 2016 been accused of highly corrosive host-guest frictions that, in addition to wide media attention, have reached the sensibilities of the scientific debate, prompting the formulation of issues such as "tourismphobia" and "overtourism" (Milano 2018). The concept of overtourism, formulated specifically to address the contemporary European urban context, is defined as the excessive growth of visitors, leading to overcrowding, in areas where residents suffer the consequences of temporary and seasonal tourism peaks that have enforced permanent changes to their lifestyles, access to amenities, and general well-being (Milano et al. 2018).

Koens (2018) summarises the consequences of this phenomenon as the following points:

1. Overcrowding of public space
2. Pervasiveness of the impact of visitors
3. Commercial touristification
4. Residential expulsion
5. Environmental pressure.

Figure 2
"Berlin doesn't love you"
Anti-tourism campaign, 2013
Photo by the author

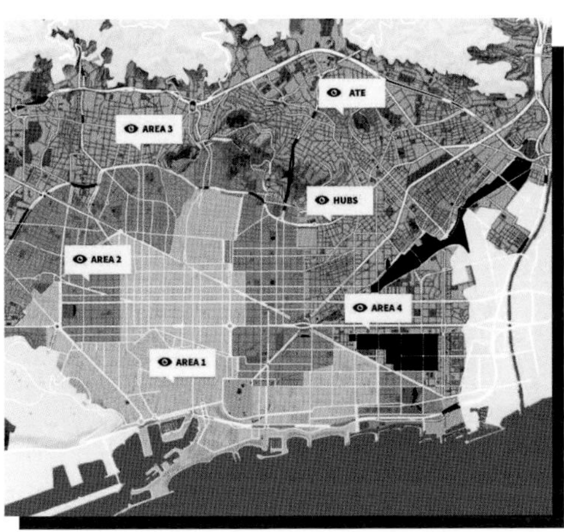

Figure 3
Special Urban Plan for Tourist Accommodation (PEUAT)
Source: Barcelona City Council (https://ajuntament.barcelona.cat)

It is clear that these consequences are not dysfunctions only inscribed within the logic of tourism management, but have massive repercussions on the city as a whole, and that tourism therefore imposes itself as an unavoidable matter of urban planning.

Old and new approaches to overtourism

Based on this complex picture of the effects linked to the problem of overtourism, the question of possible solutions arises. Although, as has been said, overtourism can be defined as a quite recent phenomenon, it is actually linked to a much longer scientific tradition that began to address the problem of tourism sustainability in the 1960s. Sprouted from the conceptual seed of Doxey's irritation index (1968) and then merged into the tourist life cycle models by Plog (1973), Miossec (1976), and the better-known Butler (1980), "carrying capacity" is a conceptual matrix for the quantitative evaluation of the impact of tourism—to which recent debates about overtourism clearly attest. Although simplistically formulated for small-scale, extra-urban tourist resorts, these models affirmed a fundamental principle that was lost in the years of deregulation that followed in the nineties (Hall 2011). These authors stated that if, on one hand, the tourist destination is comparable to a product (for example with respect to its insertion in the market), its attractive value is on the other hand strongly linked to the irreversibility of its vital, native ecosystem and to the delicate spatial, social, and economic balance that supports it. The interdisciplinary practices that have so far been experimented with in urban administrations or enunciated in academic debates measure themselves in relation to the carrying capacity threshold. On the one hand, there are practices that create a regulatory barrier to rigidly protect the threshold:

1. physical space limitations (e.g., the so-called "turnstile areas" of Venice), and
2. touristic licenses limitations (e.g., short-term rental limitations or town hall negotiations with Airbnb regarding licenses);
3. zoning regulation (e.g. the "Special Urban Plan for Tourist Accommodation, PEUAT", Barcelona; see Fig. 3);

and, on the other hand, there are practices that use the elasticity of strategic and collaborative forms of planning to instead expand the distance from this threshold:

4. dispersion of touristic pressure in the city, such as
   - congestion sensors (e.g. the Dubrovnik city council's "Respect the City" programme);
   - promotion of alternative itineraries (e.g. "Detourism: Travel Venice Like a Local", Municipality of Venice, 2014);
5. infrastructure improvement and innovation (e.g. the "Smart Parking Project", Valencia);
6. compensatory benefits to resident communities (e.g. the "Plan estratégico de turismo 2020", Barcelona);
7. integration between tourists and local society (e.g. the "My Helsinki Project", Helsinki).

This outline of an inventory of practices, in addition to not being exhaustive, certainly cannot, on its own, aspire to resolve the oxymoronic ambiguity of sustainable tourism without contextualising it in a broader vision on the role of tourism in contemporary cities.

Conclusion and outlook

The unproductiveness of the current tourism model is only one of several manifestations of a general economic paradigm based on uncontrolled consumption and the depletion of the planet's resources, whether natural or cultural. In fact, whether are we talking about desertification of land or desertification of historical fabric, whether are we facing an enlarged pluvial flow or a enlarged touristic one, this set of phenomena is attributable to the same unsustainable paradigm. These great changes, occurring on a global scale, therefore impose a new formulation of cosmopolitanism—one that clearly must detach from the distortions of Enlightenment philosophy, but also, in the face of the present complexity, requires revision of the original concepts. Urban tourism practices, in order to be able to adapt to this complexity, must move away from a purely extractive logic that, although it has usually been called post-industrial, does not really differ, even in its spatial manifestations, from the rigidity and fragmentation typical of the industrial city of the last century. The new cosmopolitan cities must therefore transform tourism from a consumptive practice into a political and participatory one (both in terms of its design processes and in distribution of the benefits it generates), calibrated on sustainable mobility and oriented towards activating metabolisms of urban proximity rather than impoverishing them. *In summa*, in the new, renovated idea of cosmopolitanism, the travelling community must constitute the materialisation of the mobile portion of an "open society" (Popper 1945) which, moreover, can no longer embody its current irrational dualism: on one hand a privileged class of travellers in the service of which urban cultural identities are immolated, and on the other hand a different class of travellers to whom cities close their physical and cultural barriers.

This complex issue raises some questions for future research: if, as mentioned above, the economic centrality of tourism is linked to the transition from the industrial urban culture to the post-industrial one, how can tourism be inserted into the new circular and productive practices required by "augmented urbanity" (Carta, 2017)? What is the role of tourism in a trend that, thanks to the smart working revolution, finally sees a chance for the revivial of internal areas and the transformation of cities into pulsating hubs of floating fluxes? Finally, in the context of a paradigm shift in anthropological and geographical studies that replaces a static reading of the urban territory with a dynamic one and sedentary inhabitants with neo-nomadic ones (the so-called "mobility turn", Giubilaro 2016), can tourists—stripped of their predatory role of cultural consumption—become real "temporary citizens", "world citizens" (Nussbaum 2019) that fully live, even with the associated rights and duties, the classic cosmopolitan ideal of the universal polis?

BIBLIOGRAPHY

Brown E. (2012) "Hellenistic Cosmopolitanism". In: Gill M.L. and Pellegrin P. (2012) *A Companion to Ancient Philosophy*. Oxford, Blackwell Publishing, pp. 549–558.

Butler R.W. and Dodds R. (2019) *Overtourism issues, reality and solutions*. Berlin/Boston, Walter de Gruyter.

Butler R.W. (1980) "The Concept of a Tourist Area Cycle of Evolution". In: *Canadian Geographers* 24. pp. 5–12.

Carta M. (2017) *The Augmented City, A Paradigm Shift*. Rovereto, List Lab.

Fougeret De Monbron L.C. (1750) *Le Cosmopolite, ou le Citoïen du Monde*. La Haye, Pierre Gosse. References are to the 2010 edition "Le Cosmopolite, ou le Citoyen du Monde" published by the Modern Humanities Research Association, London.

Giubilaro C. (2016) *Corpi, Spazi e Movimenti. Per una geografia critica della dislocazione*. Milano, Unicopli Edizioni.

Koens K., Postma A., Papp B. (2018) *Is Overtourism Overused? Understanding the Impact of Tourism in a City Context*. Basel, MDPI.

Nofre J., Sequera J. (2018) *Debates Shaken, not stirred: New debates on touristification and the limits of gentrification*. London, Routledge.

Nussbaum M. (2019) *The Cosmopolitan Tradition: A Noble But Flawed Ideal*. Cambridge (MA), Belknap Press.

Semi G. (2015) *Gentrification tutte le città come Disneyland?* Bologna, Il Mulino.

Smith A. (1776) *The Wealth of Nations London*. Strahan and Cadell. References are to the 1976 Italian edition "La ricchezza delle nazioni" translated by Bartoli F. et al and published by Newton Compton Editori, Rome.

Temas Variados by Roberto Burle Marx (detail)
Image © Roberto Burle Marx
With kind permission of Acervo de Sitio Roberto Burle Marx

Mosè Ricci ✷ Socrates Stratis ✷ Yannis Aesopos ✷ Barbara Lino ✷ Alissa Diesch ✷ Jes Hansen ✷ Cosimo Camarda ✷ Caterina Rigo

Cosmopolitan Accelerators

Activating spaces and networks

HABITAT 5.0

MOSÈ RICCI

In modern times, the *genius loci* and the *genius saeculi* have coincided. New forms of art, of the city, of architecture, and of fashion once created their respective eras. Today, this is no longer the case. While everything in our networks and connective devices changes at speed, everything in the material space of cities seems to change very slowly or to remain as it is. Rarely has the distance between the *gestalt* and the *zeitgeist* been so dramatic. The paradigm that binds aesthetics to the projection of time has crashed down, and projects that create new value for an already-existing form (to paraphrase Sullivan and then Venturi: form accommodates performances) propose overcoming the ideals of modernity and a new aesthetic of the existing. The economic and environmental crises exacerbated by the pandemic require a design logic oriented towards recycling and regeneration, and are gradually consuming interest in the new. The infinite possibilities of co-shaping virtual spaces in the Internet diminishes the originality of formal research and calls into question the concept of authorship as a brand.

Today, the relevance of our physical location seems so unimportant and unrelated to the idea of living safely and happily that one might wonder if there is still a need for architecture in Italy—or in the whole Western world. "The almost instantaneousness of the software era inaugurates the devaluation of space" (Bauman 2000). Modernity is over and has left a void. The dissolution of solid space into the network and the excess of abandoned or underused buildings almost erase the need for functional specialisations and for a new construction of physical space. If all of this is about to happen, or is already happening, it is clear that many essential paradigms of the modern age—not just that of the close relationship between the form and function of architecture or of towns—are or will become emptied of meaning. Ultimately, the revolution prompted by information-sharing technologies displaced the certainties of the modern project, suddenly making all theories and practices related to it appear out-of-date. The zoning, the functional organisation of urban contexts or that of the architectural spaces, the model theories, the best practices. They seem the manifestations of a logic that belongs to another era, theoretical and behavioural models conceived to handle a three-dimensional, solid space that is now no longer the only possible design space. This is the point. The simultaneous

Figure 1
Urbanism for the the ecological transition: Trento Leaf Plan, 2020
Source: University of Trento for the City of Trento,
Mosè Ricci (principal investigator)

nature-based solutions resilience energy-efficiency

Figure 2
Project by Maria Giuseppina Grasso Cannizzo for a former rural house in Modica: the existing as a construction material.
EU Mies Award selection 2018
Photo by Luisa Porta

Figure 3
Landscape as narrative and ecological device
FOKSTROT / Marshall Blecher, Copenhagen Islands, 2020 (ongoing)
Image by the architects

action of three key factors—the economic crisis, the environmental one, and the information-sharing technologies revolution—is so deeply changing our lifestyles and the way we imagine and want the solid forms of our future to be that all our design knowledge suddenly seems inadequate, both as an interpretative tool for the current condition and as a device capable of generating new environmental, social, and economic performances, new beauty, and happiness. Turning to the positive effects of the digital revolution, one might say that the effect of shared information in the most evolved societies is the increased possibility for people to live in much more physical space than in the past, and for them to not necessarily have to conform to specific pre-established destinies. Simply put, we have a huge amount of built-in volume that is no longer needed or that we still do not know how to use. The same is already the case for infrastructure and open spaces. This is nothing surprising. In the history of architecture and the city, great technological changes have always prompted great changes in our ways and forms of living, and consequently in the ways and forms of design.

One of the main theoretical questions of modernity concerned the best possible spatial synthesis between the function and shape of architecture and the organisation of the city in homogeneous functional areas. Today, with the revolution in information technology, we are faced with the opposite problem. That is: we need to give meaning, narrative, and uses—albeit temporarily—to spaces that already have set forms. And transform them into attractive, ecologically performing, habitable places. The dissipation of modernity requires new paradigms, such as new perspectives on the future—or on the present—and new ideas for the design of physical spaces. This is an important challenge for architectural culture: to value existing structures and resources through conceptual devices that are based on a shift of sense and on the life cycles of new habitats. It is a challenge that considers the context as an opportunity for design, the landscape as an infrastructure that produces ecological value, and the future of the city as a collective and non-authorial project. In face of global warming, low CO_2 emissions, the cost of oil, renewable energies, great social migrations, the explosion of the city, the fragility of large urban concentrations in the face of natural events that turn into catastrophes, and in face of the defence of contexts seen as bulwarks of identity, the culture of architectural and urban planning cannot remain insensitive to this challenge. It is an epochal transformation that starts from the bottom. It proceeds through quality-of-life goals, autopoietic practices, and survival strategies. The protagonists are citizens, consumers, and people focused on limiting resource consumption who feed on the products of organic agriculture and separate their recycling; they prefer public transportation or travelling by bicycle; they are attracted to low-emission cars; they appreciate bioclimatic houses, not buildings with high energy consumption; they want sustainable and landscape-sensitive infrastructures. *Habitat 5.0* is the habitat that welcomes the effects of this phase of the digital revolution and promotes the right of citizens everywhere to adapt and design their living spaces. Each *Habitat 5.0* project should be developed at least in five methodologic moves.

Co-develop the project with citizens

As local governments grow more and more interested in meaningful civic participation, it becomes important to explore available methodologies that address the challenges related to truly participatory processes. The participation of the citizens in the creation of public space is fundamental, as it leads to results in terms of the way they inhabit it, protect it and feel safe in it. Since the 1960s, games have been proposed as a means of facilitating participatory processes by enabling cooperative environments that shape and support the interaction of citizens. Gordon and Baldwin-Philippi (2014) argue that some of the main advantages in involving citizens in participatory processes through the use of video games are citizen reflection, the development of lateral and vertical trust, and civic learning. Games have the potential to foster a collaborative environment and facilitate the process of understanding by providing a framework for setting collective goals. They offer a structure based on rules and mechanisms that drive participative processes and simultaneously function as a porous communication platform. Videogames for the co-design of urban and territorial space present virtual models of real urban spaces in which the audience is involved in exploring and creating new design patterns. They engage audiences with notions of ecology, sustainability, and coexistence, encouraging the player to think creatively.

Enhance the circularity of city/space/landscape/architecture

Understanding the interactions between physical environments as diverse sets of dynamic life cycles (connecting goods, people, energy, food, information, biota, water, sediments, air, mobility, etc.), as well as appreciating their complexity and ability to adapt, requires us to overcome the relational ontology of "humanity-in-nature" and the dialectic dualism of "nature and society" (Swyngedouw et al. 2005; Moore 2011). Without discussing the trajectories in conceptualising the definition of urban metabolism, this concept is here understood as the collection of socio-technical, spatial, and ecological processes—which are ideally, but often not, equitably distributed—that shape the levels of interdependence occurring at different scales in cities and territories, sustaining the demands of a population of a certain size and affecting the surrounding environment (urban footprint). This thougth opens up new areas of applicability for the urban metabolism concept by shifting from a mere ex-post monitoring/accounting approach—which often leads to remedial approaches to urban management (sometimes unplanned and almost always reactive)—towards an ex-ante co-design planning method (pre-emptive, proactive, planned in strict sense), that is able to build alternative scenarios based on site-specific impacts and to define spaces of interactions and multi-functionality. From this reformulation of fields, three lines of research-action—flows, places, and players—can be derived, each characterised by a driver of change:

The line of adaptive dynamics identifies how the in/out flows of a system can be managed during long periods of aggregation/transformation of resources, as well as through shorter periods that create opportunities for the innovation of specific uses/life cycles. It is a vision of persistence borne out of change influencing the self-organisation and adaptation of ecosystems (Gunderson, Allen, Holling 2010);

- The line of ecological quality focuses on qualities/performances and spatial effects in places, linking multiple scales of intervention (e.g., from the territory to the urban scale, from architecture to design) and multi-targeted challenges (e.g., the EU Urban Agenda, the UN Sustainable Development Goals) to implement resilient strategies according to "productive urban landscapes" (Viljoen, Bohn 2014);
- The line of social sustainability involves the players (public, private, institutional, and economic) who take part in the transformation processes, creating networks or micro-hubs of local metabolism: site-specific flows of circularity enhancing the ecological resilience of local communities as catalysts for urban innovation and creativity (Petrescu et al. 2012).

Implement nature-based solutions; exploit the services that nature can provide to cities

Nature-based solutions are living systems that provide cities with a wide array of ecosystem services and represent a way of addressing the UN New Urban Agenda. Particularly in the last years, there has been growing recognition and awareness that nature can help provide viable solutions that use and deploy functions and services from ecosystems in a smart, "engineered" way. Ecosystem services are defined as the multiple benefits provided by nature to human beings, and are divided into four main categories: life support, such as soil formation and oxygen production; procurement, such as the production of food, drinking water, raw materials, and fuel; regulation, such as climate control and tidal waves, water purification, and pollination; and cultural values, including aesthetic, educational, and recreational values (Millennium Ecosystems Assessment 2005). These services also have a considerable impact on the social welfare, economic development, and resilience of urban environments.

Enhance energy efficiency and RES implementation

The Renewable Energy Directive establishes numerous requirements concerning the use of buildings supplied with energy from renewable sources. However, there is still a need for national initiatives in order to promote local energy conversion and to remove the barriers to their wider uptake, which remain considerable. Although the agricultural sector is relatively small in terms of energy consumption, it is quite interesting in terms of renewable energy policy.

Enhance resilience

Ecological resilience is the capacity to react to and rebound from shocks and stress, and to incorporate new information into the system itself through a capacity for independent learning and (re) adaptation. In this semantic framework, other terms can help define the different approaches of *Cosmopolitan Habitat*:

- Resilience theory offers a vision of sustainability not as stability but as persistence borne out of change—or, more specifically, out of adaptive renewal cycles able to influence self-organisation, learning, and the adaptation of socio-ecological ecosystems (the results of human/natural dynamics as a whole).

- The six main keywords for the notion of resilience can be understood, in the context of an innovative urban approach, through other synonymous terms with similar but variable potentials, linked with adapted parameters:
    a. Anticipation: linked with Pre-vision (informational and processing mapping),
    b. Adaptation: linked with Adaptability (more strategic, less categorical),
    c. Resistance: linked with Endurance (more flexible and structural),
    d. Absorption: linked with Integration (more relational and transversal),
    e. Regeneration: linked with Reactivation (more dynamic and operational), and
    f. Regeneration 2: linked with Re-information (more informational)

- Theoretical advances include a set of seven principles that have been identified for building resilience and sustaining ecosystem services in social-ecological systems. These principles build on the resilience thinking developed by the Stockholm Resilience Centre:
    a. maintaining diversity and redundancy,
    b. managing connectivity,
    c. managing slow variables and feedbacks,
    d. fostering complex adaptive systems thinking,
    e. encouraging learning,
    f. broadening participation, and
    g. promoting polycentric governance systems.

NOTE

This text is based on the studies developed for the book *Habitat 5.0: The Architecture Of The Long Present* (Mosè Ricci, Skira, Milan, 2019), on the reflections developed with Mathilde Marengo and Joao Nunes, among others, for the elaboration of a programme proposal for the 2020 Luxembourg ecological transition project, and on the author's contribution to the book *Resilient Communities and the Peccioli Charter: Towards the possibility of an Italian Charter for Resilient Communities. Volume di Approfondimento del Catalogo del Padiglione Italia alla XVII Biennale di Architettura di Venezia* (edited by Maurizio Carta, Maria Perbellini, and J. Antonio Lara-Hernandez, Springer, 2020).

BIBLIOGRAPHY

Bauman Z. (2000) *Liquid Modernity*. Cambridge, Polity Press.

Gordon E., Baldwin-Philippi J. (2014) "Playful civic learning: Enabling lateral trust and reflection in game-based public participation". In: *International Journal of Communication* 8, pp. 759–786.

Gunderson L., Allen C., Holling B. (2010) *Foundations of Ecological Resilience*. New York, Island Press.

Millennium Ecosystems Assessment (2005) *Ecosystems and Human Well-Being*. 3 Volumes. Washington, Island Press.

Moore J. W. (2011) "Ecology, capital, and the nature of our times". In: *Journal of World-Systems Research* 17(1), pp. 109–147.

Petrescu A., Vinas R., Janssens-Maenhout G., Viorel B., Grassi G. (2012) "Global estimates of carbon stock changes in living forest biomass. EDGARv4.3, Time series from 1990 to 2010". In: *Biogeosciences* 9(8), pp. 3437–3447.

Swyngedouw E., Kaika M., Heynen N. eds. (2005) *In the nature of cities: urban political ecology and the politics of urban metabolism*. London, Routledge.

Viljoen A., Bohn K. (2014) *Second Nature Urban Agriculture*. London, Routledge.

"NEGOTIATE AS YOU GO ALONG": INFRASTRUCTURES FOR SHARED, "HYBRID" TERRITORIES

SOCRATES STRATIS

This article is an investigation[1] of the infrastructural role of *Europan 13* winning projects in enhancing shared, "hybrid" territories. Such territories have multi-geographic realities, resulting from urban transport network connections and programmes relating to the incoming flows, while being transformed by location-specific characteristics. The projects demonstrate their political virtue by proposing a gradual change in the relations between the projects' actors: influencing the ways that new incoming urban dynamics, or "inputs", may transform the competition sites into shared, "hybrid" territories. Tensions may arise due to potential conflicts between the on-site urban actors' agendas and those of the incoming ones (Stratis 2006). The challenge for *Europan* projects is, therefore, to become a negotiation apparatus for the adaptable city in the hands of the urban actors. Firstly, they must foster the presence of the public domain where there is a increasing absence of the welfare state; secondly, promote sharing within an increasing segregated world; and thirdly, allow for new relations and moments of negotiation between urban actors during project making where urban fragmentation is increasing.

This article departs from the aforementioned first objective to briefly revisit the other two (Fig. 1). The *Europan 13* sites hosting such new inputs are grouped into three categories. The first category concerns large, monofunctional areas of big-box urbanism (Bondy, France; Vienna, Austria), of fossil fuel industries (Stavanger, Norway), or of former military sites now used as a centre for schools (Schwäbisch Gmünd, Germany). Most of the sites in this category have a reduced public presence and are in need of community spirit. The second category identifies areas that are part of large territorial figures, such as riverbanks (Vernon, France), former industrial waterfronts (Trondheim, Norway; Molfetta, Italy), or natural landscapes (Espoo, Finland; Landsberg, Germany) under pressure from increasing private development and threatened by their decreasing role in the local community. The third group is about rather isolated areas, some with already existing community activity (Lund, Sweden; Montreuil, France; Santo Tirso, Portugal) and others without (St Pölten, Austria), that are confronted with potentially overwhelming metropolitan flows due to imminent connection to the transport networks of large agglomerations.

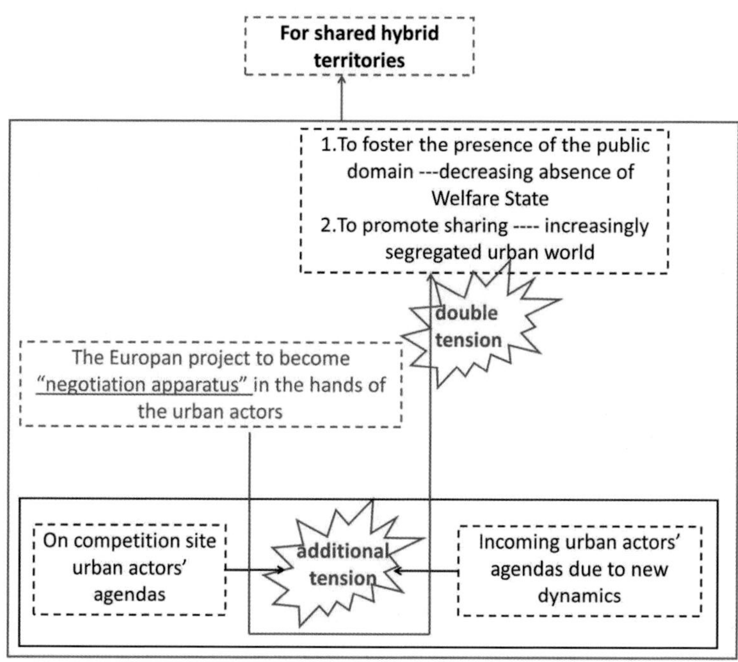

Figure 1
The Europan 13 *project as a "negotiation apparatus" in the hands of the urban actors*
Image by the author

public domain sharing negotiating

The Europan project in changing times: from participation to negotiation

The expression "Negotiate As You Go Along" draws on references to practices back in the 1960s and 1970s—such as Cedric Price's collaboration with Inter-Action, an alternative theatre collective, to build the Inter-Action Centre, which allowed him to investigate the role of architectural practice in changing times with regard to the emergence of mass media, mass consumerism, and mass housing. In fact, Price attributed negotiating capacities to architecture by opening up the design process into a collective platform, inviting participation. According to Tanja Herdt, he found himself exposed to a shift in architecture that is becoming broader in terms of communication, project development, and project outcome. Price was able to invest in participatory moments thanks to the adaptable nature of Inter-Action's infrastructure, which was based on a flexible, technical building system. However, due to the incompatibility of the high-tech building infrastructure with the low-tech labour contribution provided by the Inter-Action collective, the results were rather questionable (Herdt 2015). Going back to Europan 13, the winning teams include aspects of participation within the invisible technology of the urban project, as well as within the visible one of the architectural object—both of which are quite decisive for the co-production of shared, "hybrid" territories. "The task at hand involves working in different scales and with a diverse set of mechanisms blending urban planning, programming, operative and recreational landscapes, infrastructure and communication." In reading the abovementioned excerpt from Stavanger's competition brief, quoted by winning project *Forus LABing* by Play Studio, Spain,[2] we are witnessing a shift of architectural practice like the one confronted by Price. This new shift, however, demands complex operations and alliances beyond the field of architecture. By using the concept of "negotiation", we bring forward the aspects of participation that are internal to design processes and involve a degree of power-shifting among the project actors. We aim to surpass the pitfalls of the participatory paradigm being used to neutralise conflict and diminish the risks of investment by limiting public protest, as Jeremy Till mentions (2015). We embrace his claim that participation should be about distribution of power in the co-production of the city. Furthermore, the geographer Erik Swyngedow has addressed the myths of participation we need to be aware of. He first argues that the call for participation is a symptom of democratic dysfunction—institutions do not work, and they therefore call on citizens to find a solution. Second, he refers to a misunderstood concept of citizens' participation that addresses only a specific set of people; unlike many others, bankers and developers—who are citizens too—have plenty of access to decision-making, and would not be very happy of sharing power. Third, he refers to agents who, in the name of neutrality, are called on to articulate the demand of citizens' participation without making their own stance explicit. He goes on to state that successful citizenship demands the reorganisation of institutions to ensure that participation is embedded in their decision-making, such as in the recent case of the municipality of Barcelona.[3]

A multi-agency approach to enhancing the public: between strategies of infiltration and the tactics of revalorising the existing

The winning projects studied here employ a multi-agency approach to cope with such dilemmas, and set up negotiating frameworks to initiate sharing within "hybrid" territories (Fig. 2). The point of departure of the projects depends on the state of things with regard to the competition sites and briefs. In some cases, when the incoming global flows of people and activities are dominant—as in the first group of sites with monofunctional uses—the projects are about infiltration strategies that enhance the sites' public and collective uses, as seen in the project winners in Bondy[4] and Vienna.[5]

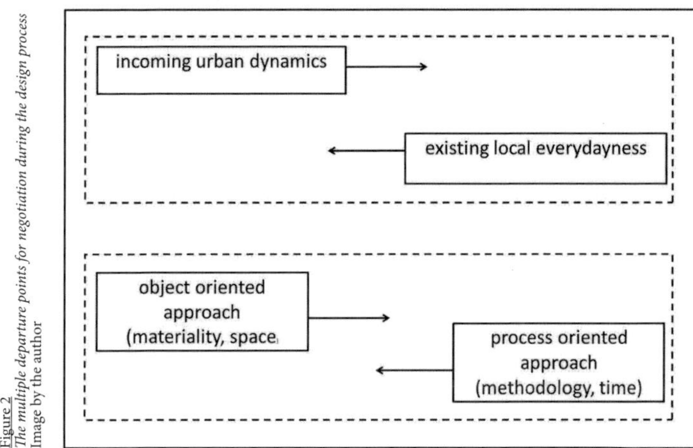

Figure 2
The multiple departure points for negotiation during the design process
Image by the author

In other cases, where there is community life that may be challenged by the incoming metropolitan flows—such as in Lund and Montreuil—the project teams chose to concentrate on the tactic of revalorising the unseen virtues of the local everyday and show how they could play a new role in such "hybrid" territories. Examples of this strategy can be seen in *Monster Planning*, runner-up in Lund;[6] *OuLiPo*, which received a special mention in Montreuil;[7] and *Insécable distance*, the winner in Vernon.[8] Beyond this, we see projects that consider the new transport nodes the initiators of such "hybrid" territories—for example, *Culture Symbiotic*, the winner in Lund,[9] and *Navigable Collections*, runner-up in Vernon. In some other cases, the project teams rely on the presence of agglomeration mobility networks to discourage the creation of isolated communities—such as in *Serendipity of Fields*, runner-up in Montreuil;[10] *Living With (In) Nature*, the winner in Landsberg;[11] and *Nodes*, runner-up in Schwäbisch Gmünd[12]—or create additional hosting space for incoming immigrant communities—as in *The Elastic City*, runner-up in St Pölten.[13]

Emerging modes of collective practices resulting from synergies between process- and object-oriented approaches

To encourage collective practices—the main ingredient of shared, "hybrid" territories—we may need to rely on new ways of negotiating, initiated through synergies between object- and process-oriented approaches. This way, we may avoid what Swyngedow warns of with regard to the never-ending processes usually employed by urbanists, as well as to the authoritarian placing of built objects by architects unaware of their political implications. Among the winning *Europan 13* projects, we can see a diversity of approaches that employ new relations between processes and objects in order to achieve sharing within "hybrid" territories by starting with either the placing of an object or the initiating of a process and suggesting exchanges among them during the design processes. In some cases, the architectural object is given a central role in defining the space for collective practices, either through its uniqueness or its repetition—as was the case, for example, for The *False Mirror,*[14] the winner in Trondheim. In other cases it is accorded the symbolic value of the community's presence along with territorial elements—such as rivers, as in *Insécable distance*, the winner in Vernon,

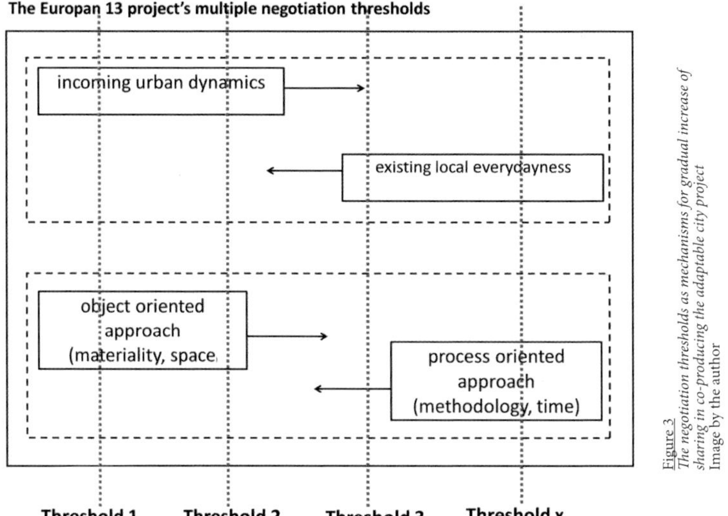

Figure 3
The negotiation thresholds as mechanisms for gradual increase of sharing in co-producing the adaptable city project
Image by the author

or *seacoasts*, as in Espoo—opening up new kinds of sharing. The winning project in Molfetta, *Hold the Line*, employs a sort of stripped-down urban Inter-Action centre to accommodate everyday activities along a public waterfront. In the case of the runner-up project in Trondheim, *More Trondheim!*,[15] we see existing industrial buildings used as shelters for public activities. In the same project, the reorganisation of space to medium-size plots becomes another way to ensure the presence of city-scale activities, keeping out "big-box" interventions. In the case of Vienna, the winning project—*Publicquartier*—re-establishes the major role of public space in the area under study by proposing the gradual demolition of a city block near the train station, adjacent to a dominating shopping mall. *Publicquartier* initiates creative synergies between the public and the collective by strategically locating a "habitat" for the negotiation of the district's urban future. The initiation of processes by the project teams may result in a playful mode of negotiation. This is the case for *Bondy's Count*, the winner in Bondy. Here, a game-like negotiation takes place, during which the city aims to infiltrate the competition site by gradually acquiring left-over spaces, as well as "left-over times" from the everyday activities. The community would initially emerge through the ephemeral activities, and through a reorganisation of the ground on a second round of the game, inviting "big-box" actors to address the intermediate scale and the introduction of a diversity of activities. To empower a structured negotiation process, a special mention for the same site, *Les nouvelles dynamiques*, offers a well-devised methodology for infiltrating the site with public and community activities, encouraging "big-box" urbanism to adapt. The team offers a "precedence catalogue", which is very handy for supporting controversial dialogues (evidence-based urbanism). *Forus LABing*, the winning project for Stavanger, encourages the development of networked collectivity guided by a complex strategy of management and design into visualising transformative processes for the urban futures of the existing monofunctional fossil-fuel industry area. The name for the 'habitats' dedicated to the negotiation processes is "Innovation Palaces". The ground is given "super-surface" characteristics to maximise flexibility, with plug-in towers to increase the critical mass of inhabitants and yield new communities.

Negotiation thresholds for increasing sharing in co-producing the adaptable city

"Negotiate As You Go Along: The Process of Making the Europan Project" is a call to all actors for the gradual increase of sharing in project making. Passing through many negotiation thresholds would alter the initial agendas of these actors towards a common final out-come. Approaches like this seem to be frequent among the winning teams, which have delivered complex proposal packages full of negotiating moments. Negotiation is ready to take place when the project teams revalorise the existing site assets—as in *Monster Planning* in Lund—and redefine the competition brief's priorities—as in *Forus LABing* in Stavanger. Negotiation is imminent when they propose roadmaps to the project actors for assisted itineraries through processes with uncertain outcomes—as in *Les nouvelles dynamiques*, special mention in Bondy—or when they make visible the complex networks of relations and the powers of the actors at stake—as in *Bondy's Count*, winner in Bondy. "Negotiate as You Go Along" is an appeal to rethink the technology of architectural practice and its contributions to urban projects operating in complex, "hybrid" territories. Issues of communication, project development, and outcome are indeed at the heart of the shift in architectural practices. *Europan* is a pertinent platform for studying for studying the tendencies not only of change, but also of the reappearance of approaches. Addressing the challenge of participation through the concept of negotiation has shown that the *Europan 13* projects could operate as platforms for changing relations among divergent urban actors in creating shared, "hybrid" territories.

FOOTNOTES

1_An earlier version of this article was published with the same title in: Rebois D. ed. (2016) *The Adaptable City 2, Europan 13 Results*. Paris, Europan Europe editions, pp. 126—129. The figures have been added for the current publication by the author.

2_http://europan.no/entries/fd970

3_References from a public presentation by Erik Swyngedow in AESOP 2015, Prague.

4_Winning Team: STUDIO DIESE, France). https://www.europan-europe.eu/en/news/e13-sites-bondy-fr

5_Winning Team: B. B. Romaniuk, A. Kravcova architects, D. Stupar landscape architect (Slovenia), https://www.europan-europe.eu/en/news/e13-sites-wien-at

6_Runner-up team: Mosaik Arkitekter, c/o Linus Mannervik (Sweden), https://www.europan-europe.eu/en/exchanges/monster-planning

7_Special mention: Ateliers George (France), https://www.europan-france.org/projet/l-ouvroir-de-lieux-potentiels-613

8 Winning Team: Adrien Rerat, architect; associate: Louise Le Penndu, architect (France). https://www.europan-europe.eu/en/news/e13-winning-teams-portraits-interviews-79

9_Winning Team: Joanna Hagstedt, urbanist; associates: David Kiss, architect urbanist (Sweden). https://www.europan-europe.eu/en/news/e13-winning-teams-portraits-interviews-49

10_Runner-up team: Florent Descolas, Mathieu Garcia, Adrien Mondine, architects urbanists (France). https://www.europanfrance.org/projets/single/611

11_Winning team: Paolo Russo, architect; associates: Antonio Cugusi, Annamaria Gaito, Fabiana Ledda, architects (Italy). https://www.europan-europe.eu/en/news/e13-winning-teams-portraits-interviews-43

12_Runner-up team: Héctor Peinador, architect (Spain); associate: Thomas Gaines, architect (UK); Swastika Mukherjee, architect (India). https://www.europan-europe.eu/en/exchanges/nodes

13_Runner-up team: Nela Kadic, architect urban planner; associate: Vera Seriakov, architect urban planner (Austria). https://www.europan-europe.eu/en/exchanges/the-elastic-city

14_Winning team: Giovanni Glorialanza, architect; associates: Andrea Anselmo, Gloria Castellini, Guya Di Bella, Fillippo Fanciotti, Boris Hamzeian, architects (Italy). https://www.europan-europe.eu/en/exchanges/the-false-mirror

15_Runner-up team: Dominique Hauderowicz, architect; associate: Kristian Ly Serena, architect (Denmark). https://www.europan-europe.eu/en/news/e13-winning-teams-portraits-interviews-11

BIBLIOGRAPHY

Note: some sources have been added to the references of the earlier version of this article in order to introduce the *Europan* context.

Herdt T. (2015) "Architecture as Negotiation: The Inter-Action Centre of Cedric Price". Paper presented at the *Architecture as matter of contention* conference, Aachen, January 2015.

Rebois D. (2004) *Implementations: negotiated projects*. Paris, Europan Europe Editions.

Stratis S. (2006) "Urban dynamics of infrastructures". In: Rebois D. ed. (2006) *European Urbanity, Europan 8 Results*. Paris, Europan Europe Editions, pp. 90–93.

Stratis S. (2014) "Architecture-as-urbanism in uncertain conditions". In: Rebois D. (2014) *Europan 12 Results: Adaptable City*. Paris, Europan Editions.

Stratis S. (Forthcoming) "Translocality as Urban Design Tool for the Inclusive City: The Case of Europan". In: *ARDETH Architectural Design Theory* 7.

Till J. (2015) "Distributing Power". In: *Participatory Urbanism: MONU Magazine 23*.

Younes Ch., Maugard A. (2019) *Villes et architectures en débat: Europan*. Paris, Parenthèses editions.

REVALORISING ATHENS

YANNIS AESOPOS

Athens became the capital of the modern Greek state in the early nineteenth century. It was a small, neoclassical city built beside the ancient one and was based on the monumental 'Triangle' urban plan of 1833 by Stamatios Kleanthis and Eduard Schaubert, which was only partly realised. However, through rapid urbanisation processes—especially those of the post-war period—Athens was transformed into a large, spread-out metropolis. These intense modernisation processes led to the "blurring" and even the erasing of fundamental elements or parts of the city's history, as well as the breaking down of its perception as a continuous, single entity. Life and urban experience became fragmentary.

Plinths / Revalorising

Large objects, in the form of a plinth (or a podium), are positioned in key locations in Athens. The plinth is a monolithic, large-scale, orthogonal prism of abstract form and particular materiality. The plinth "uplifts" and assigns value and importance to what it carries—as in the case of a plinth or a podium bearing a statue, or one in an ancient temple. Every plinth can carry different programmes and produce different mental and experiential effects. Plinths, in their different expressions, revalorise—assign new value—to parts of the city whose role and significance has been obscured, deleted, or lost. Through architecture, a reconnection of the city's history—both ancient and neoclassical—and its people can then be established. Three key locations, three public spaces in Athens, are selected: Syntagma Square, the city's political centre; Varvakeios Agora, the city's commercial centre; and Kerameikos, the entrance to and cemetery of the ancient city.

Syntagma Square: Twin Plinths / Steps and "Speakers' Podium"

Syntagma Square is the centre of Greek political life; it is the main venue for protests which, during the period of economic crisis, became massive and repetitive. The square is dominated by the neoclassical parliament building that stands on its eastern edge, designed by the Bavarian Friedrich von Gärtner in 1847. The square's longitudinal section, which starts from the austere facade of the parliament building and the Tomb of the Unknown Soldier war memorial of 1930 that is laid out in front of it, seems to "blur" as it slopes down to reach its lower, western edge, which is cluttered with

blurring erasing processes

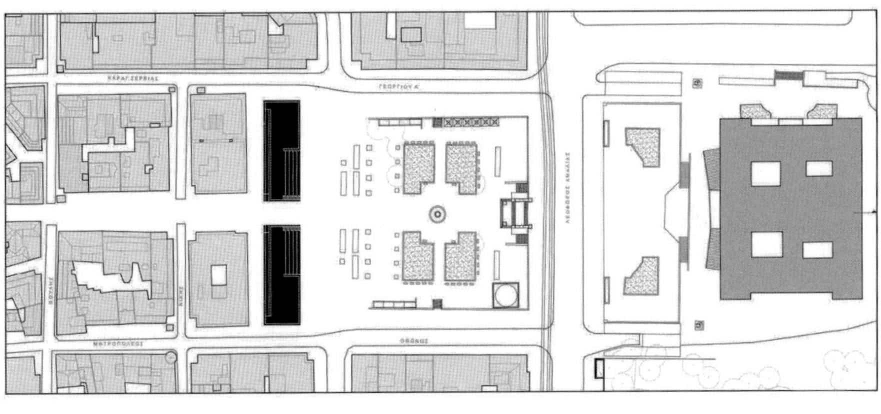

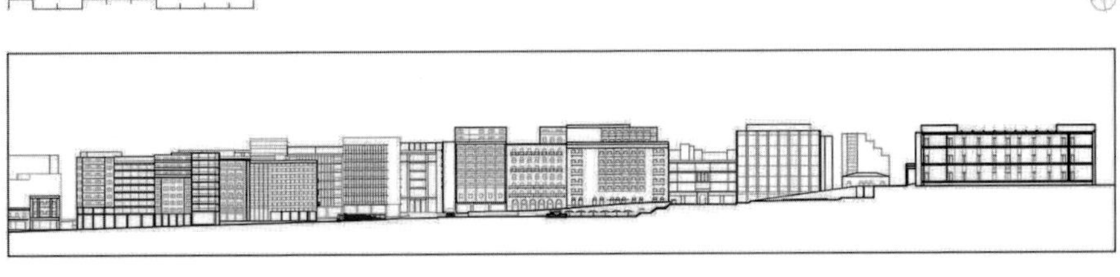

Figure 1
Syntagma Square: Twin Plinths / Steps and "Speakers' Podium"
Project by Yannis Aesopos

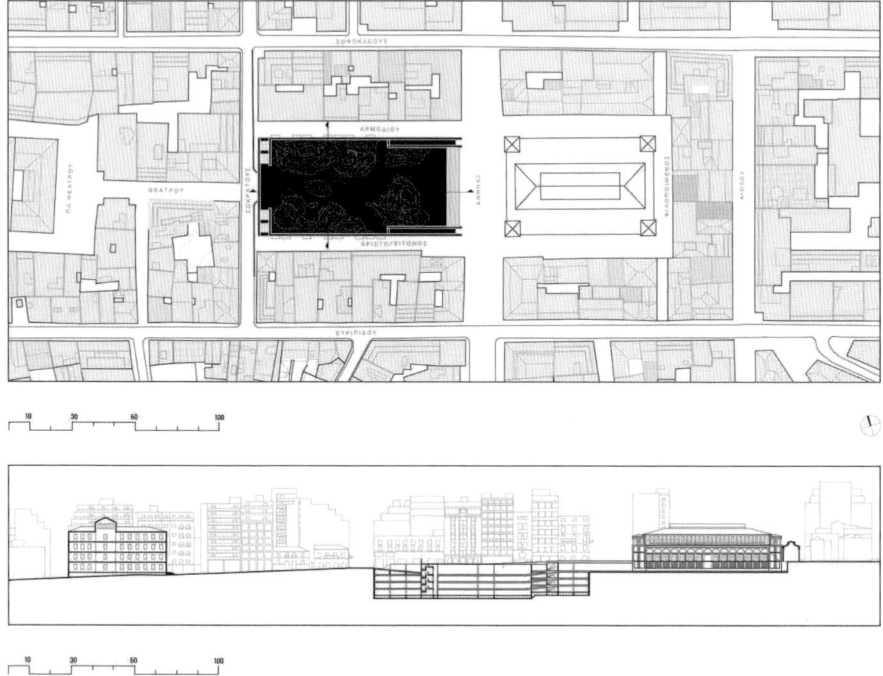

Figure 2
Varvakeios Agora Square: Planted Plinth / Attic Landscape Fragment
Project by Yannis Aesopos

"Athens was transformed into a large, spread-out metropolis... Life and urban experience became fragmentary."

tourist bus and taxi stations, as well as kiosks, cafes, and fast-food restaurants mostly populated by tourists. To counteract this, a twin plinth, made of white, Athenian Dionysus marble, is placed at the edge of the square; its two identical parts are positioned symmetrically along the square's axis. Five wide steps, which can act as benches, take up half of each of the plinths' length, functioning as viewing galleries that face out onto the square and the parliament building. The plinths' other halves remain continuous podia, and constitute a public meeting place or a "speakers' podium" facing the square. The two plinths determine the zone of tourist activities and meaningfully complete the section of the square. They allow citizens and visitors to pause and look back in order to perceive the square's layout and the various buildings that shape it, and to establish a direct visual dialogue with the neoclassical parliament building, the symbol of modern Greek democracy.

Varvakeios Agora Square: Planted Plinth / Attic Landscape Fragment

Located along Athinas Street, the Varvakeios Agora (market) and its square constitute the commercial nucleus of Athens. In the 1833 Kleanthis–Schaubert plan of Athens, a garden area was proposed for this location, while the Leo von Klenze plan of 1834 that followed it proposed a green area with market spaces. However, as the site changed use and functioned as a municipal market and a school (Varvakeios School), the use of green was forgotten and never realised. Today, the site is occupied by a poorly designed elevated square with underground parking and commercial uses along its long sides. In this proposal, a large orthogonal plinth that remodels the whole square is planted to represent a fragment of the Attic landscape, with trees (pine, cypress and olive trees), shrubs, low rocks areas, soil floor, and scattered marble benches. In reference to its green character and to architect Stamatios Kleanthis, first owner of the quarry, the plinth is made of green marble from the island of Tinos. The slope of the side streets allows for the carving of the plinth and the creation of a series of shops selling fruit and vegetables. The existing underground car park is maintained. The "lifting" of the Attic landscape, to a great extent erased during post-war urbanisation, assigns it with value and recognises its spiritual dimension.

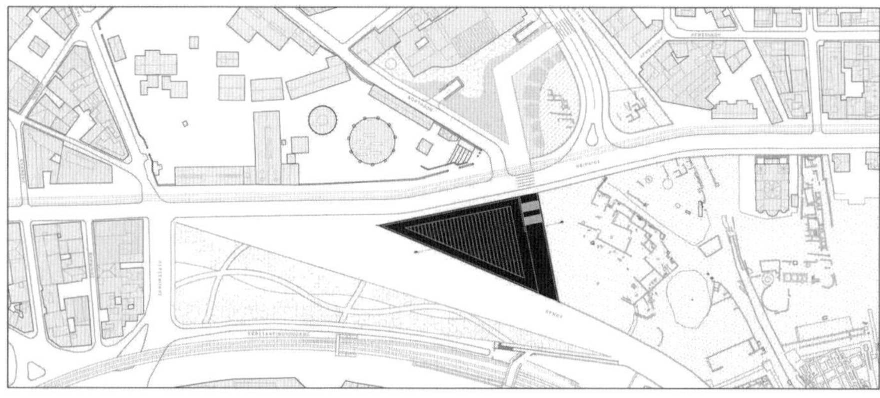

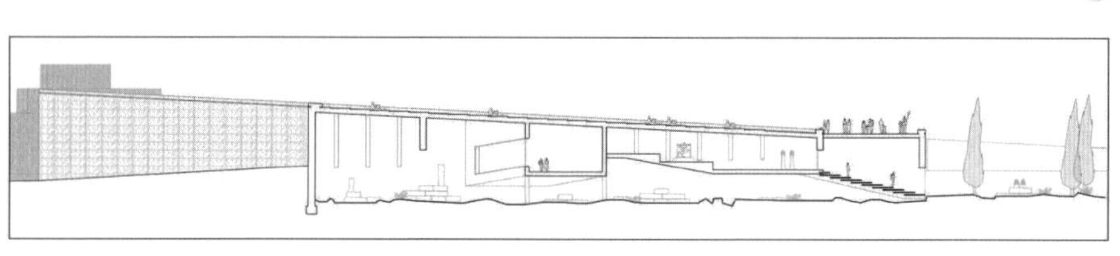

Figure 3
Kerameikos and Iera Odos: Sloped Plinth / Amphitheater and Museum
Project by Yannis Aesopos

Kerameikos and Iera Odos: Sloped Plinth / Amphitheater and Museum

References to the history of the ancient entrance to and cemetery of Athens in Kerameikos have been "blurred" by the confusing coexistence of ancient ruins and ex-industrial spaces turned cultural hubs and large-scale night clubs. At the tip of the Kerameikos archaeological site, at the point where the Ermou and Pireos streets meet, is the location of the third edge of the "Triangle" of the Kleanthis-Schaubert plan, which was never realised. Furthermore, the end of Iera Odos—the "Sacred Road" of ancient Athens that led to the entrance to the ancient city—still remains unmarked. To address these issues, a large triangular plinth, made of Mycenaean brown marble, is placed at the third edge of the "Triangle", completing the plan nearly 200 years after its conception. The plinth is angled to make it look as though it emerges from the deep soil of Kerameikos. It carries on its roof a large open-air amphitheatre that can host cultural events, creating synergies with the neighbouring Technopolis cultural centre. The roof of the plinth enables the great urban gesture of the 1833 "Triangle" that shaped modern Athens to be perceived. It also offers views of the archaeological site and the entrance to the ancient city and, further away, to the various other landscape elements that shape Athens. The large new archaeological museum of Kerameikos is laid out in the interior of the plinth. Opposite, Iera Odos is redeveloped as a linear pedestrian green-way.

Three Sites / Three Plinths: Revalorising Athens

The three different plinths revalorise and thus reintroduce into Athens' contemporary life important elements of its urban history that, over the course of time and through the intense transformation of the urban fabric, have been obscured, erased, or obliterated. These elements are now returned to the contemporary life of the city, reconnecting with history, offering continuity, providing the perception of a more uniform urban entity, and urgently re-engaging people with their city.

NOTE

Based on the project *Re-Valorizing Athens*
"Athens Regeneration", competition entry, 2019
Yannis Aesopos Architecture
Yannis Aesopos, Theodore Kantarelis, Ismini Linthorst, Lina Kakaletsi, Anna Maria Lioga, Georgia Drakou, Malvina Mathioudaki

URBAN EVENTS AS COSMOPOLITAN ACCELERATORS AND POST-PANDEMIC CITIES: REFLECTIONS ON *MANIFESTA 12* IN PALERMO

BARBARA LINO

International events are important opportunities to generate (global) open spaces and networks, and are one of the greatest accelerators of cosmopolitan networks. The global Covid-19 crisis asks us to rethink the mobility of people and the interconnections between and within cities, where networks and connections are the most powerful accelerators of what we may call the cosmopolitan dimension of urban life. How can we rethink *Cosmopolitan Habitat* in light of the pandemic? What kinds of international event will we be able to promote from an intra- and post-pandemic perspective? This contribution analyses the experiences of *Manifesta 12* in Palermo. The event is explored as field of experimentation and as a model for a capillary event based on the desire to connect and enhance places spread throughout a territory, as well as on the strong integration of the typical, art-history-driven contents of the biennial, and the cultural and political peculiarities of the city of Palermo and its cosmopolitan identity.

A "cosmopolitan" virus: will we still live in Open Cities? International events as cosmopolitan accelerators in intra/post-Covid cities

None of us can ignore the ways in which the global Covid-19 scenario that we have been living in for months now tragically redefines the concepts of *Cosmopolitan Habitat* and open cities. It is a deep economic, social, and cultural crisis that asks us to rethink the mobility of people and the interconnections between and within cities, where networks and connections are the most powerful accelerators of what we may call the cosmopolitan dimension of urban life. We have been asked to further distance the private and public spheres, with that split being continuously exacerbated. Our homes have been transformed into offices, schools, and safe shelters; some places that normally experience a high concentration of flows and people (such as tertiary places, shopping centres, and cultural services) have emptied; the system of physical relationships has been supplanted by pervasive digital connections. It is conceivable that while some of these transformations will be only temporary, others mark the future that awaits us. How can we rethink *Cosmopolitan Habitat* in the light of the pandemic? And if Harvey (2008) argues that the freedom to make and remake our cities is one of the most precious yet most neglected of our human rights, how should we manage that right?

Figure 1
Manifesta 12 *Research Studio, "Preserving Delay", Architectural Association School exposition*
Palermo, Convento di Sant'Antonino
Photo by Barbara Lino

open city urban events local resilience

If the dramatic times of Covid-19 ask us to rethink of the mobility of people in order to guarantee their right to safety, how should cities act as interconnected and open places? The Anthropocene and its expansive urbanisation have spread both the erosion of natural resources and huge social injustices (Carta and Ronsivalle 2019), and we need to review our role as citizens of the planet and urban designers—as Maurizio Carta argues in this book—by integrating ecology and rights in our plans for providing appropriate solutions to issues of climate change and social cohesion, working around the more complex dimensions of urban life and its cosmopolitan dimension. The misery of urban spaces has gradually weakened the right to the city (Lefebvre 1968)—the right to live in a comfortable, healthy, and safe city—and there can be no sustainable future without transforming the city by creating new collective spaces. In these spaces, networks become more reciprocal forms of social life, and communities can cultivate mutual cooperation. In a polycentric city, the pedestrian accessibility to services within ten to fifteen minutes' walk, as well as the porosity, connectivity, permeability, and density of public spaces (Secchi, Viganò 2009) change the forms and ways of living in domestic, collective, and work spaces, reactivating the local dimension, increasing the level of "spatial democracy", and recasting the city as an "instrument of coexistence" (Munarin and Tosi 2014). The generation of world-places such as multicultural centres, and of other places of internationalisation such as theatres, museums, or spaces for creativity and innovation, contribute to opening the city to the world through increasing locally open urban experiences. In this sense, international events are important opportunities to generate (global) open spaces and networks, and are one of the greatest accelerators of cosmopolitan networks. Internationally, urban events are important catalysts of urban transformation and effective disrupters of the international image of cities. Able to connect the "here" with the "elsewhere" and "me" with the "other" in a dimension of interrelation, they feed the cosmopolitan urban atmosphere.

However, many international experiences have revealed that the effects of events on urban transformations may be, in some cases, ephemeral: confined to the simple period of the event and incapable of generating deep, structural transformations of the territory in which they are housed. To ensure that the velocity (of transformation) established at the start of the events is maintained over time across a constantly dynamic trajectory, events must be used not as mere showcases but as instruments of urban cohesion, able to activate territorial networks between different stakeholders and to strengthen the sense of community cohesion. In the cities that used events as catalysts for innovation, it has been possible to effect transformations affecting the overall metabolism of the city and to stimulate communities, making the events important occasions in which communities perceive and conceive themselves. Which forms of international events can be considered compatible with the Covid-19 scenario? Is it possible to continue to imagine international events based not only on digital connections, but also able to feed local spatial transformations? Which of the models tested so far have proved sufficiently able to provide achievable, non-ephemeral accelerations?

Palermo Open City and *Manifesta 12*

To explore the questions raised, I will use the field of experimentation represented by the city of Palermo in recent years and, in particular, the experience of *Manifesta 12*. In recent years, Palermo has been able to condense the pulsar effect generated by multi-events that have then sown multiplier chain effects. As described by Maurizio Carta (2019), the first seed was the city's candidacy for European Capital of Culture in 2013 and the application dossier that stimulated the proliferation

"The freedom to make and remake our cities and ourselves is, I want to argue, is one of the most precious yet most neglected of our human rights."

Harvey 2008

of ideas and projects. Further results were yielded by the inclusion of the Arab-Norman sites of Palermo, Monreale and Cefalù in the UNESCO World Heritage List in 2015, and the naming of Palermo as the Italian Capital of Youth in 2017. Following this culture-sharing process, Palermo hosted the 2018 edition of the *Manifesta* nomadic biennial exhibition of contemporary art established by Hedwig Fijen. Thanks to the realisation of a system of diffused exhibitions with videos, installations, performances, and urban and literary interventions that invaded many spaces of the city, *Manifesta 12*—entitled "The Planetary Garden: Cultivating Coexistence" (Fijen 2018)—was a precious territorial laboratory for Palermo. The three main sections ("Garden of Flows", "Out of Control Room", and "City on Stage") proposed site- and community-specific artworks alongside numerous collateral events that transformed Palermo in a complex and dense laboratory for the analysis of universal issues such as climate change and migration.

Manifesta was an event that "exploded" in the city with the aim of creating a system of internal and external connections involving spaces with a strong iconic value that were often little-known. An event in which the "city has become a co-star of our wonder by showing itself from the windows, the courtyards and the terraces, often completing the sense of the artworks" (Carta 2019, p. 317). The main space regenerated by *Manifesta 12* was the Garibaldi Theatre in Piazza Magione in the historic centre of the city, which was reopened to the public and transformed into a place of meeting, discussion, and reflection, where the coexistence of citizens, cultural associations, artists, and national and international travellers nourished international connections and a cosmopolitan atmosphere. But, in addition to traversing and colonising many places in the historic centre of the city, *Manifesta 12* also chose more peripheral and iconic places for their symbolic value. At ZEN, a suburb that suffers from stigma and degradation, associations and citizens provided the impetus for a garden: the goal of the intervention by Gilles Clément and the collective Coloco was to involve the community from the beginning, building a common sense of belonging to the new garden. At Pizzo Sella, aggressive building led the hilly landscape to become known as "the hill of shame". Here, the Belgian studio Rotor intervened on one of Palermo's most complex and significant landscape contexts to address the unhealed wounds of unauthorised construction. As a further example of Manifesta 12's ability to connect diverse territorial actors, four international workshops and twelve research studios involving four major schools of architecture—the Architectural Association, the Royal College of Arts (both in London), the Dutch TU Delft, and the University of Palermo (UNIPA)—were held to investigate, study, and outline future scenarios for the city of Palermo (followed by OMA's Palermo Atlas, 2018), exhibiting their results in the former mill of the Convent of Sant'Antonino, a space owned and reopened by the University of Palermo. Concerning the event's estimated impact on the city and its perceived image, we can say the following:

- the total gross direct financial impact of non-local attendees on Palermo was estimated at 11,183,172 euros (Fondazione Fitzcarraldo 2018), and
- 42.5% of non-resident attendees went to Palermo mainly to visit Manifesta 12, and tourists spent a median of four days in Palermo (Fondazione Fitzcarraldo 2018).

Some further findings concerning non-material impacts are also relevant. Interviews aimed at assessing the cultural impact on the audience describe, on one hand, a general perception of a kind of "elitism" at the event, but on the other also revealed that the 58% of attendees who live in Palermo changed their point of view on the art, culture, and history of their town (Fondazione Fitzcarraldo 2018). Finally, as examples of *Manifesta 12's* legacy, we can mention that, after the event had ended, ten cultural producers gathered to found the new *Kalsa Art District (KAD)* association in the Kalsa

Figure 2
Installation by Per Barclay
Palermo, Cavallerizza of Palazzo Mazzarino, *Manifesta 12* collateral event
Photo by Barbara Lino

Figure 3
Casa del Mutilato
One of the *Manifesta 12* collateral event sites in Palermo
Photo by Barbara Lino

neighbourhood, where the Garibaldi Theatre at the heart of *Manifesta 12* is located. In 2019, furthermore, following the experience of *Manifesta 12*, Palermo relaunched the second edition of *BAM*, an international festival of theatre, music, and visual arts dedicated to the peoples and cultures of the countries that face the sea and focused on the themes of hospitality and dialogue.

Communities and spaces

Manifesta 12 represents an interesting field of reflection in at least two directions. Firstly in terms of legacy: as the outcome of a chain of events, *Manifesta 12* represents the capacity of some events not only to catalyse tourism but to also promote the reactivation of the city through targeted transformations of underused built heritage, unused building stock, and new forms of production. In this sense, a key element was the strong integration of the typical, art-history-driven contents of the biennial and the cultural and political peculiarities of the city of Palermo. Furthermore, Palermo has also changed *Manifesta* itself: the thirteenth edition of the biennial in Marseille continued in the wake of what was experienced in Palermo in 2018. In Marseille, in fact, *Manifesta 13* proposed increasingly rooted events, locally co-produced with cultural and social organisations in the host territory, and has increased the use of space for social purposes, for example with the Espace *Manifesta 13* venue dedicated to community functions. The event was also organised on the basis of participatory cultural democracy, starting with the commission of an urban study by the international architecture studio MVRDV (together with the think tank The Why Factory). Secondly, *Manifesta 12* is relevant in terms of its spatial model. At least in the short term, events that involve a high concentration of audience and functions, will likely be less and less thinkable (*Manifesta 13,* held in Marseilles in the midst of the pandemic crisis, proposed an intimate reception based on the format of guided tours). Instead, events must be capable of exploding their content across the city to reactivate more places at the same time. *Manifesta 12* proposed a model of a capillary event based on the desire to connect and enhance places spread throughout the territory—both well-known places and obsolete and peripheral places full of symbolic value (such as the ZEN district and Pizzo Sella). Considering the conception process of the event, its organisational modalities, and its estimated impacts, *Manifesta 12* represents a replicable model of international events that could be implemented in the intra- and post-pandemic periods, as it represents the ability of communities to enhance, transform, and share heritage with innovative tools through an exploded model of the territorial offer, keeping alive a cosmopolitan atmosphere and accelerating its processes. It is a model that strengthens community identity; one in which concentrated activities requiring massive urban transformation and infrastructure are replaced by a spread-out model of places of culture in which visitors and communities interact while immersed in a complex urban ecosystem.

BIBLIOGRAPHY

Carta M. (2019) *Futuro. Politiche per un diverso presente*. Rubbettino, Soveria Mannelli.

Carta M., Ronsivalle D. (2020) "Neoanthropocene Raising and Protection of Natural and Cultural Heritage: A Case Study in Southern Italy". In: *Sustainability* 12(10), p. 4186.

Fijen H. (2018) "Introduzione". In: *Manifesta 12 Palermo. Il giardino planetario. Coltivare la coesistenza. The Planetary Garden. Cultivating Coexistence*. Milan, Domus, pp. 12–13.

Fondazione Fitzcarraldo (2018) *Evaluation Research on Manifesta 12 Palermo Impact*. Torino, Fondazione Fitzcarraldo.

Harvey D. (2008) "The Right to the City". In: *New Left Review* 53.

Lefebvre H. (1968) *Le droit à la ville*. Paris, Editions Anthropos.

Munarin S., Tosi M.C. (2014) *Welfare Space. On the Role of Welfare State Policies in the Construction of the Contemporary City*. Trento-Barcelona, LISt Lab.

OMA (2018) *Palermo Atlas*. Milano, Humboldt Books.

Secchi B., Viganò P. (2009) "La métropole poreuse de l'après-Kyoto". In: Drevon J.-F. ed. (2009) *Le Grand Pari(s). Consultation internationale sur l'avenir de la metropole parisienne*. Paris, Le Moniteur.

POSTCOLONIAL COSMOPOLITANISMS: TWO PORT CITIES AND THE LINKAGES BETWEEN THE CARIBBEAN AND THE BALTIC SEA

ALISSA DIESCH, JES HANSEN

Harbours are important nodes in networks of exchange, connecting to large-scale and local contexts. Port cities are therefore potentially cosmopolitan spaces that need to be read relationally. They receive input from places that are far away and spread local products, people, and ideas on a global level. As such, a correlated analysis of port cities may reveal a deeper understanding of them. Flensburg and Charlotte Amalie are two very different and spatially distant harbour cities. However, they are connected by a shared history that still powerfully shapes their cultural and physical spaces. The agency of their past as two poles in the Danish colonial empire is analysed through the lens of cultural theories from the Caribbean and post-colonial urban theories. As a case study, this research frames a cosmopolitan view of the past and present relation between Europe and the Caribbean, with a particular focus on the ports as spaces of interaction and potential hybridisation.

Flensburg is a German port city on the Baltic Sea, until 1864 it belonged to Denmark. In previous centuries, it was the economic centre of the region. While it was not a formal part of the Hanseatic League, the city maintained trading relations with the League. Later, Flensburg's trading range expanded to Greenland and into the Mediterranean Sea, where merchants accessed new markets and connected the city to new ideas and cultural resources (Gesellschaft für Flensburger Stadtgeschichte 1966). Following this, Flensburg's shipping companies began their first ventures into the Caribbean, where Denmark held a colony known as the Danish West Indies from 1666 onwards. This marked the beginning of Flensburg's ascendancy as a rum and sugar trader, a role that just two centuries later would dominate the city's identity and retains a lasting influence to the present day. Many ships during this time reached Flensburg from the Caribbean harbours of Fredriksted, Christiansted, or Charlotte Amalie, importing primarily sugar and resources for the production of rum. While the city initially focused on refining sugar for the local and European markets, it began to turn to the production of rum blends after the industrialisation of sugar production in Copenhagen and Hamburg made refining sugar uneconomical (Gesellschaft für Flensburger Stadtgeschichte 1966). The absence of industrialisation and the upholding of artisanal production methods in the city had a major influence on the preservation of Flensburg's eighteenth-century cityscape, which is still visible

Figure 1
Blended Ports: Flensburg and Charlotte Amalie
Photomontage by Jes Hansen in the master's design studio "Cosmopolitan Habitat", 2020

postcolonialism historic centres harbours

today. While small-scale structures were demolished to meet the new spatial requirements in other harbour cities, the trading yards and the overall harbour structure of Flensburg survived, conserving the colonial spatial reality. Although the colonial trade lost its economic importance for the city of Flensburg more than 150 years ago, the traces of this chapter of the city's history have moulded its sociocultural self-conception and its spatial configuration in a long-lasting way. The years since the late nineteenth century have been marked by the continual reduction of connections, with the harbour almost meaningless as a trading port today. The formerly flourishing harbour is now occupied by sailing boats and historic ships that hint at its past and provide a backdrop for the touristic marketing image of the "Rum City".

Today, Charlotte Amalie is the capital of the American Virgin Islands. However, the islands were a Danish colony for several centuries. With the arrival of Europeans at the end of the fifteenth century, the Caribbean experienced a stark transformation into a territory of transit and exchange while at the same time being fully altered in terms of its population and environment. In 1672, the Danish erected the first port town to protect the harbour, and soon received African slaves in order to commence exploiting the land through the production of sugar cane and its by-product rum. Up to 50,000 African slaves arrived on the island in the seventeenth to nineteenth centuries, becoming the most important part of the local population, while the benefits of the trade remained in the hands of the European minority (Brichet 2019). Sugar was a profitable business until the end of the nineteenth century, when the abolition of slavery and the introduction of the sugar beet in Europe caused a decline in the industry. The geostrategic position of the island became a crucial asset for Charlotte Amalie again in 1917, when—at the end of WWI—the USA bought the islands from neutral Denmark in order to prevent the possible danger posed by German submarines in the Caribbean. However, the Danish West Indian Company (WICO), founded in 1905, continued owning and running the majority of the port facilities until 1993, maintaining colonially based economic relations, symbolic significance, and a cash flow back to Europe (Brichet 2019). The company's original field of action was supplying coal and water to the steamships that were used commercially in the Atlantic trade from the second half of the nineteenth century. In 1936, laying the foundation for the island's most important economic field today, WICO also started operating a tourism company. While the original intention was for tourists to stay on the islands, WICO expanded the port facilities in the 1960s in order to attract more and bigger cruise ships, meaning that tourist would only spend a few hours in the town. Even though the port is today run by a local company, the tourism scheme remains similar.

By focusing on Flensburg and Charlotte Amalie, we analyse the global, yet little-known, post-colonial constellation of two rather small cities that have not been in the spotlight. They have never become important "nodes of a globalization" (Roy 2009, p. 821) and economic power, which has rendered them less significant for the generation of urban theory (Robinson 2002). Nevertheless, they are an interesting case study that reveals the overlooked relations and dynamics of two cities shaped by globalisation for more over five centuries. The "rediscovery of places beyond the metropolis" (Schröder 2018, p. 13) is necessary in order to diversify the field of urban research, particularly as "there is still considerable work to be done to produce a cosmopolitan, postcolonial urban studies" (Robinson 2002, p. 533). Through comparative work on the two cities, one can trace back colonial agency and some "discrepant cosmopolitanism" (Robinson 2002, p. 532) outside the metropolitan hubs. At first sight, the two minor cities do not seem to have much in common; however, they would

Figure 2
Charlotte Amalie and its historic urban structure
Graphic by Jes Hansen for the master's design studio "Cosmopolitan Habitat", 2020

Figure 3
Flensburg and its historic urban structure
Graphic by Jes Hansen for the maste's design studio
"Cosmopolitan Habitat", 2020

not be what they are today without each other. They owe their cityscape, their historic urban structures, and to a considerable extent their contemporary image to the relation that connected them politically and economically for roughly 350 years. As both cities have remained small, there has been little spatial-architectural transformation of the city cores. While the historic structures have been largely reshaped in the harbour areas of big cargo ports, Flensburg's historic trading-house structure has remained mostly untouched, as has the urban fabric of the historic area in Charlotte Amalie. This makes it possible to study specific small-scale spatial structures that were shaped during the heyday of colonial exchange, as well as its effects on the cityscapes on both sides of the ocean. To analyse these continuing systems of post-colonialism, King (2009) proposes "an essentially comparative, cross-cultural, and cross-temporal perspective" (p. 5), focusing on questions of culture, heritage, and representation in a comprehensive analysis, comprising a global view. As Yeoh (2001) formulates clearly: "The 'colonial city' and the 'imperial city' [are] connected … their 'post-equivalents' … need to be analysed within a single 'postcolonial' framework of intertwining histories and relations" (Yeoh 2001). The aim is not to construct a "a strict model of cause and effect … [but] rather, the basis of a loosely comparative project" (Jacobs 1996, p. 5). The two cities make use of their colonial history through a process of reframing the past for the tourism industry, which both economies rely on today. Flensburg has branded itself as a "Rum City" and tells, as part of this marketing scheme, its colonial history as a triumphant and adventurous story of seamen, riches, and the tropics. This reveals the city's self-perception of its postcolonial understanding. The tourist relives the glorious historic chapter of Flensburg's economic rise based on the colonial seizure of lands and colonial exploitation in the West Indies. The inhuman logic of the colonial reality is suppressed through an anecdotal narrative. Charlotte Amalie, in the more difficult position of being the formerly colonised city, cleanses its history from the horrors and suffering of slave labour and reinterprets itself as a place of "the exotic" for the cruise ship tourists flooding the island on their shore excursions, with the historic city becoming a superficial backdrop to their short-lived visits. The visitors are implicitly invited to identify themselves with the position of the European colonisers, enjoying the pleasures of the fully serviced "colonial lifestyle" of the privileged class. Both phenomena, which are based on the stereotyping of the past, can be adequately decrypted and understood through Said's theory of Orientalism, the homogenisation and stereotypical depiction of the Orient by its colonisers (Said 1978). While Said's theory of Orientalism is primarily intended to analyse the Middle East and North Africa, the theory is also applicable to the representation of the Caribbean, where a similar unequal dichotomy is described as tropicalisation (Thompson 2006).

The uncritical prerogative of interpretation and usage of the historic architecture for touristic infrastructure has been hindering a discussion about the interpretation and appropriation of these sites and places. The multifaceted relations and influences between the two cities described here only reflect fragments of a dense network of globalisation. Many more encounters and continuously emerging cultures have influenced the sites. The frequently unacknowledged presence of the "other", the agency of past times, and the shifting interpretations of both create third spaces that, according to Bhabha (1994), are not of one culture or the other, but rather an entirely new concept. Bhabha states that "cultural statements and systems are constructed in this contradictory and ambivalent space of enunciation" (1994, p. 37), which includes spaces as well as the re-historisation, appropriation, and translation of their signs. Glissant (2005) refers to the creolisation in the Caribbean, based on the intertwining of cultures, places, and people with all its inadvertent and unforeseen constellations, as the opposite of planned mixing and colonialisation projects of segregation and exploitation. He proposes an archipelagic thinking—an inductive way of relational reasoning based on poesy and the imaginary—to analyse the world and its relationships. This understanding opens up a new view on how to create non-hierarchical relations based on cultural interactions and is a promising framework for pursuing and complementing Flensburg's and Charlotte Amalie's relation as *Cosmopolitan Habitats*.

BIBLIOGRAPHY

Bhabha, H. (1994) *The Location of Culture*. London, New York, Routledge.

Brichet, N. (2019) "A Postcolonial Dilemma Tale from the Harbour of St. Thomas in the US Virgin Islands". In: *Itinerario* 2. Leiden, Research Institute for History, Leiden University, pp. 348–365.

Flensburger Gesellschaft für Stadtgeschichte ed. (1966) *Geschichte einer Grenzstadt*. Flensburg.

Glissant, E. (2005) *Kultur und Identität. Ansätze zu einer Poetik der Vielheit*. Heidelberg, Das Wunderhorn.

Jacobs, J. (1996) *Edge of Empire. Postcolonialism and the city*. London and New York, Routledge.

King, Anthony D. (2009) "Postcolonial cities". Available online at: https://booksite.elsevier.com/brochures/hugy/SampleContent/Postcolonial-Cities.pdf (05.02.2019).

Robinson, J. (2002) "Global and World Cities: A View from off the Map". In: *International Journal of Urban and Regional Research* 3. Oxford and Malden, Blackwell, pp. 531–554.

Roy, A. (2009) "The 21st-Century Metropolis: New Geographies of Theory" In: *Regional Studies* 6(43). London, Taylor & Francis, pp. 819–830.

Said, E. (1978) Orientalism. London and New York, Routledge.

Schröder, J. (2018) "Open Habitat". In: Schröder J., Carta M., Ferretti, M., Lino, B. eds. (2018) *Dynamics of Periphery*. Berlin, Jovis, pp. 10–29.

Thompson, K. (2006) *An Eye for the Tropics: Tourism, Photography and Framing the Caribbean Picturesque*. Durham, Duke University Press.

Yeoh, B. (2001) "Postcolonial cities". In: *Progress in Human Geography*. 25(3). Thousand Oaks, SAGE, pp. 456–468.

THE INNER TERRITORIES: FROM THE MARGINS TO COSMOPOLITAN CENTRES

COSIMO CAMARDA

The article proposes a reflection on the cosmopolitanism linked to the "marginalised" parts of Italy, where social, economic, and infrastructural decline and the consequent abandonment of places are met with stories of renewal in which the relationship between inhabitants and foreigners constitutes the basis for starting local development processes able to activate new urban networks based on cultural interaction and to generate resilient relations, welcoming processes, and new communities. In this new "cosmopolitan nomadism", we can recognise an opportunity for territories and communities to regenerate spatial and social relations: innovation and culture, permanent exchange, and neutral enrichment have already joined in some realities of "the Italy on the margins".

Living in a small town and looking at the world

Today, we live in a situation in which material and immaterial networks and flows cross territories, places, and communities; relationships thicken and thin out around the world, following different horizons and objectives. Cities and territories, as the nodes of these networks, are constituted of the components of cosmopolitanism, in the context of which it is difficult to think of cultures as "localised" situations. As such, they represent not static identities but rather dynamic ones opened to interaction—in which migrant flows, meaning not only those relating to the last few decades, are a manifestation of this condition (de Spuches 2013). To address the issue of cosmopolitanism as it is linked to territorial systems, it is useful to ask ourselves about the actualised meaning that the concept of diaspora, which since the 1990s has been applied to the concepts of migrant, expatriate, refugee, foreign worker, as well as exiled, overseas or ethnic community (Tölöyan 1991).

These terms request a reflection on cultural interaction as a manifestation of urban cosmopolitanism, on the opportunity for growth it provides to both local and foreign communities, and on places. Reconciling local community and global community: this is the challenge for small towns that are part of a geopolitical context in which residents who are not always born in these places live in them. Considering this context, such research would ask: who are the "real" residents of the country's marginal areas? In other words, who is native and who lives in these places every day? In the next paragraph,

Figure 1
Foreign population in Italy, 2017
Graphic by the author

inner peripheries small towns nomadism hospitality

Figure 2
Welcome Garden. Green space assigned to migrants by the Municipality of Sutera
Graphic by the author, 2020

some observations on the relationship between native people and foreign inhabitants in terms of local growth and cosmopolitan opportunities for small towns and inner territories are presented; this is based on a doctoral research project in progress.

The neo-population of marginal territories

In recent years, the phenomenon of neo-population (the settlement of new inhabitants from foreign countries and regions in abandoned areas) has appeared in Italy. We can distinguish between two types of foreigners: economic migrants and forced migrants. The first group initially settled in metropolitan areas, later some have moved to the inner and mountain areas. The second group consists of individuals forced to emigrate due to critical conditions such as wars and/or natural disasters, some have been directed to stay in the inner and mountain areas (Menbretti, Perlik 2018). Taking into account these characteristics, it is necessary to consider what the inner territories offer and what the needs of foreign populations are; these both act as useful elements for defining the "marginal" territories' degree of cosmopolitanism. Here, the concept of Territorial Archipelago (Carta 2017) is useful: it represents a type of networked system in which urban tissues, infrastructures, and productive areas are multi-connected by a common identity, and in which the urban nodes of the territorial system play the role of metaphorical "city ports" and of places of interchange. In the non-metropolitan Territorial Archipelago, we can identify some attracting elements for foreigners. These elements are: 1. more affordable and competitive housing than in metropolitan areas (as evidenced by the presence of numerous vacant houses and low real estate prices); 2. a lower cost of living than in metropolitan areas; 3. quality of life in terms of social proximity, food, and environmental quality; 4. wider job opportunities. Another relevant component for analysing the "mixture" of cultures is the closeness and the sense of welcome extended towards foreigners by the native population, which is an indispensable element in building a new sense of community (Membretti, Ravazzoli 2018). The issue of the neo-population of the inner territories has assumed an important dimension in the last twenty years: the migratory balance (the ratio of immigrants to emigrants) now constitutes the fundamental component of demographic development in Europe, which was once defined by the natural balance (determined by the ratio of the birth rate to the death rate). The marginal territories, which are heavily affected by the strong influence of foreigners, benefit from these "new inhabitants", who contribute, in economic and social terms, to the preservation of communities that could otherwise disappear (Membretti 2020). Data on the presence of foreign populations in the inner territories are significant for understanding the phenomenon (Fig. 1): there are almost 700,000 foreign individuals in the Apennines (Istat 2017), equivalent to about 6.4% of the total resident population, while 1,537,410 foreigners (ISTAT 2017) inhabit the Inner Areas,[1] corresponding to 8% of the total population (Corrado, Dematteis, Di Gioia 2014).

Experiences of cosmopolitanism in smaller towns

Consequently, we can suppose that the involvement of foreign communities and the experiences of renewal in the inner territories represent a notable opportunity to ensure that smaller towns become places where urban cosmopolitanism could represent an opportunity for renewal. Among the positive practices of welcoming and involving communities in order to recover the social and then the material dimensions of small towns, some particularly beneficial solutions are described. In Ormea (Piedmont region), a community cooperative started a process of "active integration" in cooperation with La volpe e il mirtillo, a local farming cooperative, in 2015. The initiative involved asylum seekers teaching and attending a training course on the cleaning and maintenance of woodlands and the care of greenery before and after work. This has resulted in a community cooperative that works to advance both social integration and care of the territory, with the migrants involved in the project able to obtain stable work in this field. Ultimately, these migrants permanently settled in Ormea and are now working as a part of the local community, increasing the resident population and triggering new socioeconomic processes.

In Sutera (Sicily), the local branch of SPRAR,[2] the Italian protection system for refugees, hosts another virtuous example in which the welcomed people are engaged in a project aimed at restoring part of historic centre. In particular, they have contributed to the rebirth of the streets of Rabado—the ancient Arab area in historic centre—by restoring the old paving stones. The new inhabitants have repopulated the town and the alleys have been reborn; the foreign pupils who attend the primary school have increased the number of students and saved it from imminent closure; in some cases, local elders have adopted foreign children as grandchildren; and, after decades of stalemate, births are on the rise in Sutera. Despite initial distrust, the community of Sutera responded positively to the welcome project (Fig. 2) thanks to the support of the I Girasoli association, which is mainly composed of local young people. The organisation sets up many activities, such as the summer camp that involves all Sutera's children—both native and immigrant—and the annual event "Rabado embraces the world", a festival of cultures and hospitality; this, in fact, is one of the most important experiences of social innovation in Sicily (Carta 2019). Overcoming the difficulties of a peripheral area, it was possible to combine the needs of the new and old inhabitants into an effective interaction between different groups of people. It is not always easy to plan a project that leads to our centres being repopulated: sometimes there are not enough houses in good condition, or migrants prefer major cities due to the presence of relatives or other compatriots. Initially, many were reluctant—but thanks to the presence of facilities and support, the incoming foreigners opted to extend their own intimacy and accepted responsibility for advancing their own integration and the town's autonomy on all matters, even with regard to the education of children. Providing welcoming solutions in small towns is a model that allows migrants to integrate themselves in both social and work contexts.

In Riace, thanks to the NGO Città Futura – Giuseppe Puglisi, welcoming practices were established in 1999, when a large number of migrants arrived on the local beaches as potential applicants for asylum. The initial welcoming activity was based on revitalising the town of Riace. Thanks to the arrival of the refugees, many buildings that had been abandoned for years were refurbished, and are now inhabited by a new, mixed population of migrants and tourists. This has also led to an increase in new businesses. The socioeconomic context has been revitalised as a result of the new mixed community: the schools have been reopened, a multi-ethnic kindergarten and a medical clinic have been established, business activities have resumed, and local agricultural products and artefacts made by migrants are sold as far away as Bolzano. Riace's experience is significant not only because of its welcoming practices and the way they revitalised the town, but also for the way the town addressed local and international organised crime. All this ultimately resulted in a unique experience of harmony in the community. The project "Riace città futura" leverages the involvement of local actors by seeking to empower both the territory and the community; it aims to renew the sense of hospitality that characterised the ancient town by promoting innovative formulas of hospitality for both tourists and new inhabitants (Fig. 3). The project provides for the creation of a sustainable, widespread hotel industry, the recovery and enhancement of ancient crafts, and actions aimed at promoting the territory and the study of its history and culture (Esposta, Cardoni 2013). Riace's community, together with Mimmo Lucano (initially a volunteer, later mayor of the town), offered migrants—often victims of the indifference that raises walls and closes ports—the opportunity for a dignified future; these brave actions have had positive repercussions on the local economy, on places, and on people.

Conclusions

In the light of the issues dealt with and the cases examined, it is necessary to focus on policies that can be implemented in future to allow these territories, today enriched with new inhabitants, to offer themselves as places of welcome and multicultural integration in which hospitality represents a manifestation of cosmopolitanism. The watchword for action, as defined by Angelo Moretti,[3] is as follows: "community welcome … is not an innovative action in the face of the great challenges of depopulation and world migration flows, it is a quiescent heritage to be renewed, a heritage that over the centuries has created the true wealth of the territories of the Mediterranean area" (De Blasio, Giorgione, Moretti 2018). We must therefore respond to the "fear of the new" with the relationships and knowledge needed to build an "enlarged community" where diversity is seen as a benefit to places; we must go beyond imagining welcome policies for new residents and provide the opportunity and ability for them to integrate, starting from good practices already implemented as responses to this issue and useful experiences that can be used to develop a network of small, cosmopolitan towns.

Figure 3
Street art in Riace
Graphic by the author, 2020

FOOTNOTES

1_The identification of the Inner Areas, defined by the *Strategia Nazionale Aree Interne* (SNAI), is mainly articulated through a categorisation of the whole Italian territory in two phases: the first identifies the main urban nodes based on their ability to offer certain essential services; the second classifies the remaining municipalities into four groups, determined by their travel time from the nodes: peri-urban, intermediate, peripheral, and ultra-peripheral areas.

2_SPRAR's main goal is to take responsibility for those individuals accepted into the scheme and to provide them with personalised programmes to help them (re)acquire individual autonomy, and to take part in and integrate effectively into Italian society in terms of finding employment and housing and accessing local services, social life, and child education.

3_Angelo Moretti is a social planner, coordinator of the Diocesan Caritas of Benevento, and director of the NGO Sale della Terra Consortium.

BIBLIOGRAPHY

Carta M. (2017) "Planning for the Rur-Urban Anthropocene". In: Schröder J., Carta M., Ferretti M., Lino B. eds. (2017) *Territories. Rural-urban Strategies.* Berlin, Jovis, pp. 36–53.

Carta M. (2019) *Futuro. Politiche per un diverso presente.* Catanzaro, Rubbettino.

Corrado F., Dematteis G., Di Gioia A. (2014) *Nuovi montanari. Abitare le Alpi nel XXI secolo.* Milano, Franco Angeli.

De Blasio N., Giorgione G. D., Moretti A. eds. (2018) *L'Italia che non ti aspetti. Manifesto per una rete dei piccoli comuni del Welcome.* Roma, Città Nuova.

De Spuches G. (2013) *La città cosmopolita: altre narrazioni.* Palermo, Palumbo.

Esposto M., Cardoni S. (2013) "I borghi, un. nuovo modello di sviluppo e di ospitalità italiana". In: Flora N., Crucianelli E. eds. (2013) *I Borghi dell'uomo. Strategie e progetti di ri/attivazione.* Siracusa, LetteraVentidue, pp. 46–55.

Martinelli L. ed. (2020) *L'Italia è bella dentro. Storie di resilienza, innovazione e ritorno nelle aree interne.* Milano, Altreconomia.

Membretti A. (2020) "Migranti". In: Cersosimo D., Donzelli C. eds. (2020) *Manifesto per riabitare l'Italia.* Roma, Donzelli, pp. 159–163.

Membretti A., Perlik M., (2018) "Migration by Necessity and by Force to Mountain Areas: An Opportunity for Social Innovation". In: *Mountain Research and Development* 3/2018. Bern, MRD Editorial Office, pp. 250–264.

Membretti A., Ravazzoli E. (2018) "Immigrazione straniera e neopopolamento nelle terre alte". In: De Rossi A. ed. (2018) *Riabitare l'Italia. Le aree interne tra abbandoni e riconquiste.* Roma, Donzelli, pp. 333–349.

Tölöyan K. (1991) "The Nation-State and Its Others". In: *Diaspora, A Journal of Transnational Studies 1.* Toronto, University of Toronto Press Journal Division, pp. 3–7.

SLOW-LIVING HABITATS: ACTIVATING SPACES AND NETWORKS

CATERINA RIGO

Using an integrated and transcalar design approach, the *Slow-living Habitats* research project investigates a number of case studies in Italy, where recent interventions in territorial development have often been carried out with a perspective that is disconnected from local realities. In particular, this contribution aims to investigate a possible definition of "slow-living habitats" within the wider framework of *Cosmopolitan Habitat* by exploring the qualities and challenges of such habitats, particularly in relationship to the idea of openness proposed by the call for papers. These complex, hybrid territories, which should be tackled with a transcalar and integrated approach, are characterised by low density, rural patterns, multiple productive activities, and a variety of settlement typologies. This article focuses on the premises and initial results of a doctoral research project connected to a national research programme that studies inner areas and small villages as potential accelerators of "inner resilience" in four Italian regions.

Slow-living habitats

Every strategy planned from 2020 onwards, whether urban or territorial, should recognise that a deep revision of our model of living is needed. Urban design is striving to respond to the "erosive and predatory" Anthropocene that, driven by the logic of consumption, has weakened the relationship between communities and settlements (Carta 2019). The research of *Cosmopolitan Habitat* raises the necessity for a vision of openness. Cities and settlements must confront the needs of our time—particularly climate change—through processes that imagine the reuse of abandoned spaces and activate new urban networks. In response to this necessary paradigm switch, this research proposes the re-evaluation of those habitats that are certainly "moving"—though at a slower speed than others—as places that could represent an advance guard for dealing with global challenges. Europe is investing in the territories of inner areas in an increasingly structured way. In Italy, processes for the relaunch of inner areas are carried out particularly within the purview of the National Strategy for Inner Areas.[1] Relevant research reflects on new kinds of economies, based on a human scale and seeking to combat the climate crisis, generating statements of interest such as the Manifesto di Assisi, the Manifesto di Camaldoli per una nuova centralità della montagna, and the Manifesto per

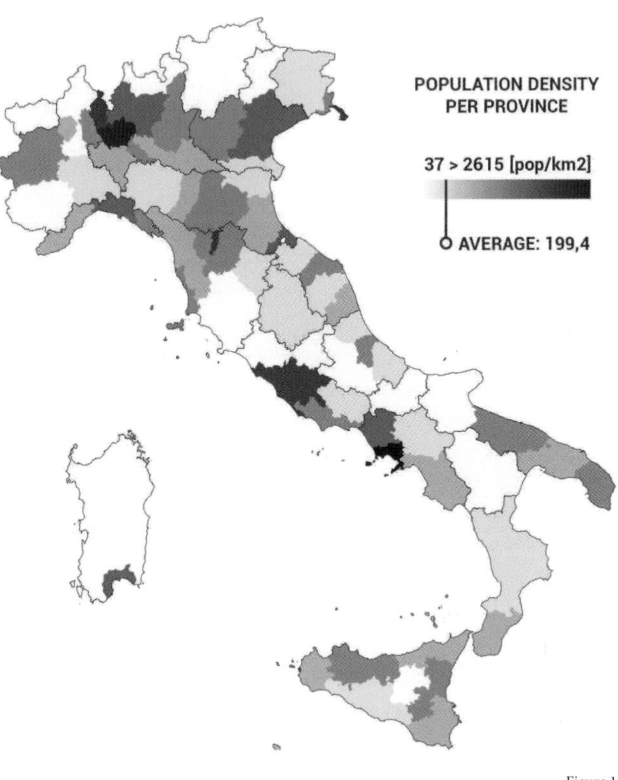

Figure 1
Population density per province in Italy (ISTAT 2020)
Graphic by the author

inner resilience hybrid territories trans-scalarity

Riabitare l'Italia (De Rossi 2018). Local administrators, local communities, and private investors sit around virtual tables structuring projects to re-enliven abandoned centres. This paper focuses on the premises and initial results of the author's doctoral research project, *Slow-living Habitats*, which is associated with the national research project entitled "Branding For Resilience".[2] The B4R project focuses on inner areas and small villages as potential accelerators of resilience in four Italian regions and promotes strategies for territorial branding. "Slow territories" are recognised as contexts that can host creative practices as "activators" for new dynamics. In our current, "suspended" time, the limits of a development model based on continuous growth and consumption have become increasingly evident. *Slow-Living Habitats* reflects on the concept of "slowness" as a human interpretation of time (Maffei 2014). The contexts studied are indeed "slow", but they are also "living"; in contemporary times, they are "territories of [the] production of new cultures, of social innovation, of knowledge and technical practices, of renewed ways of doing welfare and interacting with the environment" (De Rossi 2018). In the context of the need for a change of perspective, *Slow-living Habitats* provide a new richness to consider. The article looks at these *Slow-living Habitats* as an opportunity for reflection on the quality of space and life they provide for their inhabitants.

Rediscovering slowness in the context of the Marche region

To understand the object of this research, it is necessary to go back to the definition of "slowness" as a concept that has returned to popularity throughout different subjects over the last few decades. From the nineties onwards, the Slow Movement took place in Italy, opposing the logics of "fast" production and consumption—particularly with regard to issues linked to food and quality of life. The Slow Cities Association network today extends to an international context; slow tourism and slow fashion are responses to contemporary sustainability issues and, from a circular economy perspective, demonstrate attention to production and consumption processes (Lancerini et al. 2005, Maffei 2014). Similarly, "slow territories" have been defined as places shaped by some recognisable settlement dynamics. These habitats are characterised by an extremely varied and fragmented rural fabric; however, despite being territories strongly modified by agricultural activity, this is no longer the only aspect governing their development trends. The overall picture is completed by a multitude of productive activities, with hybrid agro-industrial economic systems and a settlement fabric that varies according to the development of the habitats—from fortified towns to linear cities—resulting from the interaction of different populations. These territories have developed along with infrastructures and river systems, but frequently in a discontinuous way, requiring infill interventions or the adaptation of structures and infrastructures. Combining local and global aspects, these habitats show that the search for quality of living is increasingly relevant in our current situation. The contemporary paradigm demonstrates once again that "being able to elaborate a different and superior quality of living is not a minor thing" (Lancerini et al. 2005). *Slow-living Habitats* will investigate some case studies in the Marche Region in connection with research projects conducted in these territories by Marche Polytechnic University. As reported in the studies developed by Arturo Lanzani in recent years (Lancerini et al. 2005, De Rossi 2018), the valley systems of the Marche region are classified as part of the widespread network of "slow territories" that characterise Italy. Considering maps of population density in Italy that refer to historical periods from the post-war years to the present day, the latest ISTAT data (Fig. 1) shows that socio-economic dynamics move at different speeds in different places and territories. The population density in the Marche region is generally medium-low (162 inhabitants per km^2), which is below the national average. Its small and medium-sized cities do not exceed one

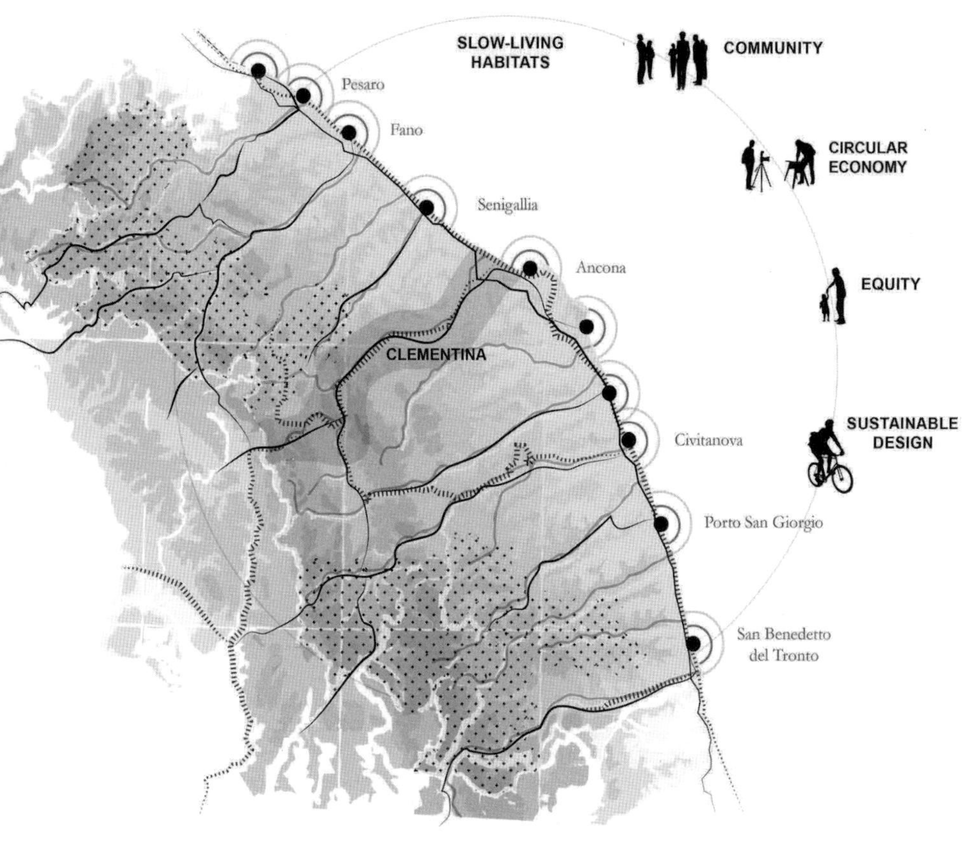

Figure 2
Slow-living habitats in the Marche Region
Graphic by the author, 2020

Figure 3
Landscape of the Aso Valley, Marche Region
Photo by the author, 2020

hundred thousand inhabitants; with the highest demographic contraction, population ageing, and declining birth rates, the Apennines are characterised by a widespread fabric of small towns and art cities. The geomorphological structure of the region, frequently described as "comb-shaped", is characterised by a sequence of waterways. Starting from the Apennines and flowing into the Adriatic Sea perpendicular to the coastline, these rivers and their corresponding basins draw a system of alternating valleys and reliefs. While the infrastructural lines continuously intersect inhabited areas and natural landscapes on the coast, the valleys appear to be characterised by open distances and "transition" landscapes (Fig. 2).

Research by design: an innovation in methodology

"An urgency emerges for the re-introduction of the territory, material and concrete, made of inhabitants and specific settlements, into the horizon of policies" (De Rossi 2018). Quoting the preface to the 2020 edition of Riabitare l'Italia, it is argued that the "spatialisation of policies" is necessary for the change of direction envisaged by the group of researchers guided by De Rossi. This study investigates an approach to research that aims to provide a theoretical framework to support and structure the formulation of operative actions in the analysed contexts—the *Slow-living Habitats*. The methodology includes an integrated approach across different disciplines and scales, but is focused on the transformation of space as a key element of future paths for development. The idea is to primarily combine layers that often remain separated: considerations of the state of the arts in the territories, along with the dissemination of scientific assessments and analyses of good practice, are integrated with an analysis of good practices, are integrated with on-site research and interaction with stakeholders involved in the project. Additionally, attention paid to the cultural transformations occurring in the contexts, as well as an insight into current policies, provides the basis for the prefiguration of new projects in order to orient the effort towards "operative action". The importance of communication—and of the representation of concepts—is central to the construction of the imaginaries and visions that form the basis on which new strategies can be structured. Novelty is needed not only in terms of topics, but in terms of method and approach—including when it comes to the integration of different disciplines. The innovative approach envisions the integration of these elements based on the interdependence and cooperation of the different territorial systems that describe the *Slow-living Habitats*. This work employs the "research by design" methodology (Viganò 2016), starting with the construction of a theoretical approach through literature review, data collection and elaboration, and the study of good practices. The use of an integrated and transcalar approach is fundamental to tying together local and global aspects that must be understood in a complementary way for the development of innovative strategies (Fabian, Munarin 2017).

Open processes

Cosmopolitan Habitat calls for a new paradigm. As Maurizio Carta, presenting the *Cosmopolitan Habitat* workshop in Palermo, said in November 2020: "Now is no longer the time for maintenance, for little, adjusting interventions: we live in times of transition". This research suggests a definition for "slow-living habitats" and their quality of life, a theme that has today become crucial in the planning and design process. With an understanding of the dynamics of depopulation and of the necessity of implementing infrastructures, abandoned spaces can become cosmopolitan accelerators within open and inclusive processes. This contribution aims to keep the attention on the relevance of a design approach that is systemic, integrated, and involves inhabitants in place-based solutions in order to identify and better address policies and measures oriented towards a paradigm shift (Ricci 2019; Schröder et al. 2018). Qualitative analysis is necessary, as is an innovative methodology that explores unconventional tools and focuses on stakeholder analysis and involvement. Urban and architectural design must include unconventional tools to reinterpret space and society. Design occasions—such as the regeneration of public spaces, the reconnection of tourist and cultural itineraries, the implementation of infrastructures, the rethinking of voids, and the regeneration of abandoned areas—can thus become a pretext to widen the view from the single lot or the single town and look at strategies of territorial reconnection (Fig. 3).

FOOTNOTES

1 The National Strategy for the Development of Inner Areas was launched in 2012 with the combined objectives of adapting the quantity and quality of education, health, and mobility services and promoting development projects that valorise the natural and cultural heritage of these areas, as well as focusing on local production sectors.

2 "Branding for Resilience. Tourist infrastructure as a tool to enhance small villages by drawing resilient communities and new open habitats" (2020–2023) is a research project of national interest (PRIN 2017 – Young Line) funded by the Italian Ministry of Education, University and Research (MIUR). It is coordinated by the Università Politecnica delle Marche (PI Maddalena Ferretti) and was developed with the following research partners: the University of Palermo (local coordinator Barbara Lino), the University of Trento (local coordinator Sara Favargiotti), and the Polytechnic of Turin (local coordinator Diana Rolando).

BIBLIOGRAPHY

Carta M. (2019) *Futuro. Politiche per un diverso presente*. Soveria Mannelli, Rubbettino.

De Rossi A. ed. (2018) *Riabitare l'Italia. Le aree interne tra abbandoni e riconquiste*. Roma, Donzelli.

Fabian L., Munarin S. eds. (2017) *Re-Cycle Italy. Atlante*. Siracusa, LetteraVentidue.

Lancerini E., Lanzani A., Granata E. et al. (2005) "Territori lenti". In: *Territorio* 34. Milano, FrancoAngeli, pp. 9–69.

Maffei L. (2014) *Elogio della lentezza*. Bologna, il Mulino.

Ricci M. (2019) *Habitat 5.0. L'architettura nel Lungo Presente*. Milano, Skira.

Schröder J., Carta M., Ferretti M., Lino B. eds. (2018) *Dynamics of Periphery: Atlas for Emerging Creative Resilient Habitats*. Berlin, Jovis.

Viganò P. (2016) *Territories of Urbanism. The Project as Knowledge Producer*. Lausanne, EPFL Press.

Piazza Marina, Palermo
Photo by Federica Scaffidi

David Grahame Shane ✳ Maddalena Ferretti ✳ Annalisa Contato ✳ Martina Massari ✳ Emanuele Sommariva ✳ Sabrina Sposito ✳ Carmelo Ignaccolo ✳ Maria Giada di Baldassarre ✳ Dalila Sicomo

Cosmopolitan Makers

Co-creating urban change

HETEROTOPIAS AS PLACES OF CHANGE IN THE COSMOPOLITAN ENVIRONMENT

DAVID GRAHAME SHANE

Throughout history, cosmopolitan cities have played a role as places of exceptional fluidity whose institutions, laws, and inhabitants facilitated the exchange of people, goods, capital, and culture. Such fluidity has taken different forms over time, but can be modelled, just as meteorologists model and measure our shifting climate and weather. This paper will look at the heterotopic systems underlying this fluidity and consider port cities in particular, using Hamburg as an example and focusing on the cosmopolitan philosophy of the Warburg Institute and its meta-historical approach to culture. Considering the cosmopolitan city as a "quasi-object"—a hybrid of events and information—in the Metacity model, the paper will conclude by examining Guangzhou (formerly known as Canton), the Hong Kong corridor, and the Great Bay project as a cosmopolitan Metacity region.

Heterotopic systems and urban modelling

Michel Foucault (1967) introduced the medical term "heterotopia" to the architectural profession as a "place of the other": an urban apparatus where supposedly incompatible life forms could live together in a mutually beneficial relationship that was dynamic and changing. He outlined the three characteristics of these heterotopic "devices" that allow inhabitants to shift and change, developing, connecting, and differentiating the living systems, and developing different models of cities: first, heterotopias reflect the structure of their host city in miniature; second, they house multiple small pockets or enclaves of space and people, allowing for multiple uses; and third, the normal codes of the host city become fluid and can be reversed. Kevin Lynch (1981), following Sebastiano Serlio (1547), proposed three city models to represent urban development: the city of faith, the city machine, and the eco city. Foucault similarly proposed three heterotopic systems that mirrored and transformed the systems of cosmopolitan cities. The first were heterotopias of crisis, where people voluntarily went to get help provided by charitable communities or faith organisations and were free to leave when they wished. The second were heterotopias of deviance, where state authorities enforced new norms to create a modern, scientific, and healthy society, preparing citizens for work in the machinic, industrial city. The third system of heterotopic devices were heterotopias of illusion, where the previous informational systems came to the fore and the free flow of knowledge and information created

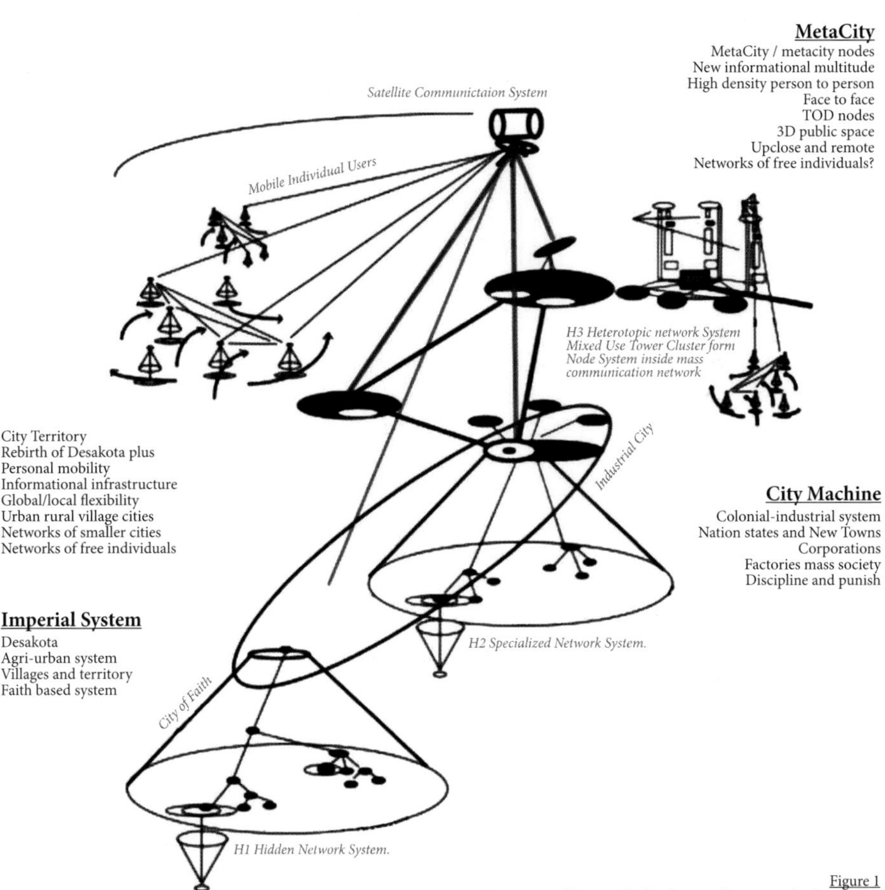

Figure 1
Heterotopic City Systems diagram and urban models
Source: David Grahame Shane, from *Recombinant Urbanism*, 2005

network heterotopic systems dynamic

a new form of fluid society, characterised by swiftly changing and shifting relationships. As examples of these heterotopic devices, Foucault referred first to the *beguinages*, or medieval hospitals inside city blocks and houses in medieval cities; second, to Bentham's Panopticon prison project at the start of the industrial age; and finally referred to a long list of museums, libraries, theatres, cinemas, world's fairs, markets, the stock market, brothels, ports, docks. and ocean liners as examples of heterotopias of illusion. All these heterotopic devices enabled cosmopolitan cities to handle the risks of infection, financial instability, social injustice, and cultural diversity while maintaining some continuity and stability over time.

The Warburg Institute and Hamburg as heterotopic and cosmopolitan systems

The methods and aims of the institute that Aby Warburg founded in 1926 anticipated many of the characteristics of Foucault's description of a heterotopia of illusion: it began as a personal library, it became a museum, it had a lecture theatre, it employed advanced media techniques and photography, it organised exhibitions and tracked the changing meaning of symbols over time, and it moved between cities. Warburg's associative and wide-ranging methodology of symbolic and formal comparisons, and his collages of photos—dismissed as madness by art historians and scholars for fifty years—have taken on a new relevance in the age of the internet. Warburg saw visual patterns within and across cultures in ways that reflected the cosmopolitan city of his birth and our current global, online, virtual culture. He studied how symbolic forms migrated between continents and cultures, inevitably changing their meanings and mutating. The hybrid structure of the Warburg Institute reflected in miniature the structure of the successful Free and Hanseatic City that had grown rich from trading in the Baltic and North Sea, with London and with North and South America through the Atlantic trade, through the activities of the Hamburg America Line, and through its links even further afield in Africa and Asia. Each system of city expansion along the river estuary added more docks, with the Atlantic ships requiring even larger moorings. Similarly, the contemporary container business made the older systems redundant, enabling the redevelopment of the Hafencity with its spectacular heterotopia of illusion: the opera house that symbolised the city's cultural and informational ambitions.

Heterotopias in the cosmopolitan world: "quasi-objects" in the informational Metacity

Foucault's category of the heterotopia of illusion and Warburg's visionary methodology both imagined a space of free-floating symbols and information that shifted and changed within a heterotopic system. The system would change like a port city or the weather. This cosmopolitan spatial imaginary depended on the ability of heterotopias to mirror systems, miniaturise elements, and reverse codes. Such operative informational systems had always been important to trade, and their acceleration shrank space and time in the twentieth century. Later, the computer revolution expanded the scope of information handled and the miniaturisation of widely available handheld devices provided access to the internet and to a vast memory system. Just as a package with a barcode could be tracked across a contemporary logistics system on a handheld computer, so researchers in India could retrieve information stored in remote server farms. In 2000, the Dutch architects of MVDR called this wealth of information the Metacity. The key to this system was the handheld device: a cell phone, a miniature heterotopia of illusion, a hybrid of the physical and virtual worlds. This hybrid object housed a search engine that processed coded metadata—the tags, descriptions, word clouds, or networks of association that made up Warburg's symbolic world. This metadata made every element of the

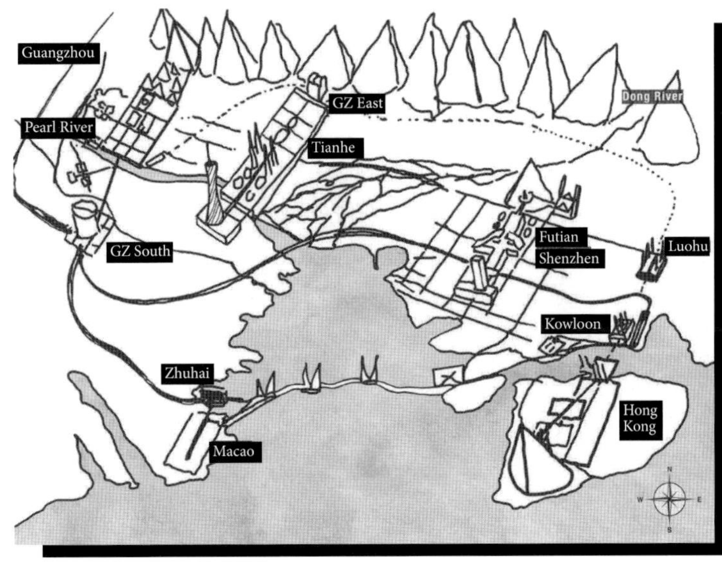

Figure 2
Pearl River Delta Megacity/Metacity.
Graphic by David Grahame Shane, 2019

city a "quasi-object", a hybrid of information, time, and space; an augmented reality. Philosopher of science Michel Serres described this new constellation of information as a system of "world objects", accessible around the globe, and "quasi-objects", hybrids of physical processes and information. Serres called for a new "contract with nature", so that humans would not be "parasites" who did not care for the world and future generations. He argued that the fingertip on the screen of the new apparatus of the handheld was the key to a new cosmopolitan sensibility.

"Quasi-objects" in the cosmopolitan Metacity; Canton, Hong Kong, Guangzhou, Shenzhen

As the imperial city of Canton, Guangzhou replicated the plan of Beijing. However, the central treasury took the place of the Forbidden City, distinguishing the port city as a logistical and trading "quasi-object"; a "world-object". For over a hundred years, the emperor licensed thirteen merchants to trade with foreigners in a tiny enclave outside the city walls. The Thirteen Hongs formed a perfect heterotopic spatial apparatus where no women were permitted, multiple enclaves housed different European nationalities, and each European factor faced, from his factory-warehouse, a public square forbidden to Chinese citizens. The British establishment of Hong Kong as a rival trading and logistical information platform, with a larger deep-water port, opened the way for the development of a modern cosmopolitan city. Like the Thirteen Hongs, it was highly compressed by site conditions, but by the 1950s it featured vertical factories, new towns, and skyscrapers in the central business district.

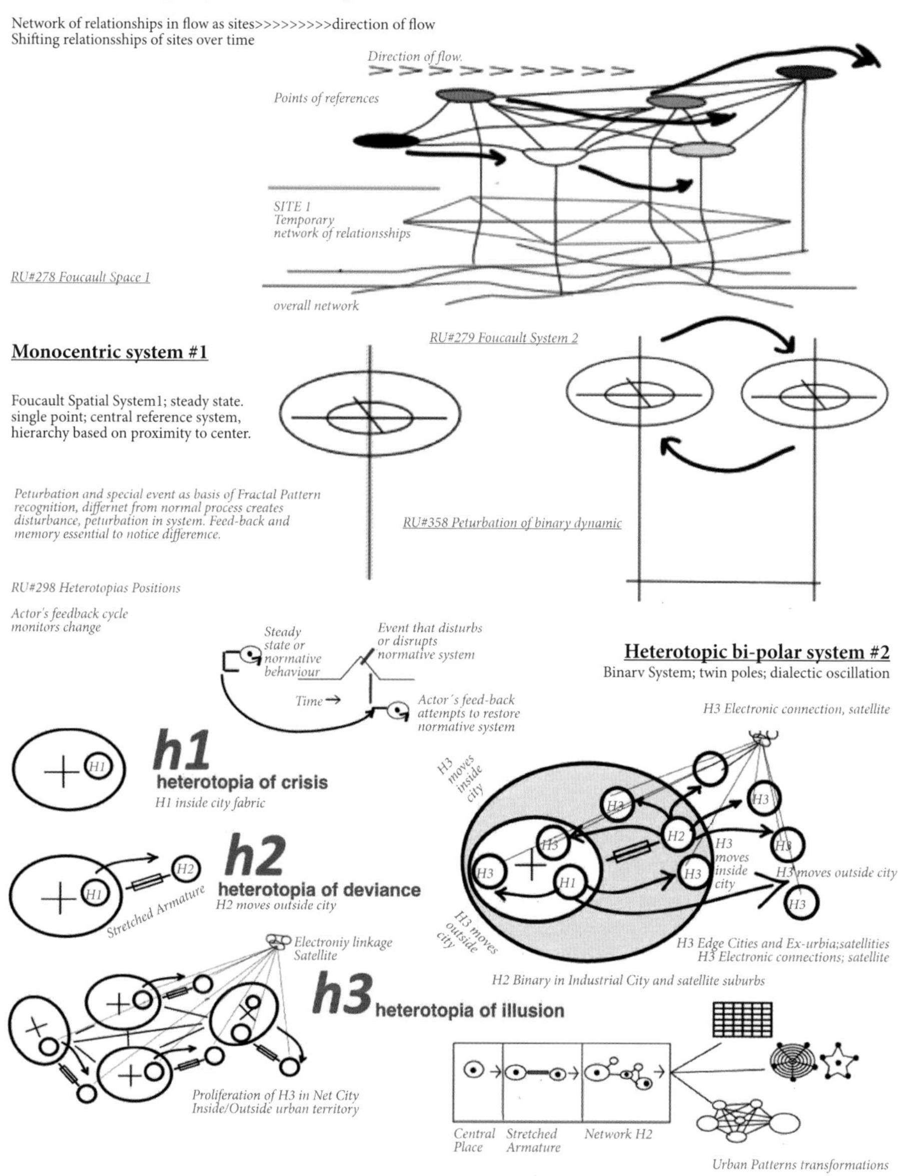

Figure 3
City systems
Graphic by David Grahame Shane

The "quasi-object" of the colonial city reversed the traditional Imperial *feng shui*-inspired plan, which had faced south to the water; instead, Hong Kong faced north, cascading down from the Peak. The Metacity informational dimension of Hong Kong expanded rapidly in the late the twentieth century, as the planned new town of Shenzhen halfway to Guangzhou became the first Special Economic Zone in China, linked to global trade for industry, then electronics, and finally for Metacity services. The recent "world-object" cultural icons of "Grand Theatre Urbanism" in the monumental civic spaces of Fuitan, Shenzhen, and the Tianhe district of Guangzhou exemplify this transformation. Despite these megastructural projects, and the high-speed rail and internet that bind them together, a resilient micro-urbanism movement with a deep local memory survives. URBANUS (2005) pioneered the recognition of the Shenzhen urban villages buried in the modern master plans as valuable heterotopic resources. Guangzhou still provides beauty products, wigs and fabrics to specialised African merchants seeking products for specialised, micro-urban, heterotopic markets, as well as provisioning Christian and Muslim religious facilities. In the Litchi Park renovation of 2019, an archipelago of imperial leisure and pleasure islands, rebuilt as a Workers' Park in the Chinese landscape tradition by Mao in the 1950s, became an eco park with restored public plazas, canals, theatres, restaurants, and pavilions: a miniature Pearl River Delta symbolic of the Metacity age.

Conclusion: Heterotopic systems and the cosmopolitan city

This brief review tracked the changing scale and nature of cosmopolitan cities powered by heterotopic systems. The Pearl River Delta has a population of sixty million people, and—as a result of SARS in 2003—has highly accelerated its Metacity public health dimension, coordinated even in the time of Covid-19 by handheld devices that track their users' every movement. Even now, new forms of micro-urban design are emerging that give weight to Warburg's optimistic hope that cosmopolitan cities will continue to produce new hybrids, innovations, and cultural forms.

BIBLIOGRAPHY

Farris J. (2007) "Thirteen Factories of Canton: An Architecture of Sino-Western Collaboration and Confrontation". In: *Buildings & Landscapes: Journal of the Vernacular Architecture Forum* 14. Minnesota, University of Minnesota Press, pp. 66-83. Available online at: https://doi.org/10.1353/bdl.2007.0000 (15.02.2020).

Feng J. and Chen K. (2019) "Cooperative Historic Landscape Rejuvenation in China: The Litchi Bay Project in Guangzhou". In: *Built Heritage* 3. pp. 76 – 90. Available online at: https://built-heritage.springeropen.com/articles/10.1186/BF03545737 (20.07.2020).

Foucault M. (1967) *Of Other Space; Heterotopias*. Available online at: https://foucault.info/doc/documents/heterotopia/foucault-heterotopia-en-html (07.04.2017).

Hafen City (n.d.) *HafenCity*. Available online at: https://www.hafencity.com/en/home.html (07.01.2021).

Lynch K. (1981) *Good City Form*. Cambridge, MA and London, MIT Press.

MVRDV (1999) *Metacity/DataTown*. Rotterdam, 010 Publishers.

Ohrt R., Heil A. (2020) *Curatorial statement on the history of this exhibition*. Available online at: https://www.hkw.de/en/programm/projekte/2020/aby_warburg/bilderatlas_mnemosyne_kuratorisches_statement/text.php (07.01.2021).

Serres M. (2014) *Thumbelina: The Culture and Technology of Millennials*. Lanham, MA, Rowman and Littlefield.

URBANUS (ed) (2006) *Village/City, City/Village*. Shenzhen, URBANUS.

Xue C. Q. (ed) (2019) *Grand Theater Urbanism; Chinese Cities in the 21st century*. Springer, Singapore.

THE AGENCY OF COSMOPOLITAN DESIGN

MADDALENA FERRETTI

Limits: how will we shape our habitats in the future?

The pandemic confronts us with the idea of limits and reminds us of their ambivalent nature: the limits of the domestic walls that protect us from contagion while simultaneously forcing us into isolation; administrative limits that can no longer be crossed for safety reasons, as well as perhaps due to the lack of a shared strategy between regions and countries that seem to be increasingly closing themselves off from one another; the limits of accessibility that, on the one hand, preserve the villages of inner areas as resilient places where contagion numbers are lower and where sociality, even if reduced, is still possible thanks to the resistance of the community structure, but that on the other hand condemn anyone without an efficient internet connection to exclusion. Reflecting on the idea of limits means first of all reflecting on identity—a controversial concept in modern thought, as it has been held historically responsible for drifts towards nationalism. According to Martin Buber, known for his philosophical work about the nature of relationships (1997), a limit establishes the distinction between "I and Thou" and is therefore the interface—the place of exchange—that constitutes the space of experience. Limit and relationship are therefore constitutively linked. The pandemic has demonstrated to us the concept of limit as distance (social distancing), as inequality (the digital divide), as the cap we must put on our ecological footprint (the limit to growth)—but it has also presented the limit as the space within which relationships exist (the balcony from which we sing together). After this emergency, there will be limits to overcome and new limits to be strategically established in order to avoid negative impacts on the future: new limits in urban settings, in public space, in mobility, in sociality, that will create new relationships and opportunities. The setting and overcoming of limits will be one of the challenges we must face in our future habitats in order to make them more resilient, sustainable, and inclusive through innovation.

Cosmopolitanism: can architecture become a tool for inclusion?

Being cosmopolitan, being a citizen of the world, first refers to the idea of globalisation, to freedom of movement, to an intensity of exchange, to the erasing of distances. Over the course of the pandemic, this perspective has been tremendously reshaped, and talking about being cosmopolitan—in this "traditional" or more commonly used sense—might seem anachronistic. But if we conceptualise

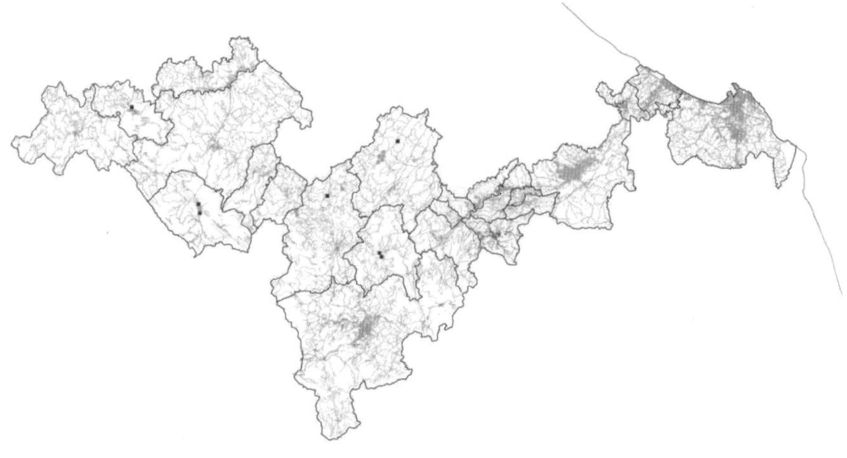

Figure 1
General mapping of the area of the Clementina road and the inner area of Appennnino Basso-Pesarese Anconetano. Spaces of opportunities in the slow territories of the Marche inner areas
Source: Master's thesis investigation by M. Campanelli and B. Staccioli at UNIVPM, supervisor: Prof. Maddalena Ferretti, tutor: Caterina Rigo

"How will we shape our habitats in the future? Can architecture become a tool for inclusion? Who are the cosmopolitan makers?"

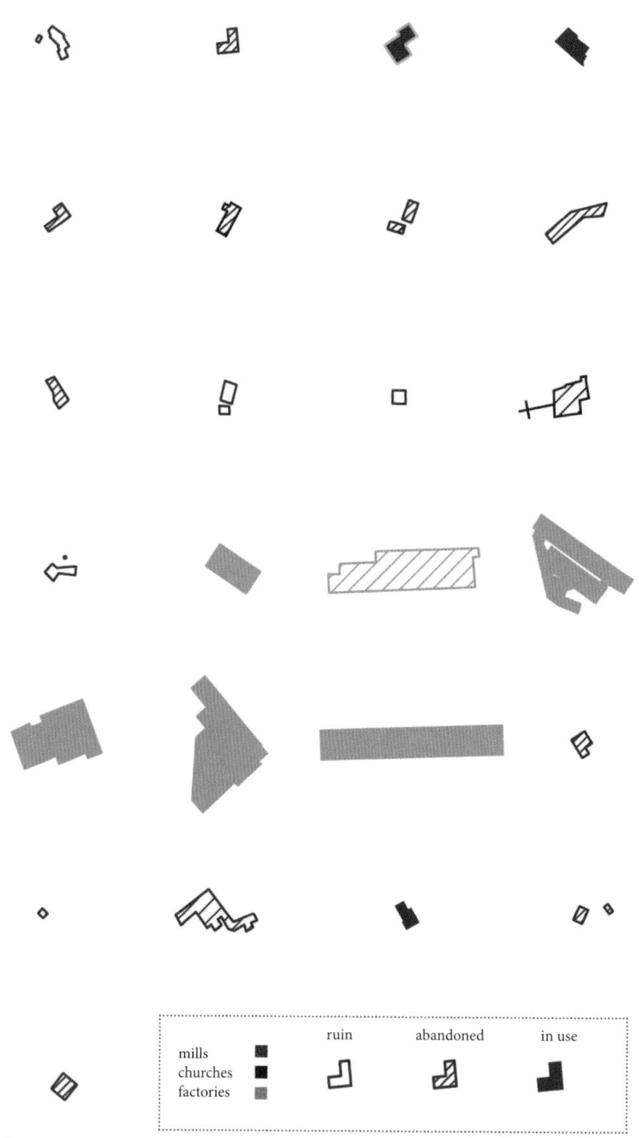

Figure 2
General mapping of the area of the Clementina road and the inner area of Appennnino Basso-Pesarese Anconetano. Spaces of opportunities in the slow territories of the Marche inner areas
Source: Master's thesis investigation by M. Campanelli and B. Staccioli at UNIVPM, supervisor: Prof. Maddalena Ferretti, tutor: Caterina Rigo

it in terms of openness, in terms of a city that welcomes differences and eases processes of inclusion, cosmopolitanism becomes instead a very real and current issue that, as experts on space, we should bring to the table and encourage action on. Particularly at this dramatic moment in time, identifying how to include people, how to not leave people behind, and how to find other ways of relating and creating connections, are crucial and decisive tasks for spatial designers. Architecture can be the place where these processes are facilitated: a space of refuge and shelter, a space where minorities can express themselves, where ideas of collectivity and reappropriation can materialise; a space that gives value and meaning to a community. Because its material nature, architecture can embody people's ideas and needs, and make them evident in the city by building real, concrete places where people can feel represented. In turn, these places may become activators of new dynamics and contribute substantially to the regeneration of derelict and fragile urban areas. *Cosmopolitan Habitat*, in this line of thinking, should provide spaces with collective and common uses in the city, in the architectures that build the urban space. Considering this shift in the meaning and scope of cosmopolitanism, we can recognise that this new interpretation does not necessarily apply only to metropolitan areas, but can be easily extended to a wider context of analysis that includes peri-urban, rural, and mountain areas. Certainly, creating *Cosmopolitan Habitat* is about setting up conditions that significantly empower people, that boost the urban inclusiveness of places, that foster people's capacity to produce more meaningful transformations, and that facilitate the implementation of community economies.

Changing economies: who are the cosmopolitan makers?

In recent years, countless experiences all over Europe have demonstrated the renewed role and engagement of communities in the care and transformation of their territories. In the 1990s, J. K. Gibson-Graham developed the "diverse economies approach" (Gibson-Graham 1996), proposing an alternative management of resources that moves away from the established capitalist system and towards shared practices of "community economies … that are based on an ethical negotiation of all the actors involved" (Elzenbaumer 2020, p. 12). These approaches embed practice- and action-oriented tools that allow for more exchange and relationality in economic processes and that include "time and repetition" as crucial factors for setting up durable transformations of spaces, productive systems, and community services, as well as the adaption of available resources to effect transformation "at the hands of everyday life" (Elzenbaumer 2020). Looking at these changing processes from the point of view of designers and spatial agents, we can identify several actions that may have disruptive impacts on habitats, such as collaborative temporary uses, tactical urban actions, and bottom-up operations. In many regeneration situations, these approaches work as a spark that triggers the interest of other stakeholders, e.g. administrations and private actors, which can then ultimately take on a more active role in the process, promoting long-term transformation. Networking between communities is a crucial aspect, as are openness and connection to international experiences that research (for example) might help to establish. But most important in these experiences of reappropriation of space, resources, and economies are the linkages with context and place-based actions that rely on the social and territorial capital at hand. The drivers behind these changing economies based on the idea of circularity, sharing, and open-source knowledge are cosmopolitan makers, in the sense that they look for interdependency more than uniqueness, aiming to create relationships and open up opportunities for the community rather than to innovate within their individual worlds. Viewed in this way, architecture and urbanism are essential to providing the frame of action within which change can happen. Designers not only help co-create transformation, providing expertise and inventiveness as fundamental tools for reconquering a space of liveability, inclusion, and welfare, but also generate the conditions necessary to support cosmopolitan-makers by negotiating meaningful strategic frameworks with relevant stakeholders. The intermediary role of designers is crucial in mediating between needs, but also in unveiling and highlighting strengths and potentials and in making them count as valuable collective resources in an interdependent system. Changing existing cultural and economic practices is a realistic and viable alternative in the global economic set-up, and design professionals should reconsider their potentially significant contribution to global challenges by readdressing their "role and agency … within shifting labor relations, … commons-oriented construction processes, [and] new commons-oriented financing and procurement methods for architecture" and by facilitating "a transition towards a commons-oriented economy based on existing peer-to-peer practices" (Alexander 2019).

Who cares? Design as an agent of collective alternatives

In dealing with the complex challenges that societies, cities, and territories are facing today, it is inevitable that we will question ourselves on the roles and responsibilities that we, as designers of space, can play in reshaping our habitats. Our goals have already been already acknowledged: high resilience, higher accessibility, more sustainable and ecological transformations, and more collaborative and transparent decision-making processes. Here, additionally, it is interesting to explore the concept of care embedded in the idea of cosmopolitanism. If society aims for more open, accessible, and democratic places, then a key concern is the care of these places, as well as the care of overstressed environments, of common goods, and, ultimately, of our territory. Who cares about these resources? The climate issue, for example, keeps being considered a matter for somebody else to worry about: "who cares?" seems to be the attitude of many people and governments. But the extreme conditions of the pandemic crisis demonstrate to us ever more clearly our inevitable obligation to take care of habitats by assuming responsibility for devising policies that firmly address the ecological transition. Taking care—as well as being cared for—raises questions about roles, about processes of interaction, co-creation, and even decision-making. Furthermore, everyday challenges should compel significant attention to practices and actions that are silently but relentlessly perpetuated by many "change-makers". The question of care is thus also a call for more horizontal, collaborative, and sustainable ways of co-existing; a call for envisaging, as architects and urban planners, more adequate and inclusive places.

New skills, knowledges, and tools must be explored in order to reconfigure the roles of expert designers in a society where non-experts have become new design agents. Design itself can become an agent of collective alternatives (Agents of Alternatives 2021), especially in the presence of co-creative processes. The "creative colonization" (Carta 2017) of places is a visible sign of the renaissance spreading throughout the peripheral inner areas of Europe, brought about by social innovators in many fields. Designers can promote processes of re-habitation by supporting these pioneering initiatives and enabling experiences of reappropriation. Design can strengthen the value of these everyday practices and provide a change of perspective by intersecting with strategic approaches for the transformation of complex territories. Seen through the lens of design, the legacy (Ricci 2019) of cities and territories is no longer exceptional or unique, but can be a common and unremarkable part of everyday life (Hartmann 2019). Legacy becomes ordinary. And such ordinary legacy makes

Figure 3
Legacy Manifesto. R.E.D.S. International Symposium Matera, 14–16 November 2019
Curated by Mosè Ricci, Chiara Rizzi, Maddalena Ferretti, Silvana Kuhtz, Ina Macaione, G. Pino Scaglione
Graphic by Woo Mezzometroquadro

Figure 4
Exchange design workshop "Ordinary Legacy" 2020–21
Curated by Maddalena Ferretti, Marche Polytechnic University, and Elena Farini, University Francisco de Vitoria Madrid
Graphic by the author

up the material of our cities, the built heritage of our historical centres, the unused buildings of our hybrid rur-urban constellations, the different patterns of our settlements, and the common resources that are enhanced by the collective action of conscious and care-taking communities. Ordinary legacy, unveiled by design, is inhabited by people. They are the actors who create new interdependencies, explore new forms of permanence, and bring about dynamics of innovation. Architects and urban designers should direct these material and immaterial potentials towards a more thorough and comprehensive regeneration of their habitats; this is the agency provided by cosmopolitan design.

BIBLIOGRAPHY

Alexander J. (2019) "Speculations on the architecture of a commons-based economy". In: Delsante I., Rong D. eds. (2019) *The City as a Commons. Research Symposium*. Pavia, 2–4 September 2019. Book of Abstracts. Pavia, University of Pavia, pp. 64–65.

Agents of Alternatives e. V. (2021) "Agents of Alternatives". Available online at: www.agentsofalternatives.com (30.03.2021).

Buber M. (1997) *Ich und Du*. Gerlingen, Verlag Lambert Schneider. Originally published in 1923 by Insel, Leipzig.

Carta M. (2017) *Augmented City. A Paradigm Shift*. Barcelona, List-Lab.

Elzenbaumer B. (2020) "Community economies. A practice exchange". *Alpine Community Economies Laboratory Snapshot Journal 1*. Berlin, Agents of Alternatives e.V.

Gibson-Graham J. K. (1996) *The End of Capitalism (As We Knew It): A Feminist Critique of Political Economy*. Minneapolis, University of Minnesota Press.

Hartmann S. (2019) *Monuments of Everyday Life. Interplays of City, Infrastructure, and Architecture in São Paulo*. Berlin, Jovis.

Ricci M. (2019) "Legacy". In: *Abitare la Terra* 3(50), p. 6.

THE COSMOPOLITANISM OF COMMUNITIES: PUBLIC SPACE AS A GENERATOR OF EQUALITY AND DEMOCRACY

ANNALISA CONTATO

The era in which we live—that of the networked society, of the knowledge society, of globalisation; the era in which everyone is connected, thanks to the annihilation of geographical distances by the dematerialisation that virtual processes allow—is the era in which the intensification of flows in every direction contrasts with the materialisation of borders and barriers and the proliferation of inequalities, social conflicts, and personal hardship. The city, which has been imagined as a place of social and cultural integration, is thus in fact "a powerful machine of distinction and separation, of marginalization and exclusion of ethnic and religious groups ... of individuals and groups with different identities and statutes" (Secchi 2013, p. 3). Cities "are also the places where inequalities and margins are emerging with increasing virulence" (Carta 2019, p. 159). The very structure of many contemporary cities proposes this urban social division, within which we find parts built on distinction and exclusion.

This factor has intensified with the increase in migratory flows, with new inhabitants finding the space in those parts of the city narrower and more degraded, further increasing the sense of insecurity—which generates intolerance—of those who still want a hierarchically divided city. These new inhabitants, not finding support in integration policies at the urban level, tend to separate along lines of ethnicity, religion, lifestyle, and the use of space. This creates a puzzle of the city with tiles whose edges are not defined in a way that allows the reconstruction of a unique and integrated design, but instead trigger strong competition when different pieces encounter one another. This competition moves into public spaces too, creating spatial tensions and, as a result, social tensions. Social separation, therefore, corresponds to spatial separation, creating stigmatised neighbourhoods and concentrations of problems in specific areas, such as (among others) the suburbs and some parts of the historic centres. These circumstances require a solution that is both political—because it deals with the coexistence and commonality of the "different"—and urban, creating spaces that promote non-hierarchical coexistence and allow people to move freely in space and generate, through horizontal interaction, the power that is created by acting in concert in public space (Arendt 1995). Because if public space is simultaneously a place of division and of community, then it must be rethought and redesigned as an "in-between"[1] that has the potential to connect people, in a non-hierarchical,

Figure 1
Palermo, Ballarò district
A city that wants to be cosmopolitan has to respond to the challenge of resolving conflicts and spatial tensions by identifying processes, practices and devices to promote and guarantee integration and plural coexistence
Photo by Francesco Bellina, 2018

social division exclusion public space human dimension

democratic form. As such, one of the main challenges that a city that wants to be cosmopolitan must respond to is that of conflict resolution and spatial tensions; it must identify processes, practices, and devices to promote and ensure integration and plural coexistence.

The role of public space

If we want the city to overcome its purely functional vision and become a "community of communities" (Carta 2019) where space and society interact and generate bottom-up virtuous processes that provide places with an identity, feelings, and the sense of a space lived by multiple communities, then perhaps it is necessary restart from the concept with which the polis was created in ancient Greece—a settlement built around the public space, the *agorà*, where free and equal men could meet at any time. "The *polis*, properly speaking, is not the city-state in its physical location; it is the organization of the people as it arises out of acting and speaking together, and its true space lies between people living together for this purpose, no matter where they happen to be" (Arendt 1958, p. 197). This is the concept of public space that we must recover and with which we must rethink our cities, from a cosmopolitan and democratic perspective, in order to give back to citizens the spaces of urban life and reconfigure social relations. So: what is needed are not only dense, private spaces with some public interstices, but large, public spaces whose "democratic use" makes them the expression of the community that lives in and around them, functioning as a meeting place, a space for intertwining, fusion, and the recognition of identities, as well as a space for the generation of new, multicultural identities. In modernist planning, the role of urban space as a meeting place has been taken into consideration poorly (Gehl 2017)—shifting the focus from interrelationships and communal spaces in cities to individual buildings, becoming increasingly isolated and introverted—with the effect of limiting the social and cultural functions of the city where urban space is a meeting place and social forum for the inhabitants. Therefore, it is necessary to create equipment and public spaces that encourage the attendance of the whole citizenship, and to construct those conditions of "porosity" within the urban tissue that enable the activation of integration and aggregation processes—even if these occur slowly. People are not interchangeable representatives of a species, but bearers of specific identities that must be maintained, handed down, recognised, and valued. To promote this perspective, those processes capable of creating a *Cosmopolitan Habitat* from the bottom up must be favoured; these are the processes in which the citizen feels they are a "world citizen" (Nussbaum 2019) and perceive a sense of being in the world ("worldliness")—as opposed to the feeling of "worldlessness"—in a city whose places are the spaces of a "shared world"; spaces of society and community.

The human dimension of urban cosmopolitanism

Unlike other issues aimed more at the logistical operation of the city, the human dimension in urban planning has often been neglected. The way in which citizens live in the urban space beyond their home and beyond their workplace has only been addressed in recent decades, during which greater attention has been paid to public space, to "non-institutional" places intended for citizens, and to places aimed at meeting and integration. The latter are the ones I would like to draw attention to. The social and cultural functions of the city are hampered both by the urban conditions (such as traffic, noise, and pollution) and by the separation of functions within cities—a separation inherited from modernist urbanism (Jacobs 1961)—to the extent that the traditional function of urban public space has been considerably reduced. These considerations have led to numerous research efforts

Figure 2
Palermo, Ballarò market
The market of Ballaro in the historical center of Palermo is a place where citizens from all over the world can meet, where everyone can find a piece of identity and where diversities mingle. This market is an "in-between" space, a nonhierarchical space—an example of a syncretic public space.
Photos by Francesca Marchese, 2018

Figure 3
Superkilen, Copenhagen, project by Studio BIG, 2012
The urban park of Superkilen is an example of urban syncretic space, a social and artistic experiment in a neighbourhood characterised by a strong cultural heterogeneity. It has created a place for a moment of dialogue and discussion between the various inhabitants of the area.
Photo by Naotake Murayama, 2015

concerning the life and death of cities, as well as to new experiments in the urban environment that aim to restore a certain level of livability and quality of life outside the walls of the private home—requiring, therefore, the restoration of urban quality. The social function of public space must be intensified: it role as a place of encounter and integration is fundamental in an era in which social injustices and urban segregation continue to exist despite the phenomenon of globalisation—which multiplies connections but pushes those who are excluded from these dynamics even more towards the margins due to their lack of access to services. It is necessary to rebuild open societies in open cities; democratic societies in places for democratic use. These must be among the main goals that today's urban planners set when rethinking the urban spaces of cities. And not just the large spaces, such as squares or promenades, but also all the places and interstices that often become hotbeds of misuse but which, if placed in the network and revitalised with new and flexible functions, can give life back to that polis in which the citizens experience the urban space as a space of their own being, of their own life, and as a space of everyone at the same time, rather than as a space that is "other" or belongs to "someone else". If the urban structure and the quality of its spaces influence human behaviour and the way the city lives, then the functional mixité becomes an important element from two points of view: firstly in terms of ensuring the continuous attendance of a place and its liveliness throughout the day, and secondly in terms of security—because a place that is lived in is a place that conveys security to its citizens. Greater connection between necessary and optional activities in urban spaces is a very important factor both in creating dynamism in relations and in promoting a greater probability of meetings between the different communities, ethnicities, and cultures that exist within the same urban environments—such as those of today's cities. We should no longer talk about pedestrian flows or the "capacities" of open spaces, but of meeting places and of paths through life that take place in the streets of the city. Not just paths from point A to point B, but porous paths; paths that interact, interweave spaces and functions, and interweave cultures, identities, and the relationships between people. In the porous flexibility of urban space, intangible relationships become tangible, take place, become matter, and create space by virtue of the relationship giving a new function, even a temporary one, to the place experienced at that time. If the pandemic we are experiencing is depriving us of the use of public community space, it does not mean that this space is no more, but rather that we must do even more to rethink it with a new dimension of security and flexibility; to rethink it in a way that allows it to be adapted to different needs, whether they are sudden or planned. Urban designers are being asked to face a new challenge: that of giving life to cities in situations where meeting is not allowed, except at a distance. So: what can "social distance" become? How can we intervene and ensure that the obnoxious term "social distancing" does not intrude on the true social sphere, but only on the spatial sphere, where the intrusion can be answered with new places?

Conclusions: the city as a spatial and social device

A cosmopolitan city is a city in which cultural and social differences are not an obstacle to overcome but a resource, a multicultural container in which different traditions, customs, and languages blend and coexist. It is a place of meetings of people where forms of communication between different cultures are experimented with. It is an integrated and inclusive city, where the sense of community is not based on your nationality of origin, but on the place where you live. As a response to globalisation, the cosmopolitan city is a city in which it is possible to feel like a citizen of the world without losing one's sense of identity; the uniqueness of different identities is recognised as containing a part of the world, not as a simple element that is added to the whole but as one that is a constituent part of the whole. We must therefore work to "[build] every day the 'city of man' that breaks the devices of control and homologation of the daily life of our metropolises, and that gives back to the citizens, increasingly pluralistic and nomadic, fluid and cosmopolitan, and times and spaces of urban living, reconfiguring social, political and economic relations" (Carta 2019, p. 160). We must work for new cities for new communities, moving towards the new paradigm of "augmented cities" (Carta 2017), whose ten components are able to respond to the metamorphosis that the current urban and human era is going through. If the cosmopolitan city is an open city, a city-world, we can no longer allow the existence of barriers or limits to the possible uses of a space by citizens, but must instead orient ourselves towards practices that tend to "urban syncretism", designing according to a logic that aggregates and hybridises the new, "contaminated" social structure of the city. The syncretic development of the urban spaces of the city can thus become an urban tactic to be pursued—one that is opposed, in a cosmopolitan vision, to the functional specialisation of well-defined parts and gentrification processes, rebalancing the entire urban system through new relationships between the space and the community.

FOOTNOTES

1_The term "in-between" is used in the sense proposed by Hannah Arendt in the 1950s, in which the "in-between" exists only when there are people using specifically that space and giving it a function, a meaning, and a social and a spatial dimension in the context. As such, a place has a real dimension only when there are people who live in it and who interact with it and with other people, creating horizontal relationships that provide the real power in a democratic society, in terms of the democratic use of the space, and in the generation of new bottom-up interventions and transformations.

BIBLIOGRAPHY

Arendt H. (1958) *The Human Condition*. Chicago, University of Chicago Press.

Arendt H. (1995) *Che cos'è la politica?* Milano, Edizioni di Comunità. A collection of unedited writings from 1950–59, originally published in German in 1993 as *Was ist Politik?* by Piper, München.

Carta M. (2017) *Augmented City. A paradigm shift*. Rovereto, LISt Lab.

Carta M. (2019) *Futuro. Politiche per un diverso presente*. Rubbettino, Soveria Mannelli.

Gehl J. (2010) *Cities for People*. Washington, Island Press.

Jacobs J. (1961) *The Death and Life of Great American Cities*. New York, Random House.

Nussbaum M. (2019) *The Cosmopolitan Tradition: A Noble but Flawed Ideal*. Cambridge, Belknap Press.

Secchi B. (2013) *La città dei ricchi e la città dei poveri*. Bari-Roma, Laterza.

AN OPEN CITY OF PRACTICES: COSMOPOLITAN INTERACTIONS IN BOLOGNA

MARTINA MASSARI

In his description of the Open City, Richard Sennett highlights two main concepts that are discussed in many of the urban studies disciplines:

- agency, referring to an increased capacity for access to resources, as well as the ability to address needs, and the exercise of these factors in the policy-making process, and
- exchange, referring to localised interaction that produces widespread value for the city.

These concepts can be found in the extensive literature on social innovation as a transformative factor for urban policies and planning (Drewe et al. 2008; Moulaert et al. 2013). For decades, social innovation has been the name given to approaches challenging the institutional mainstream (Nyseth, Hamdouch 2019) that are carried out by local communities that have activated in order to fill the gaps in the distribution of services or in the care of public spaces left by public institutions or the market. The discourse on social innovation has inherited the traditional theories and practices of urban planning, participation, and collaborative approaches (Nyseth, Hamdouch 2019), in light of which social innovation practices are described as new configurations of small-scale plans (Jacobs 2020) that are more effective in addressing global challenges than urban planning currently is.

However, as the discourse on social innovation has gained momentum, evidence has shown that the concept of local communities finding solutions for deep-rooted global challenges on their own is unrealistic (Novy, Leubolt 2005). On the other hand, the intervention of institutions can be read as stabilising the social dynamics (Savini 2019). The current, drastically changed urban context seems to call for a redefinition of this dichotomy; one aimed at reducing the distance between these dimensions, making room for practices but framing them within a planning discourse. With this in mind, considering the space of interaction between the internal agency of local communities and their more responsible exchange with governments is key to sustaining more effective social innovation

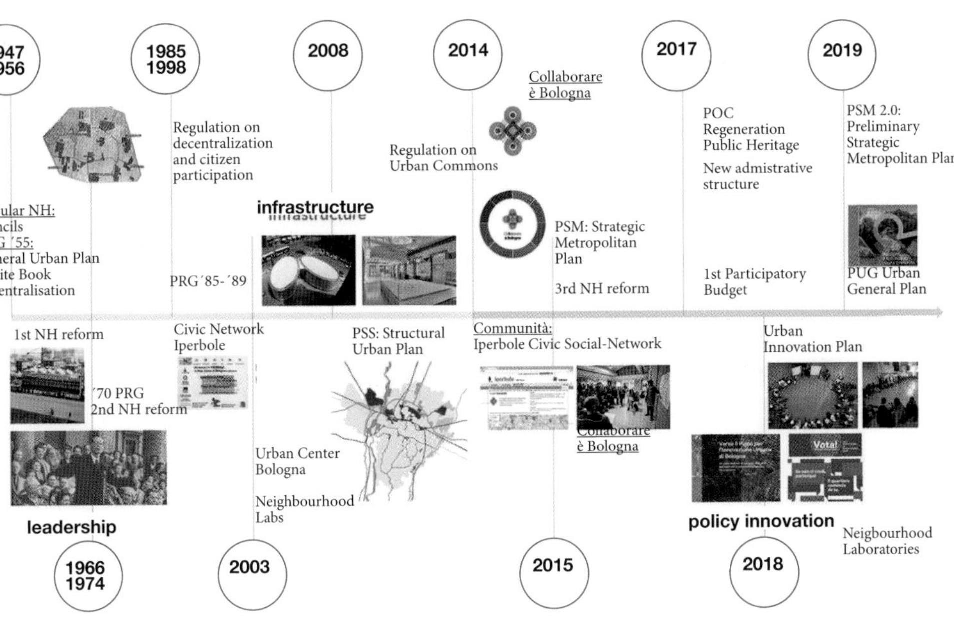

Figure 1
Timeline of policy and planning innovations in Bologna, consolidating its role as a city of exchange
Graphic by Martina Massari, 2020

interactions agency exchange planning

within urban planning (Ostanel, Attili 2018). As demonstrated by an approach that has been in use for years in Bologna, Italy, agency and exchange can be explored through the dimension of interaction between social innovation practices and institutional urban planning.

Bologna, the city of interactions

As a laboratory for innovative policies and civic oriented initiatives, Bologna is a key observation subject for urban planners. For a long time, the city has been experimenting with policies that enhance the intertwining of urban planning and social initiative, and it now finds itself renewing a consolidated tradition of cooperation. The inspirational laboratory-city model has been reinforced in recent years, with the aim of retrieving and organising the urban legacies generated by the city merging, intertwining, and creating opportunities through interaction spaces. Bologna is known for its administrative and urban model (Fig. 1), fostered by a solid political class that has experimented with innovative forms of city management in order to try to reduce the gap between planning and practices. It has deployed innovations that it has been able to renew over time, such as the civic centres, decentralisation in the seventies, and the various district reforms, all the way through to the regulation of the urban commons. The Bolognese urban planning model has always proposed that the development and maintenance of the material city go hand in hand with that of the social one (Orioli, Massari 2020). These exchanges, in the last years, have consolidated in the city in spatial form. Starting from the neighbourhood laboratories, spaces for urban co-production and stable local collaboration, the city has equipped itself with plenty of nodes of interaction. The extensive enabling infrastructure of Bologna (Fig. 2) takes the form of a distributed backbone in the urban fabric, facilitating occasions for interaction that transform proactive civic action into local and global urban value. Civic centres, social streets, collaboration pacts, community hubs, and local networks are some of the spaces of exchange that enhance skills and develop opportunities for social innovation practices, reducing the distance between local and global networks. A stable institutional presence in the territory also avoids the risk of delegating to such practices the responsibility of taking care of structural issues that are in the charge of the public actor. During the heaviest months of the pandemic, the city of Bologna saw the emergence of peculiar instances of social innovation that involved its temporary cosmopolitan citizens—its students—as agents.

Cosmopolitan agents of social innovation

The Bologna of students is itself a city, counting about 100,000 temporary inhabitants, widening the perimeter of the administrative city. One in every four inhabitants of Bologna is a student, residing there for at least three years. Many decide to continue living there permanently after the end of their studies. The student population produces about 20,000 graduates a year, who are also potentially the city's main ambassadors to the world. It is an intellectual population that is changeable, dynamic, composed of many different identities and backgrounds, and capable of interfacing with a wider global dimension. Their challenges are anchored in the local area, but they are also open to transnational models and inputs. Their permanent movement between the local and the cosmopolitan makes them intermediaries between these two scales. Further proof of the collective value of these temporary cosmopolitan inhabitants was provided during the months of the pandemic, when several practices emerged directly from the students' initiative. The projects "A un metro da te" ("A metre from you") and "OPS!" represent the initiatives of medicine and psychology students who, through student associations, made a direct contribution to improving the hospital

"In an open city, whatever virtues of efficiency, safety, or sociability people achieve, they achieve by virtue of their own agency [...] human beings create, through mutual exchange, the systems of value by which they live."

Richard Sennett, "The Open City", 2017

environment and experience. "A un metro da te" involved 250 medicine students, while "OPS!" was promoted by sixty students of sociology, anthropology, and educational sciences and focused on waiting procedures in emergency rooms from a psychological point of view. "Staffette partigiane" and "Don't panic!" involved about ninety students in a solidarity campaign created to respond to students' needs during the pandemic. This constellation of new experiences emphasised the students' agency and reinforced the disintermediation of the student citizenship in Bologna from belonging to the university to being active part of the urban community. The opportunities provided by the density of these cosmopolitan cognitive resources (both present and future), must be recognised, enabled, and strengthened in order to ensure that situated cosmopolitan knowledge becomes the key with which Bologna rethinks all its future policies and planning. In light of the new protagonism of student citizenship, the recently approved urban plan of Bologna represents a chance to put the logic of agency and exchange between social innovation practices and institutional planning into practice.

The plan as a space of interaction

Since 2018, the Municipality of Bologna has undertaken the elaboration of a new municipal urban plan (the "Piano Urbanistico Generale", PUG). The nature of the PUG is essentially strategic: it does not only have regulative value and does not localise the transformation, but instead builds a broad, coherent vision and framework for future transformations of the city. The plan is drawn to operate as a space of interaction not only between urban agents but also between planning tools, integrating both voluntary and mandatory planning instruments. Above all, it consolidates the lessons learned from the legacy of exchange and agency in Bologna, and serves as a reflection on the profile of the contemporary city. Within this framework, spatial infrastructure that enables social innovation plays a

Figure 2
Interaction of spatial infrastructure in Bologna
Source: City of Bologna, *Municipal Urban Plan*, 2020

Figure 3
General strategies of the urban plan
Source: City of Bologna, *Municipal Urban Plan*, 2020

key role. It acts as an interactive playground between the different systems, a spatial representation of the collective sphere (Avermaete et al. 2006) in which the framework of strategies can also be spatialised. Using this new dimension of the plan, urban agents can carry out proactive exchanges with one another and with public institutions in a space where the profile of the city and the plan can be verified, maintained, and updated. This allows the public administration to experiment with procedural and design alternatives, expanding the plan's field of action by also integrating globally-inspired solutions to contingent phenomena. This approach opens up opportunities to engage in proactive dialogue—including with urban agents that do not usually fit into the traditional mechanisms of city management, such as temporary cosmopolitan citizens and students.

Cosmopolitan interactions for agency and exchange in planning

The consistent incursion of planning and transformative instances by different urban actors seems to find synthesis in this dimension of the plan, which operates more through interaction than through negotiation. The plan affirms a long-term commitment, it is including with respect to emerging processes; nevertheless, it must also remain sufficiently open to incorporate small plans produced by social innovation, which represent valuable resources that unite the hyperlocal with the global. In the view endorsed here, an Open City should be receptive to unusual urban agents, especially those who are able to bring with them knowledge and experience and include a cosmopolitan dimension in their practices—whether they are permanent residents of the city or temporary ones. For all this to happen, it is necessary to remove the idea that the student citizenship is not urban citizenship. As such, the plan must be able to create spaces for interaction that strengthen the relationship between the City of Bologna and the hundred thousand student brains that populate it every year. This attitude calls for flexible planning approaches, adaptable and open enough to allow the creation of interconnected systems that observe and detect social dynamics, to translate social innovations into alternative planning trajectories, and to promote opportunities for the multiplication of urban visions. These changes to the character of planning reinstate its investigative role concerning contextual cosmopolitan knowledge; it becomes an attitude of study that, like that of the student, is endowed with a critical look at reality while remaining self-critical with respect to the proposals it generates. It is an attitude aimed at exploring the unforeseen, discovering agency through exchange, and co-learning dynamics of change.

BIBLIOGRAPHY

Avermaete T., Hooimeijer F., Schrijver L. (2006) "Editorial". In: *Journal for Architecture OASE 71* (Urban Formation and Collective Spaces), pp. 2–6. Available online at: https://oasejournal.nl/en/Issues/71/Editorial (30.12.2020).

Drewe P., Klein J. L., Hulsbergen E. (2008) *The challenge of social innovation in urban revitalisation*. Amsterdam, Techne Press.

Jacobs J. (2020) *Città e libertà*. Milano, elèuthera.

Moulaert F., MacCallum D., Mehmood A., Hamdouch A. (2013) *The International Handbook on Social Innovation, Collective Action, Social Learning and Transdisciplinary Research*. London, Edward Elgar.

Novy A., Leubolt B., (2005) "Participatory Budgeting in Porto Alegre: Social Innovation and the Dialectical Relationship of State and Civil Society". In: *Urban Studies* 42(11), pp. 2023–2036. Available online at: https://doi.org/10.1080/00420980500279828 (30.12.2020).

Nyseth T., Hamdouch A. (2019) "The transformative power of social innovation in urban planning and local development". *Urban Planning* 4(1), pp. 1-6.

Orioli V., Massari M. (2020) "Lo spazio dell'interazione: luoghi, attori e strumenti a Bologna". In: Planum (2020) *Le nuove comunità urbane e il valore strategico della conoscenza. Come i processi cognitivi possono motivare la politica, garantire l'utilità del piano, offrire una via d'uscita dall'emergenza*. Roma-Milano, Planum Publisher, pp. 173–178.

Ostanel E., Attili G. (2018) "Self-organization practices in cities: discussing the transformative potential". In: *Tracce Urbane Rivista Semestrale Transdisciplinare di Studi Urbani. Italian Journal of Urban Studies 4*.

Savini F. (2019) "Responsibility, polity, value: The (un)changing norms of planning practices". In: *Planning Theory* 18(1), pp. 58–81. Available online at: https://doi.org/10.1177/1473095218770474 (30.12.2020).

Sennett R. (2017) "The Open City". In: Haas T., Westlund H. (2017) *In the Post-urban World*. London, Routledge. Available online at: https://doi.org/10.4324/9781315672168-8 (30.12.2020).

CREATIVE FOOD NODES: INNOVATING THE ROLE OF URBAN MARKETS IN THE COSMOPOLITAN HABITAT

EMANUELE SOMMARIVA

The relations between the supply and movement of food have been crucial since the foundation of our urban society. In considering the calls for collective action to confront future territorial and societal challenges, the role of food as an urban material involves a range of factors and socio-spatial arrangements that identify resilient food systems as an integral part of Lefebvre's notion of "the right to the city". ***Food nodes*** **present an example of the spatial significance of transitional places where everyday social practices, intercultural exchanges, and creative co-creation can foster the idea of a** ***Cosmopolitan Habitat*****. Based on the research-by-design outputs of the European project "Creative Food Cycles", this paper represents a methodological reflection on the spatial implications of food-led regeneration processes alongside a collection of international practices that support the urban role of food nodes in increasing unplanned sociability and cultural** ***mixité*****, and proposes short-term actions for long-term changes.**

By its nature, the consumption of food is a cultural experience. Consuming food is recognised as a collection of contextual and evolving social practices in which food no longer merely serves as sustenance, but represents—through the processes, expressions, gestures, identities, and intangible heritages it is associated with—a way of relating to others and conveying new significances. In his famous essay "Towards a psychosociology of contemporary food consumption" (1961), Roland Barthes emphasises the role of food—in the context of cultural foodways—as a powerful vehicle for the feelings, images, usages, situations, behaviours, and communication that form the basis of our grammar of taste. At the same time, it is crucial to understand food as a phenomenon of material culture that has had the ability to direct local economies, commercial exchange, and the movements of people since the foundation of our urban society, and is a constant element in its cycles of renewal. In an augmented semiotic interpretation, eating represents the relational experience of crossing cultural boundaries and encountering other "foodways",[1] stimulating new socio-spatial practices led by the encountering of local and migrant communities (Molz 2007; Duruz et al. 2011). While the globalisation of "gastronomic landscapes"[2] and the diffusion of fake diversity (e.g., restaurants aimed at tourists, ethnic mini-stores, all-you-can-eat cuisine) pose concrete evidence of the transformation

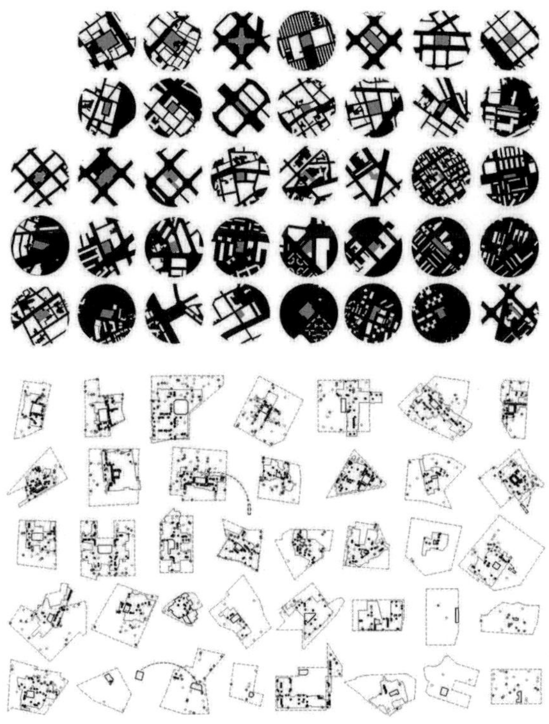

Figure 1
Market Halls as the core element for urban neighbourhood regeneration in Barcelona
Source: P. Fuertes, E. Gomez-Escoda (2020) *Supplying Barcelona*, image courtesy of the authors

urban metabolism tactical urbanism creative food cycles

of our consumer habits and domestic economies, this change of paradigm in terms of food as an urban commodity concerns a range of factors—sustainability, traceability, security, ethics, and aesthetics—in which the city is the pivotal context of action. This context has been further conditioned by the recent Covid-19 crisis, which has not only revealed the fragility of supply chains and imposed conditions of estrangement through physical distancing, but also raised questions regarding many aspects of our daily lives (such as the accessibility of urban services, the digital divide, alternative forms of mobility, the reorganisation of the labour market), and made citizens more and more dependent on big distribution players and subject to a "supermarket diet". Nevertheless, certain urban experiences offer positive examples of this intersection of food and cities: places where compact, walkable neighbourhoods centred on food markets remain or have been reconfigured in accordance with a new urban *mixité* and functional programmes aimed at counteracting the dominant model of sprawling urban conurbations. Such large conurbations are perceived as drivers of parasitic forms of collective consumption (Merrifield, 2014) and producers of the socio-economic inequalities known as food deserts or "obesogenic environments" (Townshend, Lake 2017). Against this backdrop, food nodes represent an example of the spatial significance of transitional places where everyday practices, traditional habits, intercultural exchanges, and potentials for creative co-creation can foster the idea of *Cosmopolitan Habitat*. The concept of a food node can be interpreted as an open, fuzzy-edged area in a diversified urban settlement where socio-economic arrangements interweave through physical daily routines, rituals, and micro-transformations of the open space (Parham 2013). This results in a series of human-scaled, highly mixed, walkable, and fine-grained urban morphologies that reflect the combinations of more traditional typologies, such as those of an urban market—which is not necessarily a farmers' market—at the centre of a food district.

The origins of Barcelona's food system provide an example that illustrates the polyvalent role and functions of food nodes. The first mention of the Boqueria market in Barcelona dates from 1217. In 1835 the market was fully open-air before the city gates, where street vendors and farmers gather for selling their produces. In 1840 with the construction of the first market hall, the municipality established the transition of moving markets within the city boundaries into the market hall. It represented one of the first creative reuses of historical religious complexes, namely the convents of Sant Josep and Santa Caterina. The distribution of urban market halls followed a logic of adaptation to existing morphologies, so that their service radii created a dense network —with a market hall within 400 metres of any given point— complemented by an infrastructure of nearby *food nodes* (e.g., specialty stores and groceries) that was reconfirmed as a planning standard for the Eixample district by the Cerdà Plan. During the 1970s, when the modernisation of food supply chains was leading to the disappearance of traditional urban markets in Europe, their role as extended food nodes was consolidated in Barcelona; they were the first public facility with which any new districts were equipped, even before the construction of a subway station. This organisational model, still in force today, accompanied Barcelona's expansion and its consolidation of small neighbourhood centres in the 1990s, and markets became key elements of the urban regeneration of public space. (Fuertes, Gomez-Escoda 2020). Following the example of Barcelona, food nodes can potentially become social innovation and living hubs, enhancing new forms of social encounter, education, culture, experience, and enjoyment, and drawing their mission and added values from their polyvalence of roles and functions in the context of contemporary, often non-transparent supply lines of "food cycles". (Schröder 2020). As places of exchange in the city, food nodes represent the spatial manifestation

Figure 2
Yatai Food Cart movable food stand in a renovated alley of Fukuoka, Japan.
Source: R. Kamamatsu, Note Architects, 2018
Made in Cloister temporary art-exhibition space and regional food market in Naples, Italy
Source: Rosa Alba Impronta, Davide De Blasio, Made in Cloister, 2019
Manifesto Market gastro-cultural hub for urban regeneration site in Prague, Czech Republic
Source: Radka Ondrackova, reSITE , 2018
Bergen Fish Market as an urban/harbour threshold and gastro-cultural hub in Bergen, Norway
Source: Christine Biesel, Eder Biesel Arkitekter, 2012
Nest We Grow modern reinterpretation of traditional rural hay/fish-dryers in Hokkaido, Japan.
Source: Prof. D. Buntrock, H. Chen, T. Saikawa KKAA, UC Berkeley, 2014

of an augmented dimension of conviviality, potentially enabled by the "digital milieu" (e.g. the internet of things, just-in-time logistics, e-commerce, etc.), that informs creative patterns of use, new commons, and new rituals for active public spaces. This was one of the multidisciplinary focuses of investigation developed for the European project "Creative Food Cycles"[3] to explore social perceptions, challenges, and connections around and between food, design, creativity, and space in order to enhance resilient urban metabolisms. Based on research for the *Food Interactions Catalogue*, a collection of international projects and best practices has been compiled to serve as an open repository of food-led regeneration processes and supporting and nurturing convivial food nodes in the city. Among the many entries in the catalogue, some projects emerge as particularly relevant to this paper in terms of the topics addressed and the spatial quality produced in the places affected, recalling the principles of tactical urbanism (Lydon, Garcia 2015) in order to increase unplanned sociability and cultural *mixité* and implementing short-term actions for long-term changes.

- **Manifesto Market** (reSITE) initiates new models of entrepreneurship and creative industry in Prague, bringing together cultural operators, chefs, and creatives in a cosy street-food market with twenty restaurants, pop-up stores, and gastro workshops located across twenty-seven containers. The project reclaims an abandoned area of Prague's main railway station with a strong service-design orientation that includes experiments in branding, furniture, and food fusions between different cultures.

- **Nest We Grow** (UC Berkeley and Kengo Kuma) reinterprets the traditional rural hay/fish-dryers in Hokkaido to create a new place for meditation, sharing, co-learning, and meeting activities following the time of seasonal rotation of crops that is sensitive to community rituals and life cycles. The project introduces renewable building techniques that mimic the vertical spatial experience of a Japanese larch forest where food is hung for drying.

- **Bergen Fish Market** (Eder Biesel Arkitekter) acts as both a terminal for tourists seeking fjord cruises and an urban threshold to the Hanseatic port city. Nevertheless, the large open ground floor of the market hall remains a primarily urban space for citizens, fishermen, and retailers, where new rituals—building on old traditions and new sustainable fishery practices—extend from distribution to tasting, all with a view of the city and harbour through the building's transparent walls.

- **Made in Cloister** (Rosa Alba Impronta & Davide de Blasio) forms the basis of the regeneration project of the old St. Caterina cloister in Naples. The space includes social tables with a community kitchen, an open gallery for exhibitions and music. The philosophy of work in the cloister is centred on conviviality, with events and regional markets seeking new ways to foster artisanal production and enhance the local circular economy.

- **Yatai Food Cart** (Note Architects) is part of a Japanese pop-up design movement that combines exploring new design potentials for micro-urban spaces in the megacity Tokyo with the cultural richness of Japanese temporary/traditional uses. Based on lessons learned from traditional wood construction techniques in mobile food stands, modularisation and digital design make these moving pop-up kitchens and bars suitable for self-construction.

This collection of practices demonstrates how circular design thinking and innovation in food nodes can become mutual fields of confrontation that produce visible and experienceable change in the city by using performativity and artistic languages as triggers for building up new levels of social awareness and upscaling processes. For instance, by supporting community-based initiatives that promote consumer groups, zero-kilometre food supply chains, or prosumer strategies, food nodes can become direct expressions of creativity, social involvement, and co-design with communities. In this regard, the growing digital food communities should be inspired by open-source principles like the ones adopted by the Fab City network, where the sharing of knowledge, tools, hints, and "recipes" are the norm.

However, in an era of digital knowledge during which we need to redefine the spatial requirements of the post-Covid city, we also have to reaffirm the necessity of creative disruptiveness (as a cyclical process that revolutionises economic structures from within) and spatial innovation as drivers of change that are able to reshape our social and physical relationships. The design culture associated with food nodes can contribute to exploring the spatial implications of the circular economy and the gaps between spaces of production, distribution, and consumption, moving us towards a more resilient metabolism for cities and territories.

FOOTNOTES

1_In the context of this paper, the term "foodways" defines a holistic, cross-disciplinary approach that not only applies to food, eating habits, and nourishment, but to the consumption of food as a medium that shapes our cultural, social, economic, and spatial relationships. For more information, see "Foodways: Diasporic Explorations at the Age of (Digital) Discoveries" (Sommariva, 2020),

2_The notion of "gastronomic landscapes" refers to the multiple value-chain-creation mechanisms around food cycles: from the production of foods to their distribution, from a destination's cultural and culinary identity to its tangible and intangible heritage (culinary crafts, recipes, innovation, and cross-overs, etc.) through to the meal and convivial experience itself.

3_"Creative Food Cycles" (CFC) is a European project co-founded by the European Union's Creative Europe Programme (2018–20). In particular, it elaborates on the creative actions led by the Institute of Urban Design and Planning at Leibniz University Hannover (LUH, Germany) with the Institut d'Arquitectura Avancada de Catalunya (IAAC, Spain) and the Department of Architecture and Design at Università degli Studi di Genova (UNIGE, Italy). For further information on the project's activities see www.creativefoodcycles.org.

BIBLIOGRAPHY

Barthes R. (1961) "Pour une psycho-sociologie de l'alimentation contemporaine". In: *Annales. Economies, sociétés, civilisations* 16(5), pp. 977-986.

Duruz J., Luckman S., Bishop P. (2011) "Bazaar Encounters: Food, Markets, Belonging and Citizenship in the Cosmopolitan City". In: *Continuum* 25(5), pp. 599–604.

Fuertes P., Gomez-Escoda E. (2020) "Supplying Barcelona. The Role of Public Market Halls in the Construction of the Urban Food System". In: *Journal of Urban History* November 2020.

Lydon M., Garcia A. (2015) *Tactical Urbanism: Short-term Actions for Long-term Change.* Washington, Island Press.

Markoupoulou A., Farinea C., Ciccone F., Marengo M. (2019) *Food Interactions Catalogue: Collection of Best Practices.* Barcelona, IAAC. Available online at: https://creativefoodcycles.org/food-interactions-catalogue (30.12.2020).

Merrifield A. (2014) *The new urban question.* London, Pluto Press.

Molz J. G. (2007) "Eating Difference: The Cosmopolitan Mobilities of Culinary Tourism". In: *Space and Culture* 10(1), pp. 77–93.

Oosterveer P. (2006) "Globalization and sustainable consumption of shrimp: consumers and governance in the global space of flows". In: *International Journal of Consumer Studies* 30(5), pp. 465–476.

Parham S. (2013) *Market Place: Food Quarters, Design and Urban Renewal in London.* Newcastle, Cambridge Scholars Publishing.

Schröder J. (2020) "Circular Design for the Regenerative City: a spatial-digital paradigm". In: Schröder J., Sommariva E., Sposito S. eds. (2020) *Creative Food Cycles. Book 1.* Hannover, Regionales Bauen und Siedlungsplanung Leibniz Universität Hannover, pp. 17–31. Available online at: https://doi.org/10.15488/10099 (30.12.2020).

Sommariva E. (2020) "Foodways: Diasporic Explorations at the Age of (Digital) Discoveries". In: Schröder J., Sommariva E., Sposito S. eds. (2020) *Creative Food Cycles. Book 1.* Hannover, Regionales Bauen und Siedlungsplanung Leibniz Universität Hannover, pp. 17–31. Available online at: https://doi.org/10.15488/10111 (30.12.2020).

Townshend T., Lake A. (2017) "Obesogenic environments: current evidence of the built and food environments". In: *Perspect Public Health* 137(1), pp. 38-44.

LIVING COSMOPOLITAN HABITAT

SABRINA SPOSITO

The rifts that divide the politics and economies of cities from the logics and social structures of space can be examined as distinguishing traits of the development of contemporary urban life. The spatial alienation of globalised neoliberal markets is extensively challenged by the reassertion of territorial justice, ethics, and democracy when it comes to the transformation of nature, the ways that resource streams are produced, accessed, and governed, and the specific articulation of powers and legitimation in undertaking urban actions. The "rebel cities" depicted by Harvey (2019) manifest the "revolutionary" character now growing in the everyday life of cities—a character that is bound to the very essence of feeling part of the urban society across multiple forms of social struggle, and thus also to the multiple voices arguing for the right to orient change towards better reflecting and accommodating the needs of residents so as to foster a desired urban way of living through the use of space.

In the field of urban studies, notable works discuss the emergence of a critical civic attitude in cities that is characterised by waves of vibrant activism fuelled by unchecked states of urban, ecological, and economic decay. From this analytical corpus it can be deduced that critique of the uneven organisation of space reflects, in a broader sense, critique of the bottlenecks and limits of a capitalist vision that erodes the distinctiveness of urban cultures and their regenerative capacities by inhibiting—or eclipsing—cultural processes of value-building in everyday life. The formulation by Brenner et al. (2009) of "cities for people, not for profit" seizes and interprets the strategic momentum for developing modes of urbanism inspired by an inclusive and democratic spirit, rather than by capitalist forces.

In Lefebvre's urban theories (2009 [1970]), which provide a framework for the complexities of urban life in society, space is investigated as a product of politics, ideologies, and social practices. As such, it is conflicted; a place of contradictions requiring a "dialectical method" of analysis (Lefebvre 2009 [1970], p. 172). The search for dialogic forms with which to approach tensions and struggles as they take shape and space in cities has provided the context for the production of various disciplinary foci. At the end of the nineties, Healey (1998) suggested reconciling the regulation of conflicts in the

Figure 1
Yatai Food Cart in the renovated alley, Fukuoka, Japan
Design by Note Architects (Ryo Kamamatsu)
Photo by Maki Hayashida, 2018

rebel cities creative food cycles cultural performance

Figure 2
Participants in the Firekitchen workshop, São Paulo, Brazil, 2017
Design by Johanna Dehio
Photo by André Cherry

Figure 3
PorTable
Design by Anna Pape, Josephine Arfsten,
Julia Theis, Michel Grändorf, 2019
Photo by Mohamed Hassan
for the Chair of Territorial Design and Urban Planning LUH

planning dimension with the practice of "place making", thus giving it the scope of enabling fluid collaborations across heterogeneous actors—who have "a 'stake' in a place" (p. 3)—in developing strategic objectives and giving new emphasis to the qualities and meanings of places. Thinking in dialectic terms also entails restructuring urban governance so that it can offer flexibility in the arrangements between collaborative parties, allowing creativity to spread "from experiment to governance processes and cultures" (Healey 2004, p. 19).

In the pursuit of an "open city", Sennett (2018) particularly exalts the importance of multiplying experiments and experiences in cities, arguing that openness releases nuanced possibilities for innovation—especially when it comes to dealing with complexity. By celebrating a multicultural, pluralistic imagery of urban life, he explains, "[e]thically, an open city would of course tolerate differences and promote equality, but would more specifically free people from the straitjacket of the fixed and the familiar, creating a terrain in which they could experiment and expand their experience" (p. 9). Hence, projects that aspire to true openness should, according to Brenner (2013), include dynamics of social appropriation and ownership that follow Lefebvre's spirit (1968) in reaffirming the right to the city.

The concept of *Cosmopolitan Habitat* has the ability to extend the horizon of these reflections by giving a particular cultural significance to the role of testing in the everyday city. Additionally, it can extend the domains of creative projects from everyday life to the wider, conflicted spatial geographies of territories and regions. The manifold implications of climate change demonstrate that major struggles will increasingly concern the dominant regimes around water, food, and energy infrastructures, involving the scales and settings of both the city and the countryside, understood in a mutual relationship. This requires a stronger strategic and coherent impulse for designing across various dimensions: recognising the ecological potentials of urban space; encouraging new forms of urban communities shaping more sustainable and equitable modes of production, processing, and sharing of resource streams; widening the concepts of urban metabolism through a new social imaginativeness, through cultural performances, and through artistic interventions; and co-creating new capacities and practical knowledge in society through architecture and urbanism.

NOTE

These reflections refer to the creative actions undertaken within the framework of "Creative Food Cycles", a project co-funded by the Creative Europe programme of the European Union (2018–20), at the research unit of Leibniz University Hannover. See: Schröder J., Sommariva E., Sposito, S. eds. (2020) *Creative Food Cycles. Book 1.* Hannover, Regionales Bauen und Siedlungsplanung, Leibniz Universität Hannover. Additionally, Sommariva E., Sposito, S. (2020) "Creative Food Cycles: exploring the creative dimension of regional foodsheds in Europe". In: Llop C., Cervera M., Peremiquel F. eds. (2021) *IV Congreso ISUF-H: Metrópolis en recomposición: prospectivas proyectuales en el Siglo XXI: Forma urbis y territorios metropolitanos, Barcelona, 28-30 Septiembre 2020.* Barcelona, DUOT, UPC.

BIBLIOGRAPHY

Brenner N., Marcuse P., Mayer M. (2009) "Cities for people, not for profit". In: *City* 13(2-3). London, Taylor & Francis, pp. 176–184.

Brenner N. (2013) "Open City or the Right to the City?" In: *Topos* 85, pp. 42–45.

Harvey D. (2019) *Rebel Cities: From the Right to the City to the Urban Revolution.* London, Verso.

Healey P. (1998) "Collaborative Planning in a Stakeholder Society". In: *The Town Planning Review* 69(1). Liverpool, Liverpool University Press, pp. 1–21.

Healey P. (2004) "Creativity and Urban Governance". In: *Policy Studies* 25(2). London, Taylor & Francis, pp. 87–102.

Lefebvre H. (1968) *Le Droit à la ville.* Paris, Anthropos.

Lefebvre H. (1970) "Reflections on the Politics of Space". In: Brenner N., Elden S. eds. (2009) *Lefebvre, Henri, 1901-1991. State, Space, World: Selected Essays.* Minneapolis, University of Minnesota Press, pp. 167–184.

Sennett R. (2019) *Building and Dwelling: Ethics for the City.* London, Penguin Books.

MAPPING PRACTICES FOR A COSMOPOLITAN WORLD

CARMELO IGNACCOLO

The use of maps—in forms ranging from ancient etchings in stone, papyrus-based representations, and typographic work to GPS-based info—appears to be a cultural universal (Uttal 2000). Maps are among the most effective wayfinding aids: they help us make sense of the space around us, they support our spatial navigation, and, more broadly, they have changed the way in which we see the world. Visual representations often constitute the most tangible medium of interaction across different cultures and spaces. Simply put, maps are instrumental to the notion of cosmopolitanism. The growing late-twentieth-century popularity and diverging uses of cosmopolitanism mean that the term is in danger of becoming "an abstracted discourse with no tangible meaning" (Harvey 2000). However, the challenge of cosmopolitanism does not only reside in political and sociological assertions. It can be found in a variety of forms—visual representations, aesthetics, and cultural artefacts—that continue to shape and inform our experiences as individuals navigating an interconnected world.

While we tend to take the existence of spatial representation for granted, humans lived in a condition of pre-cartographic knowledge for a long time. In the absence of these artefacts, humans used to rely on internal representations, or stored memories of experiential moments during which the presence of their bodies in space was captured by the mnemonic cells of the hippocampus. Rather than expanding on the neurological processes of map abstraction, this short essay focuses on spatial representation and critical cartography through the lenses of utility and power. What is the relationship between maps and territories? How do maps contribute to notions of cosmopolitanism and power? As Harley wrote in his "Maps, Knowledge, and Power" (1988), maps should be understood in the context of political power and with an iconological approach. Instead of being considered as inert records of morphological landscapes or spatially recorded observations, maps are to be seen as the fundamental ingredients for conducting a dialogue on what Harley defined "a socially constructed world". There is no true or false; there is no objective or subjective; and maps are not value-free representations. In short, maps are social constructions. In line with Harley's words, Crampton's piece titled "Maps as social constructions: power, communication, and visualisation," clarifies that maps are mere rhetorical devices that dismantle the "arbitrary dualism" of maps with a political

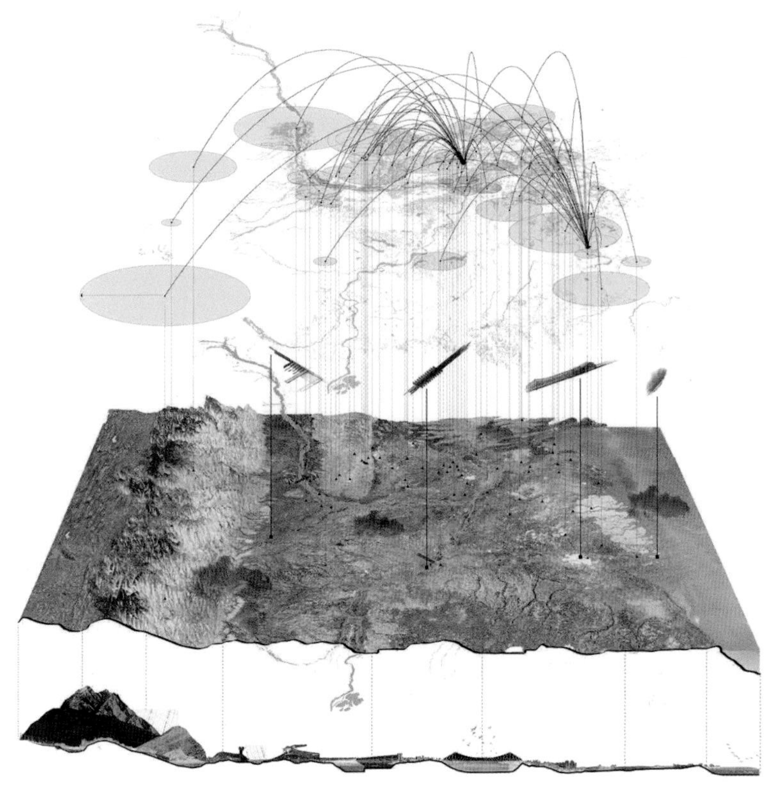

Figure 1
Despite India and Bangladesh being a politically divided region, the Bengal area experiences common environmental challenges, such as seasonal floods and large migration flows towards the metropolitan areas of Dhaka and Kolkata
Graphic by Carmelo Ignaccolo, Deniz Onder, Dissa Pidanti Raras

"What is the relationship between maps and territories?"

agenda versus merely descriptive maps, or artistic versus scientific maps (Crampton 2001). We can even advance the idea that Euclidean distance accuracy is a matter of recent technological concern, often used by designers to situate proposals in a physical landscape. More often, however, looking at a map in the past was generally motivated by the need for spatial control, which was partially achievable through better spatial accuracy. By treating maps as a visual language, scholars have advanced a critical understanding of the sociopolitical constructs embedded in these representations.

In the aftermath of WWII, as a response to modernist agendas and positivist ideals of spatial investigation, Debord and the psychogeographers advanced the troubled yet groundbreaking practice of the dérive. Their destinationless walks through city streets, detecting and mapping ambiances and "situations", became a form of political activism. However, despite being quite innovative in their psychological and sensorial readings of space, the psychogeographers and situationists remained almost constrained by their own methodological vacuum and their lack of capacity to arrange their revolutionary urban drifts into a coherent program (Sadler 2001).

In a nutshell, while the situationists' ideals remained wrapped within a veil of utopia, their claims became historically essential when the tabula rasa approach became the most common development approach to the modernisation of cities in the 1960s and early 1970s. The technocratic deployment of infrastructural arteries across hundreds of urban cores—often inhabited by minorities and migrant communities—did not at first have any vocal pushback other than that of the situationists, which was later followed by the fierce critique conducted in New York City by Jane Jacobs. The question arises spontaneously: how and why did innovation in digital representation and the distribution of GIS (Geographic Information Systems) not necessarily hamper urban renewal plans? As Sarah Williams explains in the first chapter of her book *Data Action!*, the high cost and specialist use of GIS technologies made this tool initially available only to certain groups and organisations in control of several development plans across the United States (Williams 2020). Because of this, what originally sounded like a step towards a more just representation of space inevitably became the plough with which ideological interests were sown into the city form.

The dilemma of the use of technologies is also discussed by Laura Kurgan in her *Close Up at a Distance: mapping, technology, and politics* (2013), where she argues that technologies of global positioning have become part of how we see the world. However, if modernist development models and the top-down use of satellite images were initially adopted as tools of surveillance and control, the diffusion in the late 1980s and early 1990s of GIS technologies to a broader audience (activists included) was a game-changer for the use of these tools.

In 1985, John Pickles published *Ground Truth: the social implications of geographic information systems*, which is still unanimously considered one of the most powerful critiques of technocratic GIS use. This book has been broadly recognised as a fundamental statement about GIS and society that advances an epistemological breakpoint in the use of technologies: rather than fostering technological determinacy, Pickles suggested alternative ways in which people could become active agents of spatial information (Pickles 1985). Instead of acclaiming GIS as a more objective tool for decisions, and hence extending existing technocratic ideas onto a new digital tool, Pickles planted the seed of participatory GIS and counter-cartography. He argued that defending a more efficient yet socially

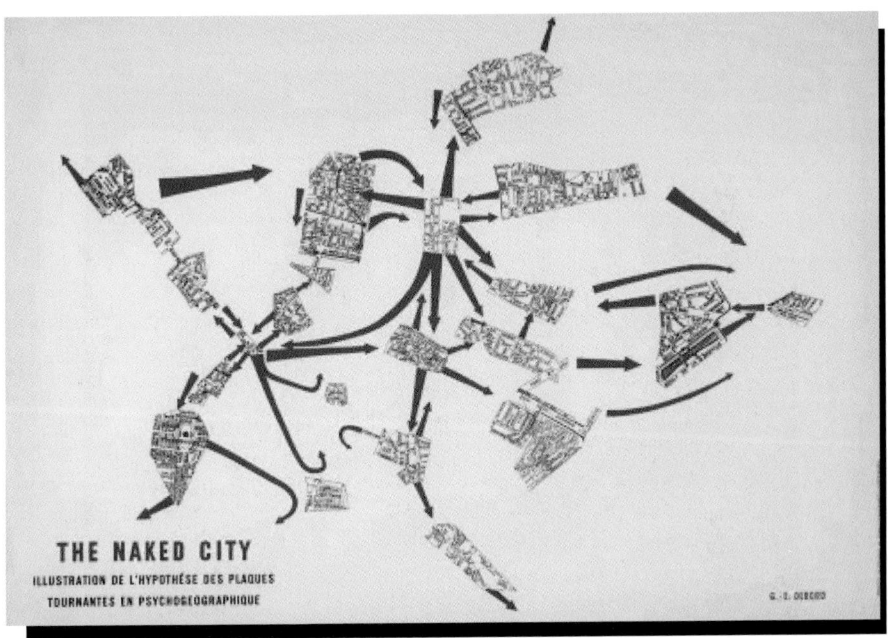

Figure 2
'The Naked City' by Guy Debord, 1957
Source: Artstor.org[1]

Figure 3
Participatory mapping session in Nairobi with bus drivers (matatu drivers), users, and researchers from MIT (Carmelo Ignaccolo) and the University of Nairobi
Photo by Sarah Williams

equitable decision-making system should not be considered as an oxymoron. Simply put, he asserted that technology was intrinsically dependent on the social world and that the system in place reflected many layers of negotiation between social goals and technical capacity. He concluded his first chapter of the edited volume by saying that GIS technology was the result of localised social constructions, rather than of a vast, superhuman realm.

The seeds planted in the academic debate by Pickles in regards to the use of GIS finally sprouted with a refreshing body of literature on critical GIS, also defined as counter-cartography or critical cartography, in the early 1990s. Lin, in her piece titled "Counter-cartographies" (2014), helps situate the development of this new body of literature within two important contexts of change: 1) the advent of participatory research methodologies; and 2) the growing affordability and accessibility of mapping technologies (Lin 2014).

Since the early 1990s, as Wilson wrote in his *New Lines: critical GIS and the trouble of the map* (2015), "critical GIS" has referred to an area of investigation at the intersection of critical geography and geographic information science (Wilson 2017). It tends to combine technical capabilities for accurate geographic representation with the critical capacities of social theory. In general, critical GIS scholarship is particularly influenced by the use of participatory action tools. In line with Wilson's points, Williams argues that Public Participation Geographic Information Systems (PPGIS) aim to address power dynamics in digital representation by involving local communities in data collection and community discussions. In the "Digital Matatus" project, for example, local communities have been involved not only in the data collection process but also in the ground-truth phase of the transit maps developed by the research team. As a result, not only do the maps and visual representations perform as community-approved images, but their ownership is seen to transition from the researchers to the community. Participatory GIS and counter-mapping techniques have interrupted the information extraction pipeline of colonialist tradition that for too long has permeated map-production processes. These tools monumentalise a new type of spatial investigation: a more inclusive, equal, and just way of inhabiting and representing the spaces and voices of our cities.

FOOTNOTE

1_For scholarly purposes retrieved from: https://library.artstor.org/asset/AWSS35953_35953_34644341 (30.12.2020).

BIBLIOGRAPHY

Crampton J. W. (2001) "Maps as social constructions: Power, communication and visualization". In: *Progress in Human Geography* 25(2), pp. 235–252.

Harley J. B. (1988) "Maps, knowledge, and power". In: Henderson G., Waterstone M. eds. (1988) *Geographic thought: A Praxis Perspective.* London, Routledge, pp. 129–148.

Harvey D. (2000) "Cosmopolitanism and the Banality of Geographical Evils". In: *Public Culture* 12(2), pp. 529–564.

Kurgan L. (2013) *Close up at a distance: Mapping, technology, and politics.* New York, Zone Books.

Lin W. (2014) "Counter Cartographies". In: Cloke P., Crang P., Goodwin M. eds. (2014) *Introducing Human Geographies.* London, Routledge, pp. 215–226.

Pickles J. ed. (1985) *Ground truth: The social implications of geographic information systems.* New York, Guilford Press.

Sadler S. (2001) *The situationist city.* Cambridge, MIT Press.

Uttal D. H. (2000) "Seeing the big picture: Map use and the development of spatial cognition". In: *Developmental Science* 3(3), pp. 247–264.

Williams S. (2020) *Data Action.* Cambridge, MIT Press.

Wilson M. W. (2017) *New Lines: Critical GIS and the Trouble of the Map.* Minneapolis, University of Minnesota Press.

DESIGNING RESILIENCE: TRANS-SCALAR CO-DESIGN STRATEGIES FOR RESILIENT HABITATS

MARIA GIADA DI BALDASSARRE

This contribution is part of the doctoral research "Designing resilience: trans-scalar architecture for resilient habitat".[1] This project presents the current situation concerning sustainable development and European Union policies for territorial cohesion in reference to the inner areas of the Marche region in Italy, and focuses on trans-scalar co-design strategies as innovative approaches for achieving resilience in inner peripheral territories. In this context, a "resilient habitat" is defined as an open and living space that responds creatively to economic, social, and environmental changes in order to increase its long-term sustainability. This contribution argues that resilience is something that needs to be designed by building on trans-scalarity and the engagement of "shareholders". A trans-scalar approach aims to integrate different disciplines, overcoming hierarchical visions and assisting with decision-making that connects top-down policies and bottom-up practices. The elaboration of common scenarios as shared visions of future development fosters engagement, participatory governance, self-recognition in the design outcomes, and social cohesion. Moreover, it produces new forms of knowledge with which to approach these types of problems in similar contexts.

In the past century, humans have changed ecosystems more quickly and widely than ever before—to the extent that several scientists and researchers have affirmed that the planet has entered a new geological era called the Anthropocene (Crutzen Stoermer 2000). The name itself conveys that humans have developed and achieved such a potential to change the environment (both social and natural) that the species has become the most important driving force of planetary transformation processes. According to the report *Our Common Future* (1987), sustainable development means "development capable of meeting the needs of the present generation without compromising the ability of future generations to meet their own needs" (United Nations General Assembly 1987, p. 43). In 2015, the United Nations launched seventeen goals known as the Sustainable Development Goals. These goals positioned the role of sustainability as central to ensuring change—not only in relation to the environment, but also in consideration of economics and policy—in order to promote development and growth in a sustainable way. The "Sustainable Cities and Communities" goal in the 2030 Agenda aims to make cities and human settlements inclusive, safe, resilient, and sustainable.

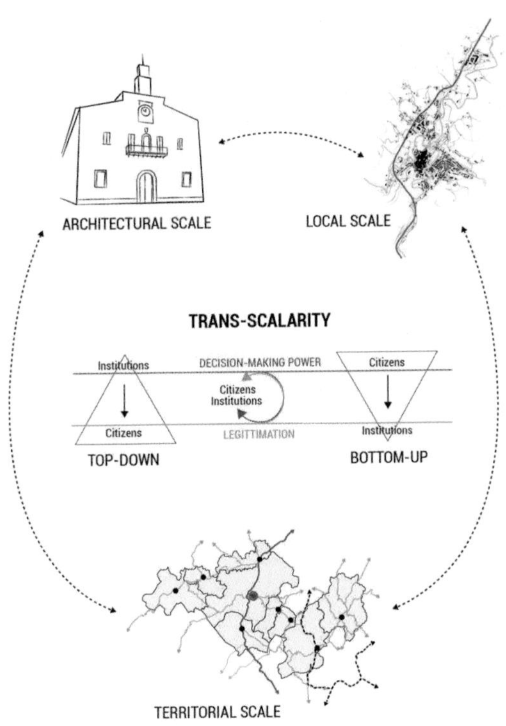

Figure 1
Trans-scalarity between top-down strategies and bottom-up practices
Graphic by Maria Giada Di Baldassarre, 2020

trans-scalarity design thinking co-design

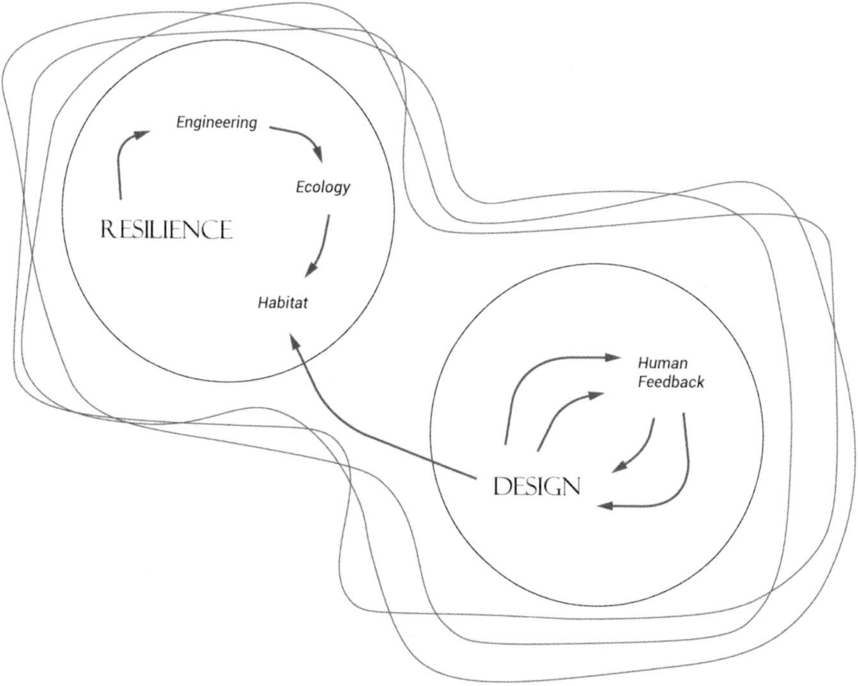

Figure 2
Infinite design loops
Graphic by Maria Giada Di Baldassarre, 2020

Within this context, the European Union has established a series of policies and devotes a significant part of its activities and budget to reducing disparities in levels of development between its regions, with particular reference to rural areas, areas affected by industrial transition, and regions with severe and permanent natural or demographic disadvantages. A *resilient habitat* is an open and living space that reduces its vulnerability to chronic stresses or dramatic and extreme events, and responds creatively to economic, social, and environmental changes in order to increase its long-term sustainability. In the past years, innovative approaches to dealing with the challenges of migration, climate change, and habitat openness have been developed in Europe. In addition to the top-down model, in which the project is the final product of institutional will and initiative, bottom-up practices have spread. This new paradigm recognises the project as the result of a true collective awareness and consequent process of self-organisation, activation, and innovation by local communities with regard to territorial policies and spatial strategies. The peculiarity of this process is that it overcomes the established approach of experts working in the interest of—or "for"—people, assuming that they intrinsically know the values and needs of the population affected and how to interpret them. Both approaches have positive and negative aspects, such as the risk that a "dropped-from-above" strategy may not be acknowledged by the inhabitants or that a bottom-up practice may not be coordinated or in harmony with institutional objectives. The ideal solution would be to adopt a combination of both systems within a cyclical approach and with a negotiation between the hierarchical levels. Designing resilience means intentionally guiding the adaptation process of a system so as to preserve

"Designing the resilience of habitats can begin at any scale and with any group of people through the discussion of needs, aspirations, and capabilities."

some of its qualities and allow other aspects to fade away, all while maintaining the identity of the system itself. The term "resilience" has its origins in ecology, where it is identified as "the capacity of a system to absorb disturbance and reorganise while undergoing change so as to still retain essentially the same function, structure, identity, and feedbacks – in other words, stay in the same basin of attraction" (Walker et al. 2004, p. 2). It is a principle that considers different scales, recognising within the analysed system a series of further sub-systems interdependent on each other and on the system itself. The relations between human systems at the various scales are not linear, but highly complex and variable, as self-organising systems operate on a range of different scales of space and time. The definition of the scale as a reference framework is a fundamental factor in designing the resilience of habitats. This designing should be based on the relationship between the scales, with their autonomy on the one hand and connectivity on the other. Understanding the relationships between habitats and scales is important to ensuring that the benefits of the intervention are maximised throughout the scales, and that negative effects, by contrast, are minimised. Trans-scalarity is a methodology that takes into account this interdependence between living systems of different scales, approaching them in a holistic way and defining design strategies that integrate different disciplines from the large scale to the small. As such, it could be the key to overcoming hierarchical visions and supporting decision-making with a continuous process that links the various scales of action, connecting top-down policies and bottom-up practices (Fig. 1). In a democratic society, the identity of a community derives from its members and represents a shared sense of its fundamental qualities. It is essentially determined by what people value about the place where they live, what they recognise as representative of their values, and what they are willing to fight for, thereby strengthening their cohesion (Lerch 2017). Since every member of society has aspirations and free will, it may be said that identity includes a shared vision of what the community should look like in the future. Identity is therefore the foundation of a community's resilience and, as a function of people living together in a community who change as society and the environment around them change, it is dynamic. For this reason, the understanding of the community identity should be constantly reviewed and refined, and planning and design activity should therefore include an iterative process in which the various scales influence each other and outcomes are adapted from time to time to suit the dynamic identity of the community. "Designing" here refers to the activity behind the realisation of any complex object, be it material or only conceptual, and whether in the form of a prototype, product, or process. It always foresees a change in regard to the status quo; moreover, it can potentially require repetitive design cycles. This tendency is presented alongside the recognition of design as a non-linear process: rather, it is a circular process, formed of a series of loops connected to each other and always symbiotically relating the object of design to the final user, the project, and the community (Fig. 2). In this context, "futuring" and "envisioning", understood as activities through which attempts are made to shape the common reality by identifying images of the future, are very effective tools for understanding the expectations and desires of the community (Dirth 2019). Creating a shared vision requires understanding people as active participants in shaping their reality and involves the ability to bring to light shared images of the future that foster authentic engagement and involvement (Senge et al. 2004). This is particularly useful for understanding the internal dynamics of a system—especially those that change over time, such as urban and social dynamics—and for predicting precisely the present and future needs of users and their desires (Fig. 3).

In the research project "Branding4Resilience",[2] innovative practices such as "co-vision" and "co-creation" represent strategies for the active involvement of the population in the design process. The process of co-design is an approach that involves both experts and the local community, channelling and aligning their ideas towards a common goal with the aim of defining some of the criteria that will affect the future development of the project. In addition to facilitating most of the processes due to their being conducted together with primary experts and representatives of the identity of the places, this produces greater support for and self-recognition in the design outcomes. It is evident that these new models of co-creation are able to engage citizens and transform them from stakeholders to "shareholders" and "netholders" (Carta 2017). One methodology that is being used more and more is design thinking. This is a human-centred approach to innovation that draws from the designer's toolkit to integrate the needs of people, the possibilities of technology, and the requirements for business success in order to come up with meaningful ideas that solve real problems, as well as with new solutions for a defined group of people. It is made up of five steps that require designers to "empathise" with the users and their needs by conducting interviews; to "define" users' actual needs by formulating a problem statement; to "ideate" several innovative ideas—not one single perfect one—that solve the problem and present them to the people for feedback; to "prototype" a solution combining the ideas, the current situation, and what has been learned from feedback; and to "test" the solution with the actual users and learn what works and what doesn't through their experiences (Friis Dam, Yu Siang 2020). It is important to point out that these five steps are not always sequential; they do not have to follow any specific order and can often occur in parallel and repeat iteratively. This non-linear process allows designers to create new interactions between theory and practice, elaborating creative scenarios for real problems and producing new forms of knowledge in order to provide transferable results.

In conclusion, this contribution argues that resilience in regard to territorial development should be designed based on the engagement of "shareholders" and trans-scalar architectural strategies, holistically addressing architecture, urban planning, and territorial governance. Designing the resilience

Figure 3
What will I be?
Graphic by Maria Giada Di Baldassarre, 2020

of habitats can begin at any scale and with any group of people through the discussion of needs, aspirations, and capabilities, after which the need to expand or contract the scale of analysis quickly becomes apparent (Lerch 2017). The co-creation of shared scenarios for future development fosters authentic engagement, participatory governance, and self-recognition in the design outcomes, as well as renewed cohesion of the community in the long term, which facilitates the achievement of common *resilient habitats*.

FOOTNOTES

1_"Designing resilience: trans-scalar architecture for resilient habitat" is the author's PhD research (still in process), carried out at the Department of Civil, Environmental and Building Engineering and Architecture of Marche Polytechnic University under the supervision of Prof. Arch. G. Mondaini (UnivPM), Prof. Arch. M. Ferretti (UnivPM) and Prof. Dipl.-Ing. Univ. J. Schröder (Leibniz University Hannover LUH).

2_"B4R Branding4Resilience. Tourist infrastructure as a tool to enhance small villages by drawing resilient communities and new open habitats" is a research project of national interest (PRIN 2017, Young Line) funded by the Ministry of Education, University and Research (MIUR) with a duration of three years (2020–2023). The project is coordinated by Marche Polytechnic University and involves as partners the University of Palermo, the University of Trento, and the Politecnico di Torino. It investigates the potential of territorial branding in promoting the resilient development of territories and communities in four Italian inner areas, starting with the introduction of minimal tourist infrastructures but with the primary goal of activating larger networks of relational systems. B4R also aims to build a shared vision of the future (co-visioning) through participatory processes (co-design), working on legacy as a memory of the past and the heritage of tomorrow.

BIBLIOGRAPHY

Carta M. (2017) *The Augmented City. A paradigm shift.* Trento, ListLab.

Crutzen P. J., Stoermer E. F. (2000) "The Anthropocene". In: *IGBP Newsletter* 41, pp. 17 – 18.

Dirth, E. (2019) *The Futuring Tool: A Toolkit for Responding to the Demands of the Fridays for Future Movement (for Governments).* IASS Brochure. Potsdam, IASS Potsdam.

Friis Dam R., Yu Siang T. (2020) *5 Stages in the Design Thinking Process.* Available online at: https://www.interaction-design.org/literature/article/5-stages-in-the-design-thinking-process (20.12.2020).

Lerch D. (2017) *The Community Resilience Reader. Essential resources for an era of upheaval.* Washington, Island Press.

Senge P., Jaworski J., Scharmer O., Flowers B. S. (2004) *Presence: Human Purpose and the Field of the Future.* London, Nicholas Brealey Publishing.

United Nations General Assembly (1987) *Report of the world commission on environment and development: Our common future.* New York, UN.

United Nations General Assembly (2015) *Transforming our world: the 2030 Agenda for Sustainable Development.* New York, UN.

Walker B., Holling C. S., Carpenter S. R., Kinzig A. (2004) "Resilience, adaptability and transformability in social-ecological systems". In: *Ecology and society* 9(2), p. 5.

TOWARDS A LIVING-ORIENTED APPROACH TO URBAN DESIGN BY COSMOPOLITAN RISK COMMUNITIES

DALILA SICOMO

At a defining moment for the future of life on Earth, active citizenship and informed communities play a decisive role in sensitising stakeholders to issues and influencing their decisions via physical and digital platforms. Anthropogenic climate change generates risks, causes migrations, expands inequalities, and mobilises people: these challenges question both the relationship of coexistence between different cultures and that between humans and other living species, such as animals, insects, and plants. If inhabiting cosmopolitan cities means living in and sharing a plural habitat, it is of utmost importance that we gather our collective expertise and rethink cities as welcoming spaces for life and species interaction in order to enhance cosmopolitan diversity. This contribution will focus on European project proposals and ongoing activities and draft a possible path to developing an empathetic, inclusive approach to urban life and living beings by building resilience through urban design.

Cosmopolitan risk communities facing global crisis

The impacts of global inequalities and world conflicts combined with the current pandemic question the compatibility between these various crises and a cosmopolitan vision of the world. Climate change and health, economic, social, and political crises form part of what has been called a "syndemic" (Horton 2020), in which the recent Covid-19 pandemic combines with the world's pre-existing conditions, interacts with them, and as a result affects a hyper-linked world whose dynamics are highly interrelated. The antidote may lie in the metamorphosis that active citizenship and what Ulrich Beck called "cosmopolitan risk communities" (Beck 2016) are triggering inside cities, questioning the notions of democracy and anthropocentrism and dealing with emergencies. Referring to Ulrich Beck's theory of "cosmopolitan risk communities"—which concerns the cooperative spirit of cities and communities in facing global challenges such as climate change—this contribution focuses on the binomial crisis/opportunity that provokes active citizenship, shaping first demands and then urban space, sometimes in a synergic way. Long before transforming urban spaces, the awareness of global risks and of the interconnection of actions throughout the world modifies people's visions of and demands on the functions and uses of space—particularly among the younger generations. All the activities, meetings, and strikes promoted by young associations and move-

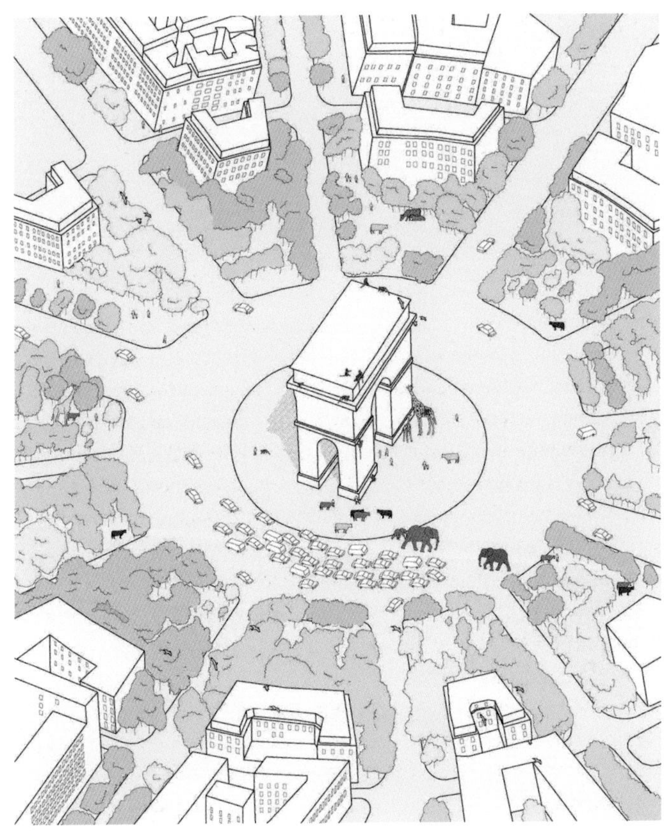

Figure 1
Concept proposal for Place de l'Étoile, Paris, by Andrea Branzi and Stefano Boeri
Graphic by Angelo Renna, 2018 (courtesy of the authors)

risk community inclusivity co-design animals

ments such as Fridays For Future and Extinction Rebellion are part of this context and contribute to shaping and creating a shared vision of the future. Today, issues of anthropogenic climate change and ecological degradation have moved to the centre of social and political discourse, stimulating the transition from the notion of the Anthropocene[1] (Crutzen, Stroemer 2000) towards what has been defined as the "Good Anthropocene" (McNeil, Engelke 2016) or the "Neoanthropocene" (Carta 2017), a new era in which humans, conscious of their impact on the Earth and its ecosystems, act with a view to their recovery. In particular, referring to the debate on environmental and ecological challenges, the sociologist John Clammer suggests that: "human civilisation, if it is to survive and flourish, needs to develop new forms of cosmopolitanism that are not purely social and political, but are rooted in an organic relationship to nature and indeed to the cosmos as the word cosmopolitan suggests" (Clammer 2018, p. 33).

As such, considering the origins of the term "cosmopolitan" (from Greek *κόσμος*, meaning world, and *πολίτης*, meaning citizen) from a Neoanthropocentric point of view, the notion of cosmopolitanism itself may evolve towards a concept that includes all inhabitants and residents of the city, including animal and plant species that no longer need to be seen as outsiders, but as an integrated part of urban design and habitat. Hence, a *Cosmopolitan Habitat* could be seen as a community that acts inside a place (such as a city and the urban environment in general), is aware of global risks, and aims to renovate its relationship with other animal species and with nature, building resilience through designing more empathetic, inclusive, and educative spaces. Developing a respectful interaction with other living species represents one way of proactively responding to climate change—this is the core objective of the author's doctoral thesis on reducing the causes and mitigating the effects of climate change in port and maritime cities, and will be explored more deeply there.

Adding a new layer to urban cosmopolitanism

Our cities are in many ways *Cosmopolitan Habitat* because they are home to a variety of ethnicities, animals, and plant species from all over the world. These elements often create syncretism and rich variations that combine and unite distant areas of the globe. The awareness of global risks and the fact that cultural exchanges lead inevitably to the ability to see the world differently assist in renovating urban theory and concepts. For instance, the influences of Indian culture and Buddhism inspired Andrea Branzi—founder of Archizoom Associati—and Stefano Boeri to design a proposal for the Greater Paris competition in 2008 that addresses the huge decline in the animal population. In their proposal, animals are allowed to roam freely in the city; they are seen as part of the urban environment and play an active role in it. The two designers proposed a non-expansive intervention programme for the metropolis based on the recovery and conversion of existing buildings and on the inclusion of 50,000 sacred cows and 30,000 free monkeys in Parisian parks and avenues. The idea used Indian metropolises, where sacred cows, camels, and elephants co-exist in cities with humans, as a reference. The presence of free animals within an urban fabric creates—in the architects' opinion—a sort of "stress reduction" effect: animals force the system to slow down, disrupt the common rhythms, and, protected by their own sacredness, are able to interrupt journeys by increasing the level of unpredictability. Branzi and Boeri's vision for Greater Paris, supported by Angelo Renna's illustrations (Fig. 1, Fig. 2), addresses cohabitation strategies between humans and the animal world for a less anthropocentric vision of the metropolis—one that would offer a "cosmic" hospitality to biodiversity (Renna 2018). On the one hand, the proposal enhances the inherent

Figure 2
Concept proposal for Greater Paris by Andrea Branzi and Stefano Boeri
Graphic by Angelo Renna, 2018 (courtesy of the authors)

contrast in the consolidated idea of western cities—historically tending to separate with borders the rural and the wild from the urban—while on the other hand, it provides a stimulus for an ecocentric approach to urban design and for rediscovering certain practices in a western urban context.[2] The thought-provoking Greater Paris proposal by Branzi and Boeri might be seen as utopian, perturbing, or even controversial during our current period of zoonosis, but its value lies in a more inclusive idea of *Cosmopolitan Habitat*; one that enhances diversity and empathy towards other species and re-interprets our relationship with nature, as suggested by Pope Francis in his encyclical letter "Laudato sì" in 2015. Two other highly topical concepts from recent years are the project for the Tour Vivante by SOA in Rennes, France (2005), and the Bosco Verticale in the business centre of Milan by Boeri Studio (2014), which both explore the theme of the vertical densification of greenery. Due to its controversial high maintenance and cost, the Bosco Verticale is still an object of debate, a number of projects and practices improving on its initial concept—such as one targeting urban forestation in Prato—have recently been started.

Towards an empathetic and inclusive approach to urban life

During the Covid-19 pandemic, we as designers have the opportunity to rethink proximity in both domestic and urban spaces, particularly in terms of adaptability, inclusivity, and accessibility. In the last years, European cities have become a refuge not only for people and temporary residents, but also for certain animals. The lockdown period offers us the opportunity to more frequently observe animals living in the city, as well as the phenomenon of synanthropy, in which wild animals move into urban spaces both due to the easier availability of food and as a result of the effective reduction of

Figure 3
Wunderbugs pavilion by OFL Architecture, Rome, 2014
Source: OFL Architecture, photo by Anotherstudio

their natural habitat caused by the rapid land consumption of human activities. A world that was previously invisible has become visible, showing us other living communities living through crises.[3] These are phenomena of very high complexity and diversity, and while they have a spiritual and religious origin in Indian culture and are foreseen and accepted there, they are still viewed as unexpected in the western world.

If inhabiting the Open City means practicing "a certain kind of modesty" by living in a world that does not mirror oneself (Sennett 2018), it is of utmost importance to gather our collective expertise and rethink cities as welcoming spaces for humans, animals, and plants, thereby enhancing cosmopolitan diversity. Nature already conquers spaces for itself in the city (think, for example, of spontaneous vegetation, birds' nests, and insects in buildings)—but what would happen if we designed spaces to welcome it?

Dominique Rouillard (2011), in her article "The Other Animal of Architecture", stresses that animals have only been included in the domain of architecture since the second half of the twentieth century, after children and women began to be considered in architecture and urban debate. More and more rooftop gardens, cat cafés (popularised in Japan), insect hotels, and urban beehives[4] have found a place in the urban context; the diffusion of urban farms into Europeans cities is an even more recent development. In particular, bees—a precious bioindicator for air quality and pollution—have become citizens of our cities, and urban beekeepers shed light on biodiversity and environmental themes in the city. Talking about bees means talking about food, economy, biodiversity, climate change, resilience, production, and incentives for micro-economies. Urban honey, such as that produced in Turin's botanical garden, could also be seen as a product composed of cosmopolitan flavours due to the variety of pollen from exotic and diverse flowers that goes into making it. Among the most interesting examples of urban architecture that caters to animals is the Wunderbugs pavilion in Rome by OFL Architecture in 2014 (Fig. 3), an interactive space dedicated to the human-insect relationship. The pavilion combines an architectural space with an educational scope, transforming our approach to the lives of insects through a friendly, curiosity-driven, and cruelty-free zone. Another ongoing project worth mentioning is Fattoria Danisinni, led by Friar Mauro and the local community of the Palermo district of the same name on a converted field that was once a confiscated property. The farm hosts a variety of plant and animal species in a mixed-use space featuring a social garden, an urban farm, a gathering space, and a circus.

By holistically considering a shared habitat that excludes single-species supremacy and welcomes different dimensions, these examples may be able to help us understand, at different scales, various elements of a living-oriented urban design approach. The reintegration of nature into cities is not a cosmetic action, but rather a way of reactivating the ecological cycles of the urban metabolism (Carta 2017) in accordance with Neoanthropocentric urbanism.

FOOTNOTES

1_The Anthropocene is assumed to be the era in which we are living and is characterised by the global effects of human activities on the Earth, our atmosphere, and on ecosystems.

2_In previous times, English lawns were maintained by the free sheep that cut the grass; Kensington Gardens, St. James Garden, and Hyde Park (London) and Central Park in New York City hosted flocks of sheep until the 1940s.

3_To further explore the topic of animal communities living in European cities, see the documentary film *Wild Amsterdam* (De Wilde Stadt) by Mark Verkerk (2018).

4_Paris counts over 300 rooftop beehives installed on top of public buildings.

BIBLIOGRAPHY

Beck U. (2016) *The Metamorphosis of the World: How Climate Change is Transforming Our Concept of the World.* Cambridge, Polity Press.

Carta M. (2017) *Augmented city. A paradigm shift.* Trento and Barcelona, ListLab.

Carta M. (2019) *Futuro. Politiche per un diverso presente.* Soveria Mannelli, Rubbettino.

Clammer J. (2018) "Cosmopolitanism Beyond Anthropocentrism: The Ecological Self and Transcivilizational Dialogue". In: Giri A. K. ed. (2018) *Beyond Cosmopolitanism: Towards Planetary Transformations.* Singapore, Palgrave Macmillan/Springer Nature, pp. 33–51.

Crutzen P. J., Stroemer E. F. (2000) "The Anthropocene". In: *Global Change Newsletter* 41, pp. 17–8.

McNeill J. R., Engelke P. (2016) *The Great Acceleration. An Environmental History of the Anthropocene since 1945.* Cambridge, Belknap Press of Harvard University Press.

Horton R. (2020) "Offline: COVID-19 is not a pandemic". *In Lancet* 396 (10255), pp. 874.

Renna A. (2018) "Andrea Branzi: bringing animals at the centre of the urban project". In: *Domus web.* Available on line at: https://www.domusweb.it/en/architecture/2018/05/31/andrea-branzi-bringing-back-animals-at-the-centre-of-the-urban-project.html (14.11.2020).

Rouillard D. (2011) "L'autre animal de l'architecture". In: *Cahiers thématiques, n. 9, Agriculture métropolitaine/Métropole agricole. Éditions de l'École Nationale Supérieure d'Architecture et de Paysage de Lille,* pp. 105–17.

Sennett R. (2019) *Building and Dwelling: Ethics for the City.* London, Penguin Books.

AUTHORS

Yannis Aesopos / University of Patras / Professor and chair of the Department of Architecture; teaches architecture and urban design and directs the "Mediterranean Futures" Master's programme in Architecture and Urban Design. Visiting professor at Columbia University and The Bartlett, UCL; research fellow at Princeton University. Commissioner and curator of "Tourism Landscapes: Remaking Greece", the Greek contribution to the 14th International Architecture Exhibition at the 2014 Venice Biennale. Co-editor of *The Contemporary (Greek) City* (Athens, 2001) and *Landscapes of Modernization: Greek Architecture 1960s and 1990s* (Athens, 1999). aesopos@upatras.gr

Angela Alessandra Badami / University of Palermo / Architect; associate professor since 2015, where she teaches urban planning. In addition to this, she has completed research and studies at universities in France and Denmark on urban regeneration, social innovation, and the enhancement of cultural heritage. She carries out theoretical and applied research on sustainable urban development and local development and has directed projects for the socio-economic and cultural enhancement of archaeological areas, to design colour plans of historical urban contexts, and for the promotion of cultural heritage. angela.badami@unipa.it

Filipe Themudo Barata / University of Évora / Historian and full professor at the University of Évora, where he specialised in Mediterranean history; now retired. Former UNESCO Chair in Intangible Heritage and Traditional Know-how: Linking Heritage. Member of several specialist academies for the subjects in which he works. Author of a few dozen articles and books on history and cultural heritage. Member and/or leader of many national and international projects, such as "Portuguese Heritage Around the World: Architecture and Urbanism". He has given a large number of lectures and seminars on these topics. ftbarata@uevora.pt

Cosimo Camarda / University of Palermo / Urban and territorial planner, PhD candidate since 2018. His research activities concern the regeneration and enhancement of historic centres, the territorial planning of marginal areas, and the recovery and enhancement of small towns as a tool for the revitalisation of inner territories. He has dealt with the relationship between port and urban systems both from a professional and a research point of view. He tutors on urban planning and territorial planning courses under Prof. M. Carta. cosimo.camarda@unipa.it

Maurizio Carta / University of Palermo / Architect, PhD, and full professor of urbanism and regional planning at the Department of Architecture. Founder and director of the Augmented City Lab, an international research agency dedicated to the cities of the future. He is a senior expert in strategic planning, urban design, and local development, and has drawn up several urban, landscape, and strategic plans in Italy. In 2015, he received an award at the International Biennial of Architecture in Buenos Aires. Visiting professor or keynote speaker at several universities and institutions. He is the author of over 300 publications, most recently *Futuro. Politiche per un diverso presente* (2019). maurizio.carta@unipa.it

Riccarda Cappeller / Leibniz University Hannover / University researcher and lecturer at the Institute of Urban Design and Planning since 2018. Her research interest is in design modes for mixed urban spaces and artistic approaches in urban design. She has been an architectural journalist since 2015 and has worked on collaborations with the collectives Exyzt/Constructlab since 2013. She has an MA in Visual Sociology from Goldsmiths University London 2017 and an MSc in Architecture from Bauhaus Universität Weimar 2015, with study periods at Universidad de Buenos Aires (2014) and ETSAM Politecnica Madrid (2012). cappeller@staedtebau.uni-hannover.de

Matevž Čelik / Future Architecture Platform / Architect, writer, editor, researcher, and cultural producer working in the fields of architecture and design. Founder and programme director of Future Architecture, a European platform for exchange and networking between architectural institutions and emerging talents. Previously director of the Museum of Architecture and Design in Ljubljana. Commissioner of the Slovenian Pavilion at the Venice Biennale in 2016, 2018, and 2020. Visiting critic or lecturer at the FA in Ljubljana, the IUAV in Venice, and Dessau Institute of Architecture. Member of the advisory board for the Archipelago festival in Geneva. matevz.celik@gmail.com

Annalisa Contato / University of Palermo / Architect, architectural engineer, PhD, and researcher in urban and regional planning at the Department of Architecture since 2020. Her research activities focus on the analysis of new territorial and urban configurations in relation to the phenomenon of globalisation and the network society, as well as on new territorial development model hypotheses. Her main topics of research concern polycentrism, city networks and gateway cities, local development strategies and inner areas, methods and tools for integrated urban and territorial planning, and urban regeneration processes. annalisa.contato@unipa.it

Maria Giada Di Baldassarre / Marche Polytechnic University / Engineer and PhD candidate in integrated facility engineering and resilient environments; she graduated with honours in Building Engineering and Architecture (2018). PhD visiting fellow at the Institute of Urban Design and Planning, Leibniz University Hannover, Germany (2019–20). She is currently focusing her research activities on the thesis "Designing Resilience: Transcalar architecture for resilient habitats" and on work within the collaboration on the PRIN "B4R. Branding4Resilience". mariagdibaldassarre@gmail.com

Alissa Diesch / Leibniz University Hannover / Architect, university researcher and lecturer at the Institute of Urban Design and Planning. PhD candidate with teaching assignments at TUM (2016–2017). Researcher, lecturer, and leader of the research group Hábitat Socio-Cultural at the Universidad La Gran Colombia, Bogotá (2015–2018). Architect at Zwischenräume Architekten (2012–2014). DAAD PhD research scholarship in Colombia 2017. Her research interests include participatory knowledge generation, post-colonial spaces, research to design concepts, and rurban-rural relations and transformations. diesch@staedtebau.uni-hannover.de

Maddalena Ferretti / Marche Polytechnic University / Architect, PhD, associate professor in architectural and urban design. University researcher and lecturer at Leibniz University Hannover until 2017. National coordinator of the PRIN 2017 "B4R. Branding4Resilience" (2020–2023). Former director of the research group for the building and settlement development project "Regiobranding", BMBF (2014–2017). Research topics: spatial ecological transformations in sensitive contexts, heritage enhancement, territorial branding. Recent book: *Scenarios and Patterns for Regiobranding* (with J. Schröder, Jovis, 2018). m.ferretti@univpm.it

Jes Hansen / Leibniz University Hannover / Student on the Master's programme in Architecture and Urban Design. Alongside his studies he works as a tutor with the Chair of Building Construction Design. He won the Laves Award 2019 for his bachelor thesis research on the Dachau concentration camp memorial site. His studies and research are focused on architectural history and the history of the city, concentrating mainly on the potentials and implications for the present and future production of architecture. jeshansen@outlook.de

Julia Hermanns / Leibniz University Hannover / Currently completing the Master's programme in Architecture and Urban Design. Alongside her studies she is a research assistant and tutor at the Chair of Territorial Design and Urban Planning and tutor at the Chair of Architecture and Arts of the 20/21st Century. In addition to her semester as an Erasmus student at the University of Antwerp, she has gained experience in architectural offices in Berlin, Hanover, and Basel. hermanns@stud.uni-hannover.de

Carmelo Ignaccolo / Columbia University / Adjunct assistant professor at Columbia University GSAPP, where he teaches a graduate-level course on digital techniques for urban design. PhD candidate in city design and development at the Department of Urban Studies and Planning at MIT. His academic research focuses on urban morphology and environmental psychology in historic cities where collective and individual mnemonic processes are deeply intertwined with the physical transformation of the city fabric. At Columbia, he was awarded a Fulbright fellowship and the GSAPP prize for excellence in urban design. carmeloi@mit.edu

Barbara Lino / University of Palermo / Architect, PhD, researcher in urban planning at the Department of Architecture. She writes about cities, the regeneration of peripheries, and local development strategies. Author of national and international articles and books, including *Periferie in trasform-azione. Riflessioni dai "margini" delle città* (Alinea, 2013), *Territories* (with J. Schröder, M. Carta, M. Ferretti, Jovis, 2016), *Dynamics of Periphery* (with J. Schröder, M. Carta, M. Ferretti, Jovis, 2018). Local coordinator at UNIPA research unit for the PRIN "B4R Branding 4 Resilience" (2017). barbara.lino@unipa.it

Martina Massari / University of Bologna / Architect, PhD, research fellow at the Architecture Department since 2019 and part of research group on Collaborative & Adaptive Cities. She teaches urban techniques. She obtained a PhD cum laude in 2020; her thesis was on the intermediate places between social innovation practices and urban planning in Bologna. She was a university researcher and lecturer at the Institute of Urban Design and Planning of Leibniz University Hannover (2018–19). Her research interests concern the interaction between social innovation practices and urban planning. m.massari@unibo.it

Marina Mazzamuto / University of Palermo / Architect, Phd student in urban planning since 2019. She achieved her master's degree in architecture at UPC University in Barcelona in 2016, where she completed a thesis on soundscapes and architectural acoustics. In 2018 she graduated from the Professional Conservatory of Musical Theatre at the New York Film Academy in New York. In 2019, she made her debut as a freelance set designer for the off-Broadway production of the musical *Spoolie Girl* at the Actor's Temple Theatre in New York. Her research explorations concern overtourism in Southern European coastal cities. marina.mazzamuto@unipa.it

Anna Pape / Leibniz University Hannover / Currently completing the Master's programme in Architecture and Urban Design. Alongside her studies she is a research assistant and tutor at the Chair of Territorial Design and Urban Planning. In addition to her experience in several architecture and urban design offices in Hanover and Berlin, she is part of the art collective Betz°3, which devises projects in urban space and light installations. She is pursuing a second qualification with the aim of becoming an urban planner. anna.pape@web.de

Mosè Ricci / University of Trento / Emeritus of the Italian Republic for art and culture since 2003; full professor of architectural design and urbanism. Fulbright scholar at GSD, Harvard (1997) and visiting professor at UM Lisboa (2006–7), TUM (2008–9), IAAC, BCN (2015), and MAUD Athens (2018). His books include *Habitat 5.0* (Skira, 2019), *New Paradigms* (List, 2012), *UniverCity* (List 2010), and *RISCHIOPAESAGGIO* (Meltemi, 2003). He has received prizes in international competitions, and participated in the 1996 and 2012 Venice Biennales. He received an award from the Italian National Academy of Sciences for his "MedWays" project and served as a member of the advisory board for the Italian Pavilion at the 2021 Venice Biennale. mose.ricci@unitn.it

Caterina Rigo / Marche Polytechnic University / Architect, PhD candidate in architecture, teaching assistant, and research fellow for the PRIN "Branding 4 Resilience". She graduated with honours from IUAV University of Venice in 2016. Since 2017, she has been a freelance architect in Ascoli Piceno, following a number of training experiences at international workshops and an internship at TAMassociati. She has participated in architectural competitions and won a special mention at Europan 15 in 2020 as coordinator of a group of students. c.rigo@pm.univpm.it

Daniele Ronsivalle / University of Palermo / Architect and associated professor since 2019, where he teaches urban design. He is a member of many research project groups and is teaching on the topics of landscape preservation, urban regeneration, and strategic planning for sustainable development. He was recently a member of the research project "Playground per architetti di comunità" on urban regeneration in the peripheries (funded by Con i Bambini / Fond.Sud), as well as of the research project "ENSURE: European Sustainable Urbanisation through Port City Regeneration" on waterfront regeneration (ESPON 2014–20). daniele.ronsivalle@unipa.it

Federica Scaffidi / Leibniz University Hannover / Architect, PhD, and university researcher and lecturer at the Institute of Urban Design and Planning since 2018. Visiting scholar at Polytechnic of Turin (2015–2016), ETSAM in Madrid (2016), and LUH (2017). PhD and Doctor Europaeus from University of Palermo (2019). Her research is based on qualitative and quantitative methodologies. Her research interests to date have addressed territorial development, social innovation and recycling, and how creative cycles are driving new urban communities and social entrepreneurship models. scaffidi@staedtebau.uni-hannover.de

Jörg Schröder / Leibniz University Hannover / Architect and urban planner; full professor and Chair of Territorial Design and Urban Planning. He focuses on urbanism and architecture for sustainable transition and territorial innovation as well as on design research, particularly regarding new metropolitan and peripheral spatial constellations, emerging creative habitats, and circular dynamics. Recent R&D projects include "Rurbance" (EU Alpine Space Programme), "Regiobranding" (BMBF), and "Creative Food Cycles" (EU Creative Europe Programme). Recent books: *Territories: rural-urban strategies* (2017, Jovis), *Dynamics of Periphery* (2018, Jovis), *Creative Heritage* (2018, Jovis). schroeder@staedtebau.uni-hannover.de

David Grahame Shane / Columbia University / Adjunct full professor in urban design. Diploma from the Architectural Association (AA) (1969); Master of Architecture (Urban Design) (1972) and PhD in Architectural and Urban History (1978) at Cornell with Professor Colin Rowe. He has taught at the AA and at Columbia. He has lectured widely and published in Europe, the USA, and Asia. He co-edited *Sensing the 21st Century City: Close-Up and Remote* (Architectural Design 75, 2005) and is the author of *Recombinant Urbanism: Conceptual Modeling in Architecture, Urban Design and City Theory* (Wiley, 2005) and *Urban Design Since 1945; a Global Perspective* (Wiley, 2011). grahameshane1@mac.com

Dalila Sicomo / University of Palermo / Architect and PhD student in urban, regional and landscape planning since 2019, where she graduated the same year. Previously, she was an Erasmus student at ENSA Paris-Malaquais in France, where she worked as an architectural intern. She took part in the *Manifesta 12* Research Studios and has carried out research on the history of contemporary architecture, gardens, and landscape. She is currently a member of the AugmentedCity Lab coordinated by Prof. M. Carta. Her research project focuses on the proactive responses of port cities to climate change. dalila.sicomo@unipa.it

Emanuele Sommariva / University of Genoa / Architect, PhD, assistant professor of urban design and planning at the Department of Architecture and Design since 2020. He was a university researcher at the Institute of Urban Design and Planning of Leibniz University Hannover from 2012–2020. His research interests include urban recycling, the evolutions of settlements and landscapes, urban-maritime regions, urban-rural strategies, urban agriculture, and food and the city. Scientific Manager of Local Research Unit in EU project "Creative Food Cycles" (2018–20), "Regiobranding" (2017–19), PRIN "Re-Cycle Italy" (2013–16). emanuele.sommariva@unige.it

Sabrina Sposito / Territorial planner; PhD, researcher at the Institute of Urban Design and Planning of Leibniz University Hannover for the EU project "Creative Food Cycles" (2018–20). Recipient of the AESOP YITP research award (2019) and a DAAD research grant for postdoctoral scientists (2017–18). Postdoctoral research fellow at the Institute for Advanced Studies on Science, Technology and Society (IAS-STS), Graz (2016–17). Member of the PRIN "Re-Cycle Italy" (2013–16). Her research interests include urban resilience and circular urban metabolism, hydro-based scenarios, urban-rural settings, and culture-led urban regeneration. sposito.sabrina86@gmail.com

Socrates Stratis / University of Cyprus / Associate professor in the Department of Architecture; PhD; architect, urbanist, and activist for the urban commons. His research focuses on the political and social agencies of architecture and urban design. It oscillates between critical urban practice and practice-based research, thanks to many entanglements between teaching, practicing, curating, and writing. Founder of the agency AA & U, Cyprus. Publication: *Guide to Common Urban Imaginaries in Contested Spaces* (Jovis, 2016). www.socratesstratis.com; www.aaplusu.com; stratiss@ucy.ac.cy

COSMOPOLITAN HABITAT

A Research Agenda for Urban Resilience
Edited by Jörg Schröder, Maurizio Carta, Federica Scaffidi, Annalisa Contato

Funded as Higher Education Dialogue with Southern Europe 2020 by the DAAD German Academic Exchange Service, financed by the Federal Ministry of Foreign Affairs.

A cooperation between the Leibniz University Hannover Institute of Urban Design and Planning and the University of Palermo Department of Architecture.

Organising committee:
Leibniz University Hannover: Prof. Jörg Schröder, Federica Scaffidi, Riccarda Cappeller, Alissa Diesch, Anna Pape, Julia Hermanns, Marie Schwarz, Rebekka Wandt
University of Palermo: Prof. Maurizio Carta, Prof. Angela Alessandra Badami, Prof. Daniele Ronsivalle, Barbara Lino, Annalisa Contato, Cosimo Camarda, Marina Mazzamuto, Dalila Sicomo

Scientific board:
Prof. Yannis Aesopos (University of Patras), Prof. Filipe Themudo Barata (University of Évora), Prof. Maddalena Ferretti (Marche Polytechnic University), Prof. Manuel Gausa Navarro (Institute of Advanced Architecture of Catalonia), Prof. Mosè Ricci (University of Trento), Prof. David Grahame Shane (Columbia University New York), Prof. Socrates Stratis (University of Cyprus).

Editors: Jörg Schröder, Maurizio Carta, Federica Scaffidi, Annalisa Cantato
Copy Editing: Jessica Glanz
Design and Setting: Anna Pape
Cover: Murales in Palermo by Alessandro Bazan (detail), photo by Barbara Lino, design by Anna Pape

Printed in European Union

Bibliographic information published by the Deutsche Nationalbibliothek
The Deutsche Nationalbibliothek lists the publication in the Deutsche Nationalbibliografie
detailed bibliographic data are available on the internet at http://dnb.d-nb.de

jovis Verlag GmbH
Lützowstraße 33
10785 Berlin

www.jovis.de

jovis books are available worldwide in selected bookstores. Please contact your nearest bookseller or visit www.jovis.de for information concerning your local distribution.

ISBN 978-3-86859-690-8 (Print)
ISBN 978-3-86859-962-6 (PDF)